The Essential Guide to the
STEEL SQUARE

The Essential Guide to the
STEEL SQUARE

KEN HORNER

Fox Chapel Publishing
1970 Broad Street • East Petersburg, PA 17520
www.FoxChapelPublishing.com

Fox Chapel Publishing Company, Inc.

Alan Giagnocavo
President

J. McCrary
Publisher

Gretchen Bacon
Editor

John Kelsey
Series Editor

Troy Thorne
Creative Director

Lindsay Hess
Design & Layout

ISBN 978-1-56523-342-3

Publisher's Cataloging-in-Publication Data

Horner, Ken.

    The essential guide to the steel square : facts, short-cuts and problem-solving secrets for carpenters, woodworkers & builders / Ken Horner. -- East Petersburg, PA : Fox Chapel Publishing, c2007.

        p. ; cm.

    (Woodworkers essentials & more)
    ISBN: 978-1-56523-342-3

      1. Carpenters' squares. 2. Carpentry--Tools. 3. Woodworking tools. 4.Woodwork. I. Title. II. Steel square. III. Series.

TH5619 .H67 2007
694/.2/0284--dc22   0710

To learn more about the other great books from Fox Chapel Publishing, or to find a retailer near you, call toll free 1-800-457-9112 or visit us at *www.FoxChapelPublishing.com*.

Note to Authors: We are always looking for talented authors to write new books in our area of woodworking, design, and related crafts. Please send a brief letter describing your idea to Peg Couch, Acquisition Editor, 1970 Broad Street, East Petersburg, PA 17520.

Printed in the United States of America
10 9 8 7 6 5 4 3 2 1

Because working with wood and other materials inherently includes the risk of injury and damage, this book cannot guarantee that creating projects based on the information in this book is safe for everyone. For this reason, this book is sold without warranties or guarantees of any kind, expressed or implied, and the publisher and the author disclaim any liability for any injuries, losses, or damages caused in any way by the content of this book or the reader's use of the tools needed to complete the projects presented here. The publisher and the author urge all woodworkers to thoroughly review all content and to understand the use of all tools before beginning any project.

The Essential Guide to the Steel Square is printed on Williamsburg brand paper produced by International Paper Co. at its Ticonderoga, N.Y., plant. IP has earned chain-of-custody certification from the Sustainable Forestry Initiative for all of its brands of paper, which means all trees used to manufacture its products are replaced through reforestation or natural regeneration. The certification also ensures harvesting practices that are used protect the air, water, soil, and wildlife. SFI is the largest of two primary independent forest certification standards in North America, and is the recipient of the United Nations Environmental Program/International Chamber of Commerce's 2002 World Summit Business Award for Sustainable Development Partnerships.

Dedication

This book is dedicated to everyone who likes to collect and use old tools. You spend time at garage sales and at flea markets peering into rusty buckets and scratching among the junk—trying to find a gem. You look for a name you know—Stanley or Starrett or Eagle. It's a good feeling, peering into the past by rescuing tools most people don't want and wouldn't know how to use. It doesn't really matter what the tool is—a plane, a hammer, or a saw. The beauty is apparent—you can see the shape and how it was made by mentally wiping off the rust and dirt.

The framing square is one of those old tools. It first came into use about 1820 and soon became indispensable. Carpenters, roof framers, staircase builders, sheet metal benders—all of the trades—used the square to build things and to figure complex angles and miters. Not many woodworkers today know how to use a steel square—other than to draw a 90° angle. I hope you rescue one from the rust heap and then read this book to learn all of the magic it holds.

Acknowledgments

This book was complicated. It has history, angles, miters, roof framing, and staircase layout. Linda Salter read every page, worked through every problem, and checked every drawing. She noted where I was wrong, put question marks when I wasn't clear, made comments about my conclusions, and helped to make this a better book. Thanks a lot, Linda.

As in my other two books, anytime I had a tough math problem I turned to my brother, Byron Horner. He always came through.

—Ken Horner, Sunnyvale, CA, June 2007.

Preface

This book started as a chapter in my second woodworkers' math book—*More Woodworkers' Essentials*. It was going to be just another 10-page explanation of how to use the scales on a framing square. But as I got deeper into the subject, it became obvious this should be a separate book on the steel square.

About a year ago, I was driving through western Vermont and saw a road sign that read "South Shaftsbury." I remembered South Shaftsbury was the village where the framing square was born, and I wanted to visit the museum and check out the buildings. Linda, my good friend, and I got off at the next exit and we drove into the little town (population about 700); there were only a few stores plus a cemetery. This was the home of the Eagle square. Silas Hawes made the first all-steel square here in 1814 and then patented it. This is where a small company cornered the market on steel squares for nearly a century; Stanley never even carried a framing square until it purchased Eagle in 1916.

We asked about a museum at the gas station and learned there wasn't one; the young fellow had never heard of Eagle. We asked at the real estate office and got the same reaction. The lady at the lone grocery store in town (which also sold antiques) had never heard of Eagle, but on the wall I spotted a faded old map. Sure enough, there it was: Eagle Square Co.—only a few blocks away, just off the short main street. Once there, all we could see was a tall brick wall. Parking, we walked over and looked beyond to discover a large metal casting of an American eagle and on the wall behind it, in big black lettering, Eagle Square Manufacturing Co. The sprawling building was mostly empty, but we found an unlocked door and went inside; it was obvious that Eagle didn't live there anymore. The manager told us the building was mostly empty and a small part was being used by a company making plastic mannequins. What a letdown.

The first reason I wrote this book was to show woodworkers how to use the steel square; the second reason was to preserve the history. There should be more than just a near-empty building and a few molded dress forms.

Eagle Square Manufacturing Co.

The Eagle Square factory in South Shaftsbury, Vermont, closed in 1983, but the building still stands. Here, Ken Horner poses with the company's trademark eagle.

Table of Contents

CHAPTER 1

Introduction

Of all of the tools used by a carpenter, there is none so useful as the framing square. To those who have mastered its use, it is an incredible tool. Until 200 years ago, a square was used only as a guide for laying out and marking work; finding complex angles and degrees was far beyond the ability of even a master woodworker. With the advent of steel, however, it finally became possible to manufacture precisely made squares that would remain true and upon whose surfaces and edges a variety of lines, scales, and tables could be permanently marked (see **Figure 1-1**).

In the Middle Ages, carpenters made their own squares with varying degrees of accuracy. The homemade, wooden squares were adequate for stone masons and rough carpenters, but the serious furniture maker, forced to make his own square, was greatly handicapped because of the inaccuracies inherent in a handmade tool. The local smithy could make a metal square, but his accuracy also was spotty.

In about 1820, a small Vermont company began to manufacture steel squares with inch graduations and useful scales stamped on the tongue and body. The Eagle square was manufactured to exacting standards and quickly came into general use. It became known as a framing square and was universally used to ensure accuracy for measuring lumber and in determining roof angles. New uses for the square were discovered continually, and the markings were constantly updated until they became standardized in the trades.

With the square, a workman could measure in 10ths, 12ths, 25ths, 32nds, 50ths or 100ths of an inch. By using the various scales and tables inscribed on the framing square, the savvy woodworker could determine board feet, figure

Figure 1-1. The Steel Square

The modern steel square has inch graduations on the edges, tables engraved on both sides, and a precise 90° angle at the heel. For those who know how to use it, the steel square is a sophisticated measuring and calculating tool.

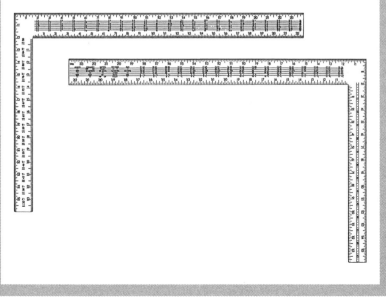

the bracing for post and beam construction, change hundredths of an inch to fractions, convert a square beam to an eight-sided post, and figure the rise and run of a complicated staircase. The framing square made it easy to find the length of common, hip, and valley rafters and to mark the complex ridge and top plate angles. Until that time, such tasks might have required a degree in math, but armed with a framing square, the ordinary workman could now do all of it without consulting trigonometry tables. It was all done using the lines, numbers, and scales on his framing square, which became, for the intelligent carpenter, a calculating machine of most remarkable usefulness. The steel square was what the slide rule was for the engineer, and what handbooks and tables were for the office worker.

Square and True

Throughout history, a woodworker's prestige and livelihood always have depended upon his ability to build both square and true. To find angles and miters and do complicated layouts, a thorough knowledge of mathematics is necessary. The framing square changed the way the common woodworker approached the job—the square became a calculator. Without it, the woodworker was just a person who could hit a nail and saw to a line. By knowing how to use the square, the woodworker now had the ability

to make the lines, and that was the mark of a real craftsman.

The framing square especially changed the way a carpenter approached house framing. No other tool could be applied so easily to the quick solution of the many difficult problems of roof construction. In the hands of one who knew how to use it, the framing square became a calculating device of amazing capacities—lengths and compound miters of rafter layout were easy to figure. One hundred and fifty years ago, a builder-architect wrote, "In the whole course of practice in the building arts, there is no tool the artisan possesses that lends itself so readily to the quick solution of the many difficult problems of laying out work as the steel square."

Today, there is a general feeling among woodworkers that the framing square is antiquated, that the intricate markings, figures, and tables inscribed on the tongue and body are from another age and learning to use it is too complicated. It's true the scales are old; they were first introduced some 200 years ago, and to the uninitiated, they may seem bewildering. However, the tables are fairly easy to understand and, once learned, open a whole world of knowledge for a woodworker. How else can a woodworker easily and quickly determine the length of any common, hip, valley, or jack rafter for any slope of roof? How else can a woodworker make the proper top and bottom cuts, as well as side and cheek cuts, for any rafter? And all of this with nothing but a framing square.

Perhaps the proudest day in the life of a beginning carpenter is the first time the foreman asks him to lay out rafters for a roof. The young carpenter uses a framing square and measures and marks and finally cuts a couple of 2x4s and, lo-and-behold, they fit. The top plumb cut snuggles right up to the ridge beam, the bird's mouth sets precisely on the top plate, and the ridge is the height the blueprint calls for. By mastering the scales and tables on the framing square, the apprentice has started his move into a higher realm, that of master craftsman.

The Modern Steel Square

There are many different squares used in woodworking and building today; however, they all are based on just four types of squares—the try square, the combination square, the triangular miter square (speed square), and the large framing square. *Essential Guide to the Steel Square* will be concerned mostly with the framing square for two reasons. First, it is the most useful square to a woodworker who wants to do more than just measure and make some marks. The figures etched on the framing square provide a wealth of useful information. Second, the same tables and scales make the framing square the most difficult

to understand and use. *Essential Guide to the Steel Square* can make everything clear.

In his 1903 book, *Practical Uses of the Steel Square*, Fred T. Hodgson gave advice to the young woodworker concerning the carpenter's square. "It is not necessary for me to remind the young workman of today of the necessity of arming himself with all of the resources of modern methods and appliances for the performance of his work, if he desires to stand in the front rank of his trade. It is the bright, well-informed young man who wins the race, and the fellow who drops his tools at the first clang of the bell at quitting time and gives no further thought, either to his work or his tools, until the commencement of work again the following day, who always remains at the foot of the ladder, and wonders how it is he does not prosper and thrive at the same rate as his more energetic and studious fellow workman. A few hours' quiet study each week during the winter nights may make the difference between poverty and sufficiency, for be it known, the employer soon discovers the superior qualities of the man who employs his brains as well as his hands in the performance of his duties, and advancement and higher pay are sure to follow sooner or later."

Today's young, and not-so-young, woodworkers could not hew to better advice.

CHAPTER 2

History of the Steel Square

Anthropologists posit that because man has opposable thumbs, only he is able to make and use tools and thus is able to harness the forces of nature for his own benefit. In the Stone Age, man used stones for hacking meat and sharpened sticks for grubbing roots. The first man-made tools, other than weapons such as spears and clubs, were the hammer, knife, saw, and bow drill. All were crude devices made from wood, stone, and bone to build shelters and fashion weapons.

Figure 2-1. Old Squares

The large all-wood square (a), 52" x 86", has a cross brace probably more for strength than for layout since it is set at 38° and 52°. The wooden square (b), 35" x 66", has a semi-circular brace. The square (c), 27" x 44", has one arm thicker than the other and so forms a shoulder or fence. The thicker arm is made of wood and the metal blade is unscaled—much like a modern try square.

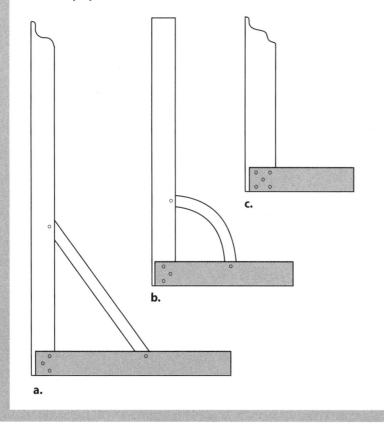

At some point, crude furniture was needed and the square was born. It can be seen in museums resting proudly with axes, chisels, hammers, and saws. Ancient drawings show both the L-type and the triangular-type square being used in building construction. Ruins around the ancient world from Mesopotamia (Iraq) to the Mediterranean (Italy and Palestine) show evidence squares have been used for thousands of years to set out timber work and to face stones for masonry projects.

A bag of carpenter's tools, with a square included, was found in an Egyptian tomb, dating four-to-five thousand years before Christ. The ancient square was a right triangle made of three pieces of wood (two sides each about 12-inches-long and a crosspiece 17-inches-long) and was carved with a hieroglyphic inscription. Some 2,000 years ago, the Romans used several versions of the L-shaped square (or *norma* as they called it), some with a thin strip along the narrow edge to act as a fence. Triangular squares have been found made of flat pieces of board with stops along one edge (for framing?), and with a right angle cut out of the middle to mark out a miter (for box construction?). One Roman triangular square (6 inches x 8 inches x 10 inches) was made of three strips of iron welded together to form the familiar 3-4-5 right triangle, perhaps used for squaring inside corners. **Figure 2-1** shows some old squares.

The purpose of a square in ancient times was, as it is today, to ensure the different parts of a work were true and square and, further, that the pieces would fit together properly. The early squares were made of wood or a crude metal, such as bronze, but whatever they were made of, it is evident squares have been used by carpenters and masons for thousands of years.

Squares of both the L-type and the triangular-type continued to be used throughout the Middle Ages. Because they were handmade by the carpenters themselves, they varied in detail and accuracy. The markings often were irregular and probably not reliable. Some that still exist were made of hardwoods or a few of recycled oak barrel staves.

As craftsmen became more skilled, buildings became more complex and furniture more delicate with more complicated joints. An accurate square became one of the most useful and valuable tools in the carpenter's kit, and especially so for the more advanced workman who laid out the work for others less clever or less ambitious.

Because the square had straight, true edges, it came to be used also as a measuring tool with each craftsman making his own marks depending upon the trade he was practicing. Some squares had marks like a story-pole for a specific job, and others were marked off in inches and subdivisions of inches for general use. Because the square had broad, smooth sides and was made of wood, it became the custom among builders to mark down or inscribe, on those smooth surfaces, certain rules, notes, and tables they found useful. As the square was passed down from father-to-son or given to apprentices, so also were the rules and knowledge passed on, long before books and printed guides became common.

Making Tools in Colonial America

In 1620, the Pilgrims brought tools with them on the Mayflower knowing they would need to build houses and furniture when they landed in the New World. Among the tools belonging to Francis Eaton, a carpenter of Plymouth Plantation in 1627, was a metal square. When Governor Theophilus Eaton of New Haven, Connecticut, died in 1657, two iron squares were among his many tools. These squares probably were made in England and brought to the colonies. **Figure 2-2** shows four wooden squares made by colonial woodworkers. They all are constructed with a common joiner's technique: the tenon of the thin blade is mortised through the thicker handle and held in place with pegs. They were made of American beech and maple, and none have graduations on them.

One reason the government of England finally allowed the Puritans to leave was economic: they would not only colonize the New World, but also would help to meet England's expanding need for raw materials. However, the harsh climate, the total lack of preparedness among the newcomers, the high death rate, and the hardships of their first years made these goals impossible. There was little time for mining or cutting timber for the mother country. The days were devoted to work and religion; survival was the goal of both body and soul.

Figure 2-2. Wooden Squares 1650–1700

Woodworkers often made their own squares out of wood. The ornate shaping of the blade end, common at the time, was mostly decorative. The blades were all joined to the body with pegged mortise-and-tenon joints. These all-wood squares were made here in the American colonies.

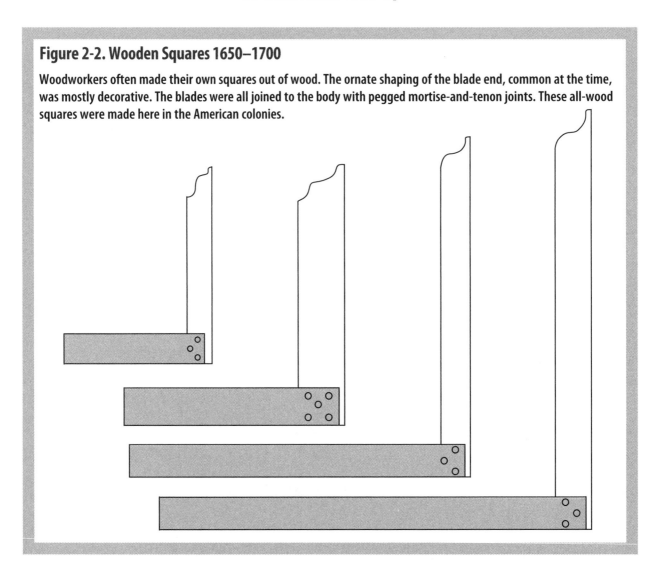

Three interdependent, inseparable factors–transportation, manufacturing, and distribution– were responsible for the establishment and growth of the tool industry in the American colonies.

Transportation

An urgent need for more tools and utensils paved the way for colonial hardware manufacturing. Axes, hatchets, knives, traps, and kettles not only were essential to the settlers but also quickly proved themselves basic requirements for barter with the Native Americans, and initial supplies were insufficient. Early colonists put in their orders, then waited a year or more for the return of sailing ships from England, knowing full well that when the ship finally did arrive, they would receive inadequate quantities of merchandise and equipment. Thus, transportation, or the lack of it, had a great influence on the American tool business. Blacksmiths, who were a part of each company of settlers, made many crude tools and implements that substituted for factory-made products until those items were available.

Manufacturing

Eventually the iron and steel orders of American blacksmiths presented a problem in England, where the ever-increasing demand for charcoal used in the smelting of iron ore was depleting British forests. Deposits of iron ore had, by that time, been discovered in most of the colonies where forests were considered inexhaustible and water power was plentiful. Why not allow the colonies to make iron? For some time the preservation of its British forests battled with the firmly established Crown policy of discouraging manufacturing in the colonies. The increased needs of the British sailing fleet for timber to make masts and spars finally tipped the balance, and iron making in America received the blessing of the Crown.

Distribution

The colonies exported iron to England and bought British steel. The agreement was an admirable arrangement until the colonial appetite for things made of iron became insatiable and our iron export stopped almost completely.

Steel differs from iron in that it has a lower content of carbon. The manufacture of steel is really nothing but the removal, by combustion, of the carbon contained in the iron. The process makes the structure of the metal more resilient, more flexible, and—what is more important—the metal can be cut without breaking. In addition to carbon, pig iron contains other admixtures such as sulfur and phosphorus. All these impurities can be removed by bringing the molten metal into contact with air so the impurities are transformed into their oxides by the oxygen in the air. The resulting slag is lighter than the molten metal and can be drained off before the steel itself is poured.

Making Iron and Steel

The first successful ironworks in the colonies was built in 1644 on the Saugus River near Lynn, Massachusetts, and the first product was a small cast-iron pot. Ironmaking soon spread to Connecticut and then quickly to the other colonies. Lack of transportation localized the industry, and eventually most thriving colonial communities had their own ironworks and blacksmiths. While colonial production of iron increased rapidly, progress in steelmaking was slow. Steel is preferred for tools, being stronger and easier to work than iron.

Making iron from ore (smelting) was a tedious process. Horses pulled ore wagons from open-pit mines or hauled ore from underground tunnels to the surface via shafts and a windlass. The ore was washed in water to remove dirt and clay, and then moved to a smelter.

Meanwhile, charcoal was prepared. Hundreds of acres of hardwood trees were cut, and 30 to 40 cords of four-foot logs were piled in a kiln. The logs were set afire, the door closed and sealed with small openings left for draft. The kiln was watched carefully for a week to ensure that the wood didn't burn too fast, otherwise the only thing produced would be ashes. The resulting charcoal was taken to the furnace in wagons with five-foot-high sides. About one-third of the wood by weight was converted to charcoal.

The furnace was charged at the top every hour and a half, around the clock, with each charge being 30 bushels of charcoal, 1500 pounds of ore, and 150 pounds of limestone. Every eight hours, the furnace was tapped and the molten iron drawn off into molds to create pigs weighing about 80 pounds each, thus converting 4 tons of ore into a little more than 3 tons of pig iron. The men worked 12-hour shifts, seven days a week, and 250 pigs, or 10 tons of iron, was thought to be a good day's work. Every nine months it was necessary to shut down the furnace to reline the hearth with new sandstone.

Making Steel Tools

Hammering metal by hand can be dated back more than 4,000 years. The purpose then, as it is today, was to change the shape and/or properties of the metal. Blacksmiths used a forge and an anvil to make useful implements such as horseshoes, nails, wagon tires, chains, household goods, and tools.

Politics Interfere

In 1735, serious opposition developed in England to the fledgling colonial steel industry and its offspring, tool manufacturing. A depression had closed many British tool factories, but English steel makers still needed customers. The inopportune arrival of colonial-made steel aroused resentment, enhanced by the publication of

British Navy tests declaring the quality and output of colonial furnaces to be the equal of higher-priced Swedish steel and of better quality than English steel.

Hungry British factories complained they were being deprived of the important American retail market because colonists were using their own iron to manufacture steel tools and hardware—we were becoming self-sufficient. The climax was reached when the owners of colonial schooners were reported to be selling hardware to former customers of English factories. For the next 15 years, protests and counterprotests were bandied about. Then, in 1750, the British Parliament passed laws limiting colonial production of iron and steel and forbidding colonial manufacturers from installing additional equipment to roll, plate, slit, or hammer steel. Even though the mandate was largely ignored, resentment grew and less than 25 years later, the American Revolution began. The revolt wasn't specifically about iron, steel, and tools—but they were certainly a part of the general dissatisfaction.

The British Parliament's attempts to restrict colonial iron and steelmaking failed miserably, and at the beginning of the American Revolution, the output of colonial ironworks exceeded that of the mother country. The colonial hardware and tool-making industry, which consumed much of the output, was also producing more tools than its British counterpart. The restrictive laws of 1750 had a most unintended result: when English hardware manufacturers restricted shipments of British steel to America, colonial furnaces increased their output to take up the slack and the colonies no longer needed or depended on Britain for steel.

Starting in 1760, there occurred in the colonies a remarkable series of inventions in cotton spinning, weaving, coal mining, iron smelting, earthenware manufacturing, road construction, and canal building—all substituting machines for human muscles.

Canals Enable Expansion

Beginning with the American Revolution, the iron and steel industry expanded rapidly. In every country during each armed conflict, factories expand to meet war effort, especially for making steel and converting it into war material. Afterward, the same machinery is used for tools, implements, and utensils of peace. This beating of "swords into plowshares" accompanied great surges of growth in the colonies. Finally, the discovery of vast deposits of rich iron ore in the Great Lakes region, and in the Southern states, and finally in the West made the United States the world's largest producer of steel. There was a problem—the iron ore from Minnesota and Michigan could not be easily transported to the smelters in Pennsylvania because of rapids in the St. Mary's River between Lake Superior and Lake Huron.

The St. Marys River, 63 miles long, is formed by the flow of water from Lake Superior to Lake Huron; the level of the former is 23 feet higher than the latter. Early trappers and traders found the sault, or rapids, some 49 miles upriver, made free navigation impossible. At this point on the river, the descent is 18 feet in one mile. The Sault Ste. Marie Canal, with one lock, was built in 1797 by the Northwest Fur Company. U. S. troops then destroyed the lock during the War of 1812. Finally in 1853, the State of Michigan, on land granted by the transportation, manufacturing, and distribution U. S. government, started a ship canal completely within the borders of the United States. In 1855, the Soo Canal opened, allowing ore from Minnesota and Michigan to join West Virginia coal and coke in the Pennsylvania steel furnaces.

Making Metal Squares

The metal framing square with permanent markings and tables, as we know it, is of comparatively modern development. The first metal squares of fairly exacting standards were made in the United States. Vermont legend has it that one day, soon after the War of 1812, a peddler stopped at the

blacksmith's shop of Silas Hawes in South Shaftsbury to have his horse shod. In payment for this service, the peddler left Hawes some old saw blades. The story goes on to assert that Hawes, with typical Yankee ingenuity, hand-welded two blades together at right angles, thereby producing the first metal carpenter's square. According to the legend, up until that time all squares had been made of two lengths of wood, joined together at a right angle with a piece of metal. An anonymous cynic suggested that while the story "has charm," it is of dubious authenticity and "probably not true."

We do have records that show inventor Silas Hawes was granted in 1814 a patent for "Cutting Files"—possibly an early metal file-cutting machine. In 1817, Hawes hired Stephen Whipple, a fellow Shaftsbury blacksmith, to help him make squares, and on December 15, 1819, Hawes received a patent on the "Carpenter's Square."

A fire in the Washington Patent Office in 1836 destroyed most of the records, so the exact nature of Hawes' patent is not known and perhaps never will be. However, the simple act of welding two pieces of iron or steel together at right angles to make a square was hardly new or patentable. Many blacksmiths were doing it, and such squares had been made for hundreds of years. Experts surmise Hawes' patent was for tapering the thickness of the square from the heel to each end to improve the "hang," making it lighter and saving scarce metal. Balance was important when a tool was used hundreds of times a day. The nicely balanced tool may also have had the brace scale inscribed on the blade. Both of the features are found on some early squares marked "Hawes Patent." Tapering improves maneuverability of the tool in the carpenter's hand, and the brace scale gives the length of braces for known lengths of rise and run. The blade and tongue of the early squares were graduated on the inside edge in inches, and on the outside edge in quarter inches.

Eagle Square Company

In 1820, a year after Hawes received his patent, he and Stephen Whipple went into business as the Eagle Square Company. Hawes and Whipple hired a few laborers to work in the shop for 75 cents to one dollar per day. There was such a demand for the new square that in 1823, the company leased land in the center of town near the grist mill, built a dam on Paran Creek, erected a shop, and built a waterwheel. Eagle Square Company began making squares from bar stock by drawing and welding the metal under a water-powered drop hammer.

Forge welding bonds two pieces of metal by heating them to a high temperature approaching fluidity, treating the surfaces to be welded with a suitable flux so that oxides will be fluid, and then pounding the pieces until they fuse together.

The advantage of a drop hammer over the hammer and anvil is the physical properties of metal are improved by severe mechanical working. The operation is fast, a lesser amount of finishing is necessary, and internal defects are eliminated. Also, the welded joint is stronger and there is less internal stress on the metal. Until the innovation, squares had been welded by hand. By changing to the drop hammer, output was doubled.

In 1825, Silas Hawes signed a ten-year lease on the land where the shop was situated for $106 per year. For nearly ten years Eagle Square Co. had a virtual monopoly on the steel square. Hawes retired in 1827, reputedly a rich man, and by the time his original patent expired in 1834, many shops in southwest Vermont were engaged in making squares. In 1838, Dennis George purchased a one-quarter interest in the Eagle Square Co. and in 1845 became sole owner. By 1850, quite a few of the smaller concerns were still making squares; however, Eagle dominated the square industry in the valley.

Mechanical Graduators

What gave Eagle the lead over all competitors and finally put all others out of business was the invention, in 1849, by Norman Millington and Dennis George, of a "New and Improved Method of Graduating and Figuring Carpenter's Squares by Machinery" (U.S. Patent 6,684). (See **Figure 2-3**.)

Until then, the graduating marks —the inches and fractions of an inch—had all been cut by hand with a graving tool. That meant—for a square graduated in eighths—marks had to be cut with an incising chisel exactly one-eighth of an inch apart, on each edge of the square. Because there are eight edges (four edges on both sides of the blade and four more on the body), that meant cutting 1,264 graduations on a single 24-inch x 18-inch square—assuming both face and back and all edges were calibrated with $\frac{1}{8}$-inch marks.

With the Millington graduator, the metal square blank was clamped onto a bed that moved longitudinally via a rack and pinion. The square blank on the carriage was made to pass under a roller having sufficient pressure to make a full impression on one side of the blade. When the square passed out from under the roller, the lever was raised by a foot treadle and the square was removed from the machine. Another die was placed in the chase and the other side of the blade and the two sides of the

tongue were stamped in like manner. Because one complete side of the blade or tongue was done at one time in one pass, only four die sets were needed for the entire square.

In 1849, Jeremiah Essex, who owned a blacksmith shop in North Bennington, just a mile or so south of Shaftsbury, patented his Essex Board Measure, a set of tables that could be used to determine board feet, and he started graving this scale on his squares. In 1854, Essex became a partner in Eagle Square Co.

In 1852, Rufus Bangs who, like Essex, was making squares in North Bennington, invented the "Eccentric Rolls" machine which could taper square blanks. Before then, the taper had been made by drawing out the metal strips under a drop hammer. The eccentric rolls machine made a square that was thick at the angle (heel) and tapered toward each end, giving the square better balance than one made untapered.

It is necessary to heat steel to about 2200°F for forging. A natural consequence of heating is the formation of scale, a coating of oxides that must be removed. Bangs also invented a method for removing scale by using large grindstones, six feet in diameter. Another improvement in the manufacturing of the steel square during the period was a jointer that could finish and make parallel two edges of a square in one operation.

Other tool makers in the United States were just as busy. In 1840, Henry Disston in Philadelphia started a saw manufacturing plant that was destined to become the largest of its kind. In 1859, the predecessor of what now is the Stanley Works in New Britain, Connecticut, started a mill designed to cold-roll steel for the manufacture of butts and hinges, and lowered the cost of many items made for the hardware trade. Stanley started making try squares in 1857—four squares were available in eight sizes with nongraduated blades measuring from 3 inches to 18 inches long, with rosewood handles and brass trim. For many years after the 1860s, there was one area in which the Stanley Rule and Level Co. could not compete—in the manufacture of carpenter's squares. Stanley produced levels, miter squares, and try squares, but these were not the large framing squares, precisely cut and welded and inscribed with divisions and tables for computation of board measure and rafter length.

In 1857, Heman Whipple received two square patents—one for improvements in the graduating machine (U.S. Patent 16,857) and a second for an improved machine for stamping the figures on squares (U.S. Patent 16,817). In 1859, Dennis George, Norman Millington, Jeremiah Essex, Heman Whipple, and others formed a partnership as owners of Eagle Square Co., with capital assets of $17,000—this when wages were $1 per day for common laborers, $1.50 per day for carpenters and masons, and $2.50 per day for a teamster who brought his own horse and wagon. In 1860, they purchased large tracts of land and began a manufactured lumber department; the company name was changed to Eagle Square Manufacturing Co. Sixteen years later, in 1874, when it was incorporated in the state of Vermont, the company had a capital worth of $60,000, and not one of the original partners from 1859 was still

Figure 2-3. The Millington Graduator

The Millington Graduator, patented in 1849, automated the graduation of the carpenter's square, a tedious and inaccurate chore when done by hand.

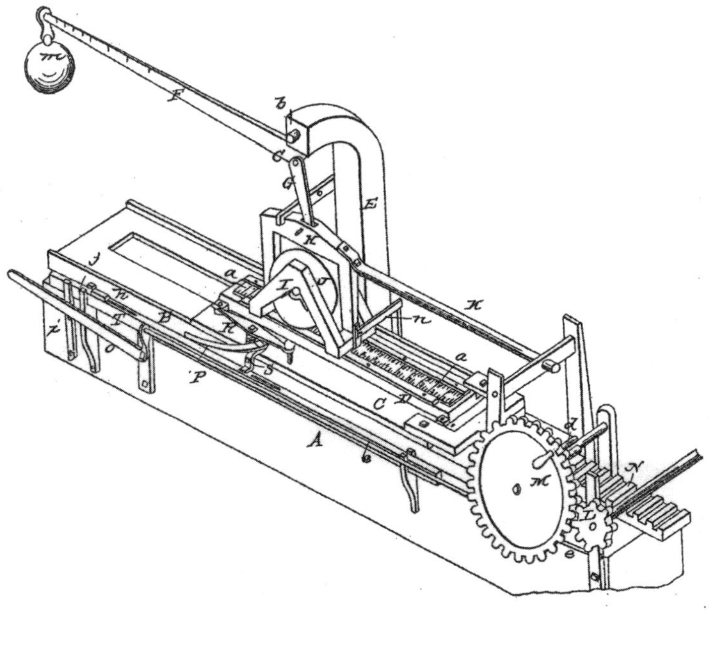

listed as a major stockholder.

Sears, Eagle, and Stanley

The 1897 Sears, Roebuck & Co. catalog ("Cheapest Supply House on Earth, Chicago") advertised "Carpenter's Squares—both body and tongue are tapered, the ends being thinner, which gives strength where it is needed, and makes the square lighter than it would otherwise be. We guarantee the squares to be equal to any made, and exactly as represented." The cheapest iron square (24-inch x 1½-inch body, 12-inch x 1-inch tongue, spaced in eighths on both sides) was 20¢. The more expensive, and warranted, steel square with 24-inch x 2-inch body, 16-inch x 1½-inch tongue with Essex new board measure, was 40¢. The same steel square with Essex and brace measure was 45¢, and the same square with Essex, brace, and 8-square octagon scale was 75¢. Sears was not yet selling a square with rafter framing scales.

In 1906, when Eagle Square could buy steel sheets in 24-inch widths, powerful machines were developed that could cut a blank from a sheet so welding was no longer necessary. Later in the twentieth century, when scientists better understood the properties of steel, squares again were welded at the heel so the grain of the metal ran the length of the tongue and of the blade. A square so constructed was more stable and the taper was more uniform. Also in 1906 the "take down" square was developed and patented by Henry Harris, a plant supervisor at Eagle. The take down square could be taken apart at the angle (heel) and carried in a tool box.

For almost 100 years, Eagle Square had practically the whole market. In the early 1900s, Eagle owned hundreds of acres of rock maple trees and had a prosperous side business supplying ready-cut lumber for building projects. Eagle passed through several hands, and in 1916, Stanley Rule and Level acquired a majority interest in the company. Stanley not only got the right to put its trademark on the finest framing square known, but also acquired Eagle's vast acreage and wood processing facilities.

It wasn't until Stanley acquired Eagle that they finally brought a carpenter's square to the product line. In 1937, the Eagle Square Manufacturing Co. facility in South Shaftsbury employed 100 people and was shipping 190,000 squares per year. The facility was closed in 1983, and operations were moved to Puerto Rico. Today, Stanley ships more than one million steel squares each year.

CHAPTER 3

A Close Look at the Steel Square

The framing square has a body (the wider part) and a tongue (the narrow blade), set at 90° to one another, but it's much more than just a 90° reference guide. When you're building a roof, a flight of stairs or any sloped structure, it can be used to lay out angles from 0° to 90°. However, to use it, you must learn a different kind of "angle language" than you learned in geometry class.

A roof angle is expressed as a slope (rise-over-run) instead of as degrees of a circle, so the angle is easy to lay out with the framing square. A carpenter will say that a building has a ⁵⁄₁₂ roof or a 5-in-12 slope, which means the roof rises 5 inches for every 12 inches of horizontal run. Although any combination of numbers can be used to express slope, it's convention to express angles in terms of a 12-inch horizontal run. That's why 12 always forms the denominator, or the lower half, of the fraction.

A right triangle is a figure having three (tri-) sides: base, altitude, and hypotenuse. The hypotenuse is the longest side of the triangle and is always opposite the right angle (**Figure 3-1a**). The speed square, or 45° framing square, is actually made in the form of a right triangle (see **Figure 3-1b**).

In diagram **Figure 3-2a**, note that because angle b is a right angle, the triangle is a "right triangle," or "right-angled triangle." The speed square, (**Figure 3-1b**), the framing square (**Figure 3-1c**), and all roof framing are based on the geometry of a right triangle.

Figure 3-1. Framing Squares Are Based on the Right Triangle

The steel square, (c), and the speed square, (b), are based on the right triangle, (a).

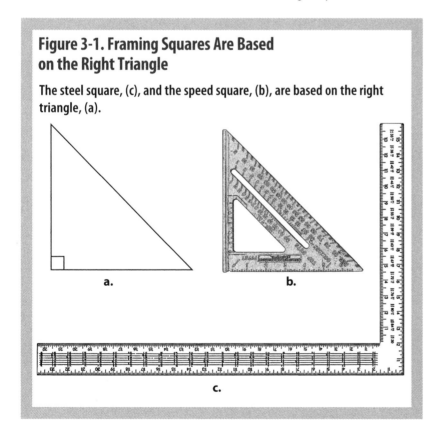

a.

b.

c.

Figure 3-2. Right Triangle

The right triangle (a) is the basis for calculations done with a speed square or a framing square. The calculations and estimates can be verified with an electronic calculator, (b).

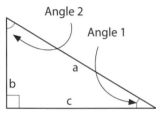

a.

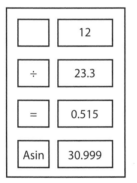

b.

Find Angle 1 when Side a = 23.32 and Side b = 12.

Sin = b ÷ a

Arcsin = 30.999° ≈ 31°

Right Triangle

A = area, a = hypotenuse,
b = height, c = base

Example: b = 12 inches,
c = 20 inches

Area

When any rectangle is cut in half by a diagonal, two right triangles are formed. The **area** of any triangle can be thought of as one-half of the area of the rectangle it was formed from.

Area Right Triangle:
A = ½ bc

Problem 3-1. Area of a Right Triangle

Find the area of a right triangle (see **Figure 3-2a**) where Side b = 12 and Side c = 20.

Solution 3-1
Area = ½ bc

A = ½ (12 x 20) = ½ (240)
= 120 square inches

Diagonal

The **diagonal** (hypotenuse) (see **Figure 3-2a**, **Side a**) can be found by using the Pythagorean Theorem:
Diagonal $a = \sqrt{(b^2 + c^2)}$

Problem 3-2. Length of Diagonal

Find the length of Diagonal a where Side b = 12 and Side c = 20 (see **Figure 3-2a**).

Solution 3-2
Diagonal $a = \sqrt{(b^2 + c^2)}$

$a = \sqrt{(12^2 + 20^2)}$
$a = \sqrt{(144 + 400)}$
$a = \sqrt{544} = 23.32$ inches

Length

Using the above equation, the **length** of any one side may be found if the other two sides are known (see **Figure 3-2a**).

$a = \sqrt{(b^2 + c^2)}$
$b = \sqrt{(a^2 - c^2)}$
$c = \sqrt{(a^2 - b^2)}$

Circumference

The **circumference** of a right triangle is the sum of the three sides.

Circumference = a + b + c

Problem 3-3. Circumference

Find the circumference of a triangle when the sides have lengths of 23.32, 12, and 20.

Solution 3-3
Circumference = a + b + c

Where a = 23.32, b = 12, and c = 20
C = 23.32 + 12 + 20 = 55.32 inches

Angle

To figure the **angles** of a right triangle, use the sine, tangent, or cosine formula.

Sin = opposite ÷ hypotenuse
Tan = opposite ÷ adjacent
Cos = adjacent ÷ hypotenuse

Problem 3-4. Angles on the Calculator

Use a calculator to find Angle 1 (see **Figure 3-2b**) when Hypotenuse a = 23.32, Side b = 12, and Side c = 20.

Solution 3-4
Sin Angle 1 = b ÷ a

Sin = 12 ÷ 23.3
Sin = 0.515
Arcsine 0.515 = 30.99 = 31°

Describing the Square

Most framing squares have a 16-inch or 18-inch tongue and a 24-inch body. The squares come as polished nickel plate, copper, galvanized steel, polished steel, or steel with a blued finish. The figures and marks are filled with red, white, or yellow enamel to make the etchings more readable. Squares made of aluminum and light-weight plastic are also available now.

Better squares are made from high-grade tool steel and are carefully tested for trueness and accuracy of marking. The squares are welded at the junction of tongue and body so the grain of the metal runs with the length of the tongue and body, instead of across the tongue as it would on a square cut from a single piece. The welded construction method makes a more durable square and also one that tapers more evenly.

The steel square consists of two parts: the body and the tongue or blade. Measurements are etched onto all eight edges of the square, as detailed below, and useful tables are etched on both the face and the back of the tool. (Use of each of the tables will be explained in later chapters of this book.) **Figure 3-3** shows the parts of the steel square:

1. Body

The body is the longer and wider part. On most squares, the body is 2 inches wide and 24 inches long.

2. Tongue or Blade

The tongue (or blade) is the shorter and narrower part, and usually is 18 inches long and 1½ inches wide.

3. Heel

The section where the body and tongue meet on the outside edge of the square is called the heel. If it becomes necessary to alter the square to make it a true 90°, the joint is the area of attention. (See Chapter 6, "Truing a Square.")

4. Face

The face of the square is the side with the manufacturer's stamp. The face is upright when holding the body in the left hand and the tongue in the right hand. (See **Figure 3-3**.)

5. Back

The back of the square is the side opposite of the face. (See **Figure 3-3**.)

6. Measurements

Measurements and graduations are found on the outer and inner edges of the square:

Face of body — outside edge: inches and sixteenths.

Face of body — inside edge: inches and sixteenths.

Face of tongue — outside edge: inches and sixteenths.

Face of tongue — inside edge: inches and eighths.

Back of body — outside edge: inches and twelfths.

Back of body — inside edge: inches and thirty-seconds.

Back of tongue — outside edge: inches and twelfths.

Back of tongue — inside edge: inches and tenths.

7. Hundredths Scale

The rafter table gives lengths in hundredths of an inch. The scale is used to convert the readings to fractions. It is located on the back of the tongue near the heel. The hundredth scale consists of one inch divided into 100 parts.

On some squares, directly below the hundredths scale, one inch is divided into sixteenths, which makes it easy to set dividers to hundredths and to transfer the measurement.

8. Rafter Table

The rafter table is found on the face of the body and is used to find the lengths of common, valley, hip, and jack rafters, and also the angles at which they must be cut to fit. The rafter table consists of six lines; their use is indicated to the left end of the table. The use of this scale is described fully in Chapter 11, "Laying Out the Rafters."

9. Octagon Table

The octagon scale or the "eight square" scale is found on the face of the tongue. Using these graduated marks, one can shape any square into an eight-sided figure (octagon), as for a pillar.

10. Brace Measure Table

The brace measure table is found on the back of the tongue. Mathematically, it is a series of numbers showing the length of the hypotenuse (brace) for certain right triangles. Practically, it is used to find the length of braces in post-and-beam construction.

11. Essex Board Feet Table

The essex board feet table is on the back of the body and is used to find the number of board feet in lumber of common lengths and widths.

Figure 3-3. Face and Back of Framing Square

There are four main tables—rafter length, octagon scale, Essex board feet, and brace length. Using the square, you can determine rafter lengths and cut angles, cut a square pole into an octagon, determine board feet, and find the length of a brace. The edges are divided into various increments, as shown.

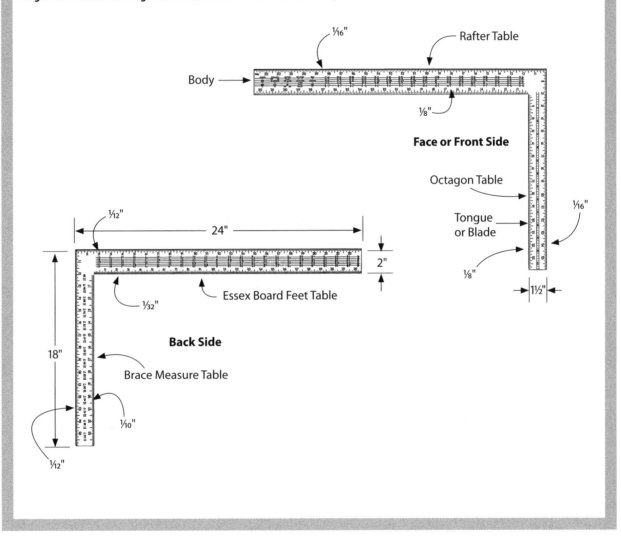

Chapter 4

Types of Squares

The five most popular squares today are the try square, the try-miter square, the combination square, the speed square, and the large framing square. The main functions of the three small squares are to make sure something is at 90° from some reference and to make marks on a board. They are mostly used by cabinetmakers, general woodworkers, and machinists. The speed square is useful as a saw guide and for house framing. The framing square has multiple uses: to determine angles, to set out the rise and run for stairs, and to determine rafter angles and lengths for house framing.

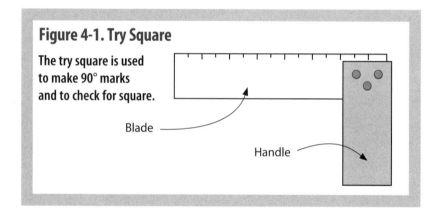

Figure 4-1. Try Square

The try square is used to make 90° marks and to check for square.

Blade

Handle

Try Square

The try square, (see **Figure 4-1**), is a fixed-blade tool used for checking and marking 90° angles. The blade is available in lengths ranging from 3 inches to 15 inches. The try square has two parts: the handle and the blade. The blade is made of tempered steel, and the handle or stock is made of a hardwood. A brass face is attached to the inside edge of the stock to ensure a straight edge and to resist wear.

The try square is made to the most exact tolerances of the five squares. Woodworkers use it to check whether the edge of a board is square with the face and to mark short lines across a narrow board.

To "try" a board edge for square, place the handle firmly along one surface, sliding the blade into contact with the board edge. If light shows between the blade and the board, the edge is untrue, that is, not 90° or square.

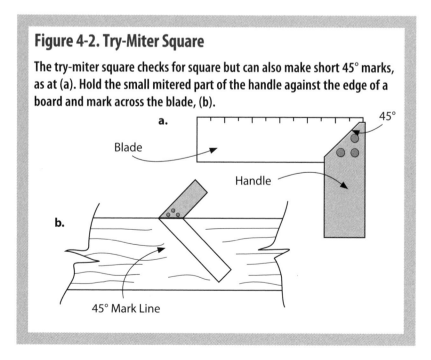

Figure 4-2. Try-Miter Square

The try-miter square checks for square but can also make short 45° marks, as at (a). Hold the small mitered part of the handle against the edge of a board and mark across the blade, (b).

a.

Blade

Handle

45°

b.

45° Mark Line

Figure 4-3. Combination Square

The combination square is used to set out 45° and 90° angles, check for level and plumb, and gauge depth. It is extremely useful in cabinetmaking and general woodworking.

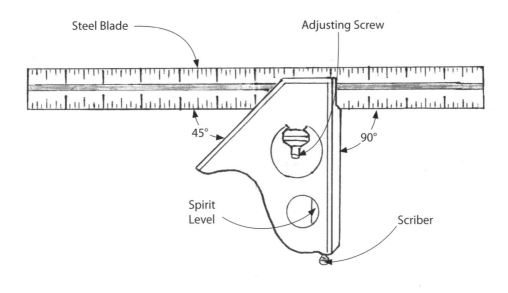

Figure 4-4. Combination Square with Three Heads

The centering head is used to find and mark centers. The protractor head rotates to any angle from 0° to 180°. The squaring head has both 90° and 45° faces.

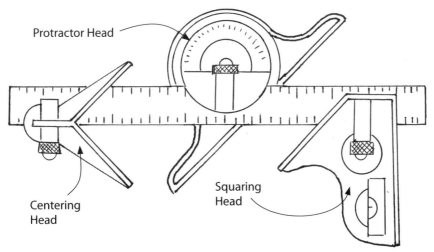

Figure 4-5. Using the Combination Square

The combination square can be used (a) for layout, (b) for gauging depth, (c) as a level, (d) for transferring duplicate measurements, (e) as a miter gauge, (f) as a height gauge, and (g) as a try square.

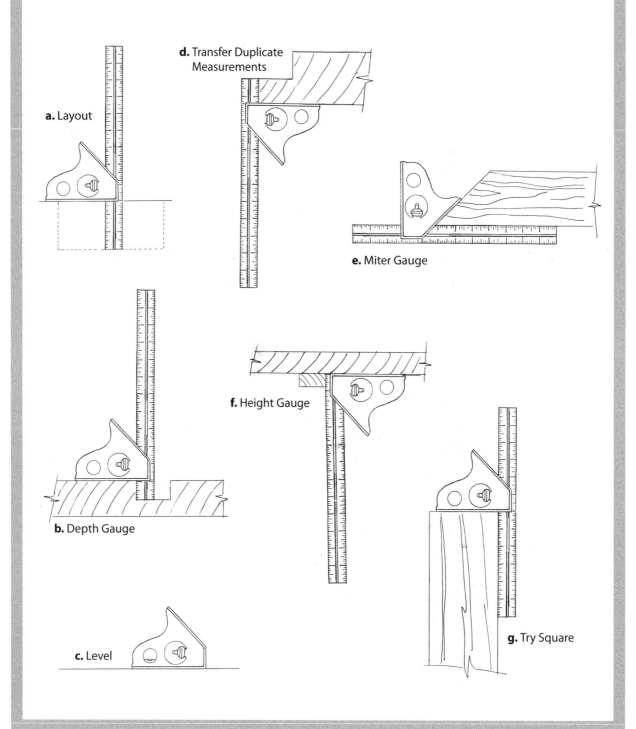

a. Layout

d. Transfer Duplicate Measurements

e. Miter Gauge

b. Depth Gauge

f. Height Gauge

c. Level

g. Try Square

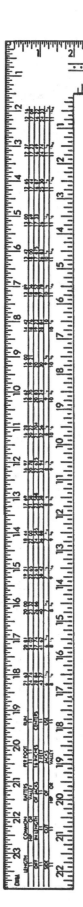

Figure 4-6. The Framing Square

The carpenter's framing square or rafter square can be used to calculate and to lay out. It is the most useful square for house construction.

Try-Miter Square

The try-miter square is a combination of a try square and a miter square. (See **Figure 4-2a**.) It has a 45° bevel cut into the handle, allowing the layout of both 90° and 45° angles. Because the bevel is short, the resulting line isn't accurate for more than a few inches. **Figure 4-2b** shows the try-miter square in use.

Combination Square

The combination square was invented in 1877 by Laroy Starrett. He was working as a pattern maker and disliked what he called the "clumsy, fixed-blade try square" in use at the time. After he patented his square, Starrett quit his job and began selling his combination square full-time. Today, L. S. Starrett Co. still makes squares and is well-known for its high quality.

The combination square (see **Figure 4-3**) differs from the fixed-blade type try square because 45/90 head is made to slide along a precision 12-inch steel rule. The reversible etched steel rule is graduated in eighths, sixteenths, thirty-seconds, and sixty-fourths. The head has a 90° face, a 45° miter face, a built-in bubble level, and a scriber. The accuracy of the adjustable square is due to the spring-loaded, adjustable tab in each head that engages a groove and runs the length of the blade. Starrett developed improvements over the years: a sliding centering head and a protractor head. (See **Figure 4-4**.) The three heads can be interchanged by sliding them on and off the rule.

Figure 4-5 shows some of the uses of the combination square. The detachable blade doubles as a ruler or straightedge.

Framing Square

The framing square, **Figure 4-6**, is the most versatile tool in a carpenter's box because it can be used both to calculate and to draw lines. The framing square is the best way to lay out rafters, compute board feet, figure out the bracing of post and beam construction, lay out eight-sided figures or other polygons, and to measure in tenths or hundredths of an inch.

Figure 4-7. Speed Square

The speed square with all the degrees and marks first appeared in the 1930s. It is used mainly as a saw guide and to mark rafters. While not as versatile as the framing square, it is considerably more convenient because of its small size and built-in fence.

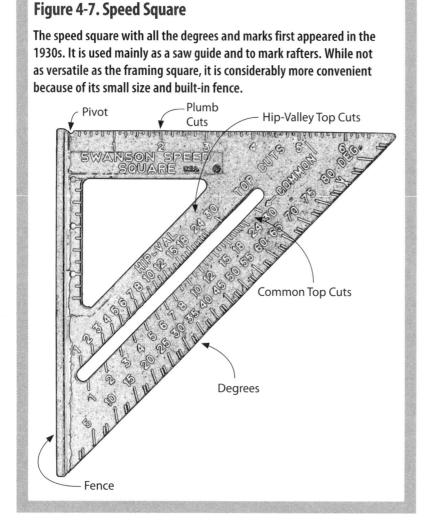

Framing squares scaled in centimeters are commonly used in Europe and Japan, but metric squares are rarely seen in the United States, where we are still firmly rooted in the feet–inches system.

Speed Square

Carpenters have been using triangular squares (see **Figure 4-7**) since Noah used his to design and build the ark. The three-sided square is strong—it's fairly easy to fasten three pieces of wood together—and it has a fence.

The modern speed square was designed specifically for laying out rafters and stairs. Its small size and the T-shaped fence allow a carpenter to work faster than one could with a regular framing square. The slope markings are easy to read, as are the angles. It can be used to mark common, hip, valley, and jack rafters, as well as simple angles and miters. A small book with slope tables must be used to find rafter lengths. The 12-inch version of the speed square also is very useful as a crosscut guide for the portable circular saw.

Chapter 5

Testing for Square

A square should be accurate, but just how accurate? Should a 24-inch framing square have the same accuracy as a small, metal machinist's square or a 4-inch try square? Probably not. How square is your square, and how square should it be?

The U.S. General Services Administration (GSA) requires try squares bought for government use must not have a run-out of more than 0.0010 inch per inch of blade length (or 0.0120 inch run-out per foot) on the inside edges. This last distinction is important—most try squares are designed to be used, and to be square, only on the inside edges. However, any good square I've ever tested was equally accurate, or inaccurate, inside and out. Maintaining accuracy only requires the manufacturer make the two edges of each blade parallel. Some manufacturers of try squares have a go-no-go gate set at 0.002 inches per 12 inches of blade length. (See **Figure 5-1**.)

Manufacturers of large steel framing squares shoot for an accuracy of 0.003 inches to 0.008 inches per foot along the arms, depending on the grade and price of the square. For general carpentry and house framing, either is sufficient. And so how do you check your square for accuracy? It is quite easy, and over the years, woodworkers have devised quite a few ways.

Figure 5-1. Square Tolerances

With a run-out of 0.0033 inches per foot, a 24-inch framing square would be off by 0.007 inch. This is a little more than the thickness of a sheet of paper or the width of a pencil line.

	Try Square Tolerance		Carpenter's Square Tolerance	
	Inches per Foot	Inches per Inch	Inches per Foot	Inches per Inch
Manufacturer	0.002	0.000	0.003	0.000
U.S. Govt. GSA	0.012	0.001	0.012	0.001

Figure 5-2. Check Using a Standard

Use a flat surface such as a jointer bed and a machinist's square. With a light source in the back, bring the two squares together. It is easy to see any deviation.

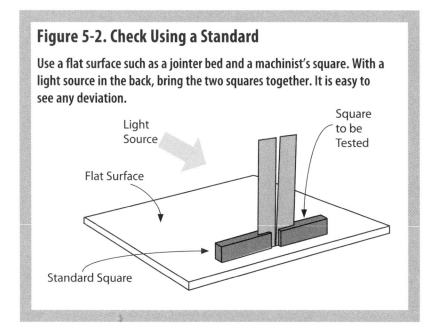

Figure 5-3. Checking a Steel Square for Accuracy

Hold the square against the straight edge of a piece of plywood and scribe a line with a sharp knife, as in Position 1. Reverse the square and scribe a second line, as in Position 2. The two lines will coincide if the square is dead-on. If the lines don't match, see Chapter 6, "Truing a Square."

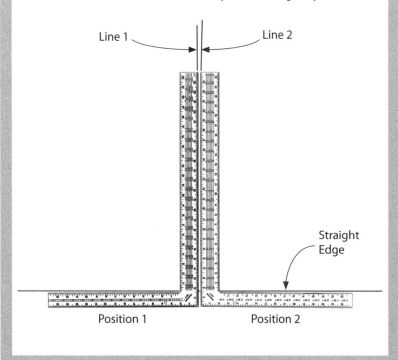

Check Against a Standard

To determine if a square is accurate, the suspect square is checked against a known standard. (See **Figure 5-2**.) This is the test square manufacturers use to ensure accuracy. It requires a flat surface, a 90° standard, and a light source. In the home shop, use a jointer bed, a table saw surface, or a piece of plate glass for the flat surface. The 90° standard can be a machinist's all-metal square or a 6-inch engineer's square—both are made to great precision and can be purchased for about $15.

With a light in the back, the suspect square is brought blade-to-blade against the standard square. As the blades converge, the light should be extinguished evenly and instantly from top to bottom. Measurements show the human eye can detect a difference as small as 0.0001 inch using this method. The method described only checks the outside edge of the square. Try square manufacturers shoot for a run-out of no more than 0.0002 inch per foot of blade length.

Use a Straight Edge

The diverging-line method requires only a sharp knife and a straight line such as the factory edge of a piece of plywood. Place the square on top of the plywood with the blade or tongue snug against the straight edge, with the length of the body extending away from you across the board. Use a sharp knife to score a line on the face of the board along the body. (See **Figure 5-3**, **Position 1**.) Now, turn the square so the blade points the opposite direction and again hold it tight against the board. (See **Figure 5-3**, **Position 2**.) Scribe another line along the body, trying to match the first line.

Compare the two lines. They should match exactly if the square is indeed square. If they don't match, decide whether the square needs to be closed or opened, and follow the directions in Chapter 6,

"Truing a Square." Remember, the difference between the two lines, if any, is double the true error in the square itself.

To check both inside and outside edges of the square, follow the same procedure but scribe two lines and label them "inside" and "outside."

Checking Two Squares

You can check two unknown squares against one another. Nest the two squares—first, A under B, and then B under A, as in **Figure 5-4a** and **Figure 5-4b**. If they meet precisely, you know the two squares are identical and they could be square, but they also could both be off in the same way.

Next, test the two squares back to back (see **Figure 5-4c**). By nesting the squares, you only prove they are identical. By comparing them back to back, you can be assured they are also square—or not.

Figure 5-4. Checking Two Squares

First, nest Square A under Square B, (a), and then Square B under Square A, (b). If they are identical, then check them back-to-back (c) to see if they are square.

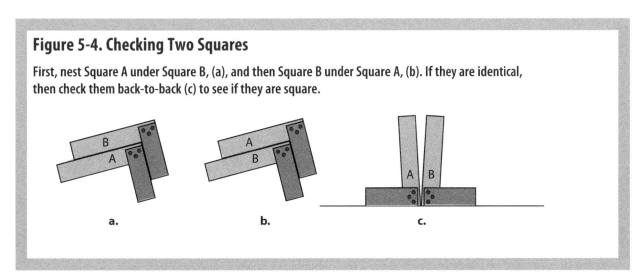

a.   b.   c.

Figure 5-5. Use a Mirror to Check for Accuracy

Stand a mirror up between two boards, and place the square on one board with the handle flat against the mirror, (a). Sight along the top edge of the blade into the mirror, (b). If the blade and the mirror image coincide, then the blade is at 90° with the mirror and also at 90° with the handle.

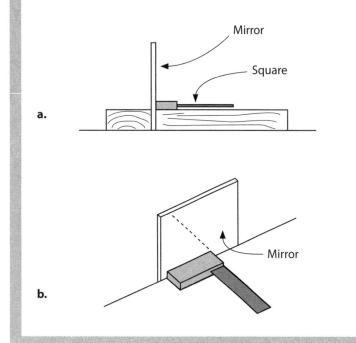

Use the Mirror Image

Another method of checking either a try square or a steel square for trueness is with a mirror. To check the square, lay it on a flat surface with the handle pointing either left or right and with the blade pointing toward you. Place a small mirror flat against the handle, and sight along the blade while also looking at the reflection of the blade in the mirror. (See **Figure 5-5**.) If the blade is set exactly 90° from the handle, the blade and its mirror image will form a straight line. If the line bends at the glass, the square is off.

Check a 45° Speed Square

To check a 45° speed square, first find a straight line such as the factory edge of a piece of plywood or the body of a large steel square. Use a drafting triangle purchased from an art supply store as the standard, and put small pieces of double-stick tape on its three corners. Place the 45° speed square with its fence against the straight edge and snuggle the drafting triangle up tight against it, as shown in **Figure 5-6**, **Position 1**. Fasten the drafting triangle to the board using the double-stick tape. Now flip the speed square over and slide it against the other side of the triangle, as shown in **Figure 5-6**, **Position 2**. Any difference between the square and the triangle is twice the actual error. The method described assumes the drafting triangle is true.

Rule of Thumb: Care of Squares

You should treat a good square as you would a precision instrument, because that's what it is if you learn to use it and take care of it. Never use it as a pry bar or as a hammer. After each use, wipe the square with an oily rag to keep it from rusting during storage.

If the numbers and lines become hard to read, clean the surface with paint thinner and then wash it with soap and water. Dry it well and then rub a little contrasting paint along the body and blade; use white or yellow on a black surface and black on a light-colored surface. Wipe off the excess with a rag, rubbing across the lines. Enough paint will stay in the embossed figures to make them easily readable again.

Figure 5-6. Checking a 45° Speed Square for Accuracy

Hold the speed square against the straight edge and bring the drafting triangle up against one edge (Position 1). Tape the drafting triangle down. Flip the miter square over (Position 2) and bring it snug against the other side of the drafting triangle. The edges should align exactly.

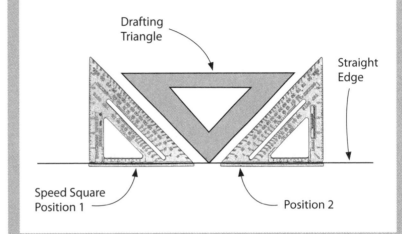

Drafting Triangle

Straight Edge

Speed Square Position 1

Position 2

CHAPTER 6

Truing a Square

A square should be true—the arms exactly at a 90° angle to each other and the edges of each arm parallel. If the square isn't true, throw it away and buy another, or, if it's only a little off, fix it. Some woodworkers have suggested truing a square to thousandths of an inch is ridiculous. We often read tape measures to only the nearest sixteenth inch, table saws and other shop tools aren't set up to cut to the nearest thousandth, and wood expands and contracts according to the relative humidity and temperature—sometimes ⅛ inch per foot. All this being true, it still makes sense for a woodworker to make his joints and cuts as accurate as he can, and a good square is the starting point.

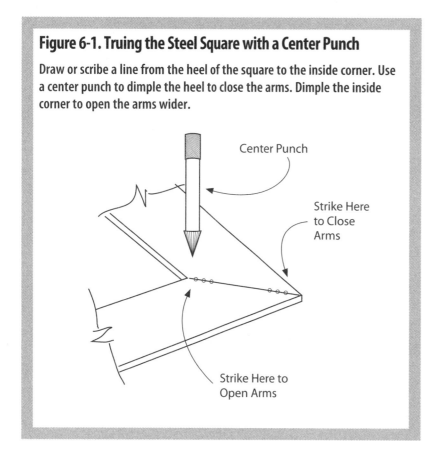

Figure 6-1. Truing the Steel Square with a Center Punch

Draw or scribe a line from the heel of the square to the inside corner. Use a center punch to dimple the heel to close the arms. Dimple the inside corner to open the arms wider.

Center Punch

Strike Here to Close Arms

Strike Here to Open Arms

After you've checked the square (see Chapter 5, "Testing for Square") and found the body and the blade need to be opened or closed, use the following methods.

Steel Squares

Truing steel squares involves expanding the metal at the heel to either open or close the arms. Making small dimples in the metal with a center punch causes the arms to move outward or inward depending on which correction needs to be made. The angle of the square is reduced when the dimples are on the outer part of the heel, and the angle is widened when the dimpling is on the inside of the heel.

Begin by lightly incising a straight line from the heel of the square to the inside corner. The line can be a light scratch with an awl or a line drawn with a pen. Do the dimpling on a hard surface such as an anvil or a steel vise.

If the square needs to be opened, that is, its angle is less than 90°, then the arms of the square will have to be moved further apart. Use the center punch and a hammer, and tap in a series of dimples on the 45° line near the inside corner of the square, as shown in **Figure 6-1**. Check progress frequently.

If the angle is more than 90°, move the body and the tongue closer together, that is, the arms of the square need to be closed. Use the center punch and tap at the outside corner of the 45° line.

During manufacture, if a square is slightly off, a quality control worker corrects it with a ball-peen hammer by tapping the face of the square either close to the outside corner or near the inside corner (see **Figure 6-2**). Both corrections are done on the blade instead of on the body. Work carefully and check progress often if the ball-peen hammer method is used.

Machinist's Square

A machinist's all-metal square can be corrected, but it should come from the factory at a perfect 90°. Machinist's squares are purchased because the user wants perfection and needs at least one tool that's dead-on accurate. If it isn't, send it back. Manufacturers shoot for a run-out of less than 0.0002 inches per inch of blade length on the square.

Figure 6-2. Truing the Steel Square with a Hammer

Lay the square on a flat, metal surface and strike near the inside corner of the blade to open the arms. Hammer near the heel of the blade to move the tongue in.

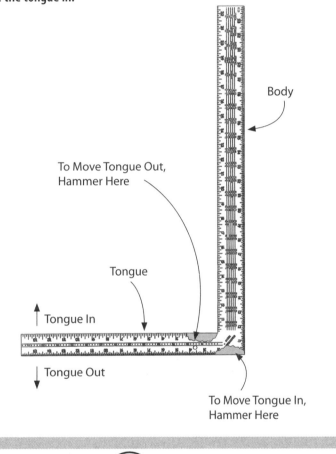

Body

To Move Tongue Out, Hammer Here

Tongue

Tongue In

Tongue Out

To Move Tongue In, Hammer Here

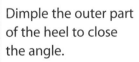

Rule of Thumb

Dimple the outer part of the heel to close the angle.

Dimple the inner part of the heel to open the angle.

Try Square

Wood-handled try squares cannot be opened or closed by dimpling like steel squares. If you find yours off by just a hair, you can true it by carefully removing small amounts of material from the handle. Leave the blade alone—it's important the two edges of the blade remain parallel. Start by determining whether you're going to correct toe-out, that is, the square reads more than 90°, or toe-in, it reads less than 90°. Note the methods in **Figure 6-3** only fix the outside of the square—it's almost impossible to fix the inside angle.

Figure 6-3a shows the area of the wooden handle to sand to make the outside angle larger. To make the outside angle smaller, sand the end of the wooden handle. (See **Figure 6-3b**.)

Use a black marking pen to blacken a 2-inch spot on the area to be sanded. Hold the square firmly on 120-grit sandpaper glued to a flat surface. Rub the square across the sandpaper, putting pressure on the area to be sanded. (See **Figure 6-4a**.)

Another method of truing a try square is by holding the blade in the wooden jaws of a workbench vise so the outside surface of the handle is facing up. (See **Figure 6-4b**.) Use 120-grit sandpaper wrapped around a flat surface (I've used a 1-inch wood chisel) and carefully remove material from the proper handle area. The ink should help you remove material flat to the surface while keeping the handle edge square. Test often using a machinist's square—it shouldn't take much.

Speed Square

The speed square is used primarily as a rough saw guide and to mark rafter angles. Neither job requires great precision. If you do decide to true an errant speed square, you can easily remove material from either the long edge or the short 90° edge. Leave the fence side alone.

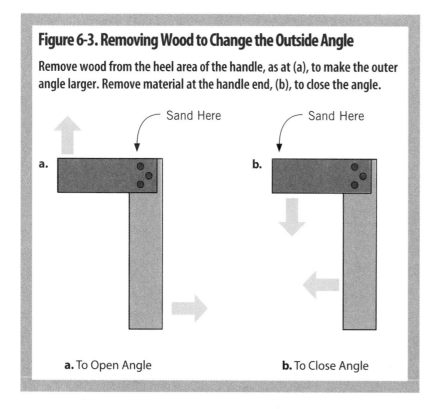

Figure 6-3. Removing Wood to Change the Outside Angle

Remove wood from the heel area of the handle, as at (a), to make the outer angle larger. Remove material at the handle end, (b), to close the angle.

Sand Here

Sand Here

a.

b.

a. To Open Angle

b. To Close Angle

Figure 6-4. Truing a Try Square

If the try square is just a little off, the outside edges can be trued by removing material from the handle. In (a), put pressure at area 1 and sand lightly if toe-in is the problem. Put pressure at area 2 to make the angle smaller. In (b), the square is held in a wood vise and sanded to make it true.

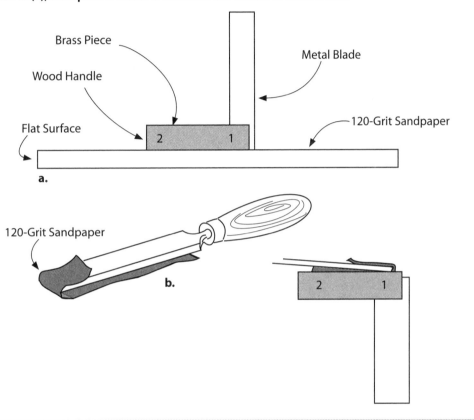

Brass Piece

Wood Handle

Metal Blade

Flat Surface

120-Grit Sandpaper

a.

120-Grit Sandpaper

b.

CHAPTER 7
Problem-Solving Techniques

In the middle of the nineteenth century, when the modern steel square was first introduced, carpenters and other building tradesmen soon realized the steel square is actually a right triangle and could be used to find angles and degrees. Similar right triangles bear a direct relationship to one another, thus the square could be used to multiply, divide, and do proportions. In short, it could help solve complicated math problems on the job.

Figure 7-1. Right Triangle

The steel square represents a right triangle. Different-sized triangles with equal angles are said to be similar, and their sides are proportional to one another.

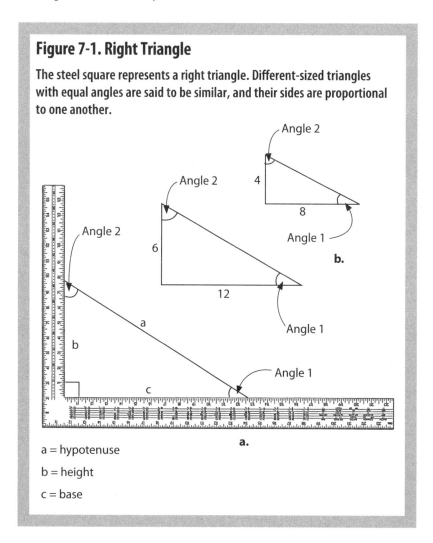

a = hypotenuse
b = height
c = base

Carpenters soon were using the square to mark degrees and bisect angles. Sheet metal workers used the square to find the size of the junction when two pipes converged. At the lumber yard, a buyer knew how to figure the price of a load of lumber using only his steel square, and a mason could use his square to lay out an elliptical arch.

By the early 1900s, the steel square was the one tool all trade craftsmen had to have, and its intricacies were carefully nurtured and then carefully passed on. A carpenter taught his apprentice how to find the rise and run of a flight of stairs. A sheet metal man taught his son how to cut a raised conical cover to cap a round pipe. Both projects were accomplished using just the steel square. Today, most of these secrets have been lost, except to you. Once you understand the steel square and the basic techniques for using it, these secrets will be yours and you can pass them along, too.

The Right Triangle

As discussed in Chapter 3, "A Close Look at the Steel Square," the steel square represents a right triangle. The two arms, the base and the altitude, make an angle of 90°. The hypotenuse, or diagonal, is measured. (See **Figure 7-1a**.)

It's a fundamental geometric law that any right triangle bears a direct proportional relationship to other similar right triangles. **Figure 7-1b** shows two right triangles where the small angles are equal, as are the large angles. Mathematically we say they are "similar triangles." The smaller triangle has base = 8 and height = 4. The larger but similar triangle has base = 12 and height = 6. The triangles have the following relationship:

Four is to eight as six is to twelve.

$$4 : 8 = 6 : 12$$

Mathematically this is the same as:

$$4 \div 8 = 6 \div 12, \text{ or } 4 \times 12 = 8 \times 6$$

By knowing any three values, we can find the fourth value:

$$4 \times 12 = 8 \times X$$
$$X = (4 \times 12) \div 8 = 48 \div 8 = 6$$

Problem 7-1. Ratio and Proportion

Four boards cost $8. What is the cost of six boards?

Solution 7-1

As in **Figure 7-1**, 4 is to 8 as 6 is to X

$$X = (8 \times 6) \div 4 = 12$$

Thus six boards will cost $12.

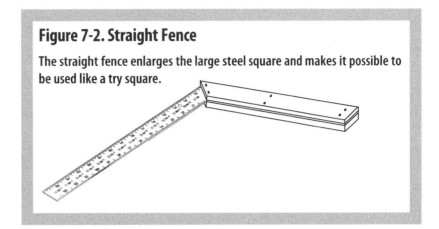

Figure 7-2. Straight Fence

The straight fence enlarges the large steel square and makes it possible to be used like a try square.

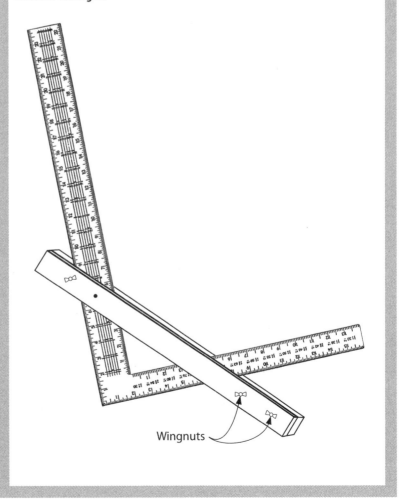

Figure 7-3. Adjustable Fence

The adjustable fence is useful for repetitive marking, such as when laying out stair carriages.

Wingnuts

The relationship between two similar triangles can be used to solve many problems with the steel square.

Fences for the Steel Square

Many of the problems in this book, like the ones encountered on the job site and in the workshop, will be easier to solve if you make a fence for the steel square. Three useful fences are detailed below.

Straight Fence

A carpenter's square is frequently needed just because of its size. The key drawback of such a square is its lack of a supporting fence or ledge. (See **Figure 7-2**.) An aftermarket or shop-made fence can be attached to either the body or the blade. The fence extends the square for use on big jobs, and also makes it easier to use the square for right-angled lines.

Adjustable Fence

The adjustable fence (see **Figure 7-3**) can be set as the hypotenuse of a right triangle, allowing you to hold the square in a fixed position on a board and to draw an angled line. It does the same job as a set of stair gauges (see **Figure 7-8**) and makes repetitive work for stair stringers and rafters a snap.

Fence with Adjustable Arm

The framing square is often used to find proportions. Once the adjustable-arm fence shown in **Figure 7-4** has been set, it can be moved along the body of the square, similar triangles of different sizes may be drawn or measured, and proportional data can be read easily. The adjustable arm represents the hypotenuse of a right triangle. The fence is very useful for calculations involving proportions and worth the trouble to make well.

Figure 7-4. Adjustable-Arm Fence

The adjustable-arm fence is used to make calculations using proportions.

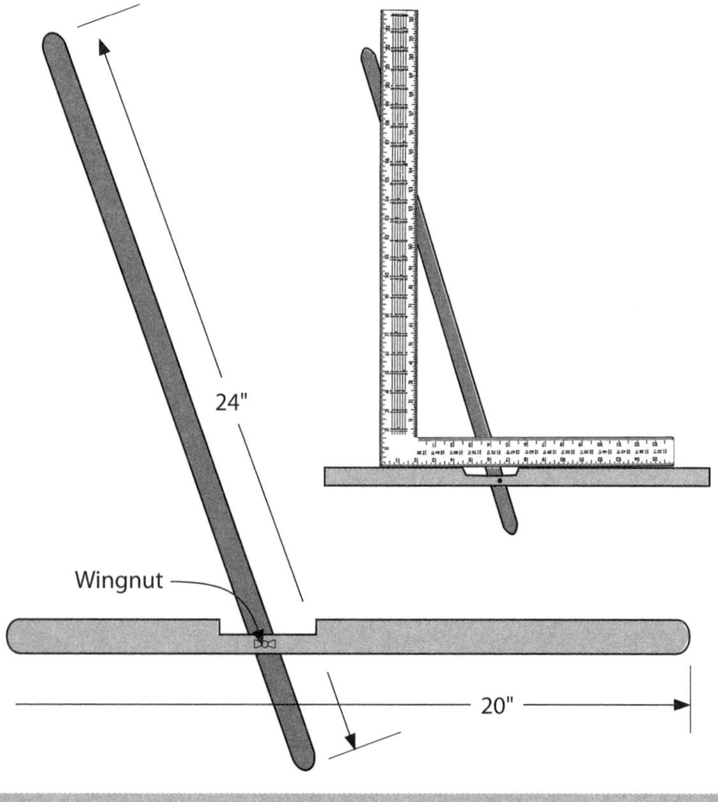

24"

Wingnut

20"

Using the Adjustable Arm

Instead of drawing triangles as in **Figure 7-1** or doing multiplication and division, carpenters use the adjustable-arm fence to make calculations. **Figure 7-5** shows the adjustable-arm fence in use. The key to this is sliding the fence along the blade or body of the square, without changing the angle of the adjustable arm—in effect, maintaining similarity between the triangles formed in **Position 1** and **Position 2**.

Problem 7-2. Pulley Sizes and Speed

On a given motor, the speed of a pulley is proportional to its diameter. With a 4½-inch pulley, the lathe speed is 850 rpm. What speed will we get with a 7-inch pulley?

Solution 7-2

The problem is a typical one involving proportions or ratios, where three values are known and the fourth is unknown. Set the arm (see **Figure 7-5**) to the initial ratio 4½ (pulley size) and 8½ (lathe speed of 850 rpm). Slide the adjustable-arm fence to 7 (new pulley size) and read 13¼. The new speed will be 1325 rpm.

Math

$$7 \times 850 = 4.5X$$
$$X = (7 \times 850) \div 4.5 = 1322$$

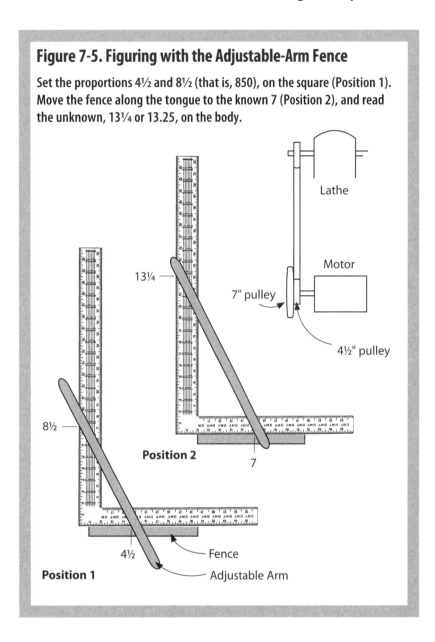

Figure 7-5. Figuring with the Adjustable-Arm Fence

Set the proportions 4½ and 8½ (that is, 850), on the square (Position 1). Move the fence along the tongue to the known 7 (Position 2), and read the unknown, 13¼ or 13.25, on the body.

Why It Works

We are using the steel square to construct two similar triangles (**Position 1** and **Position 2**) and then using the ratio of one triangle (4.5 is to 8.5) to locate a new pulley size (7) on the second similar triangle and find the unknown value (1325).

Figure 7-6. Figuring Area of Square and Circle

To compare the area of a circle and a square, set the known ratio along the edge of a board, and draw a proportioning line. Then slide the square along the proportioning line to find the new ratio.

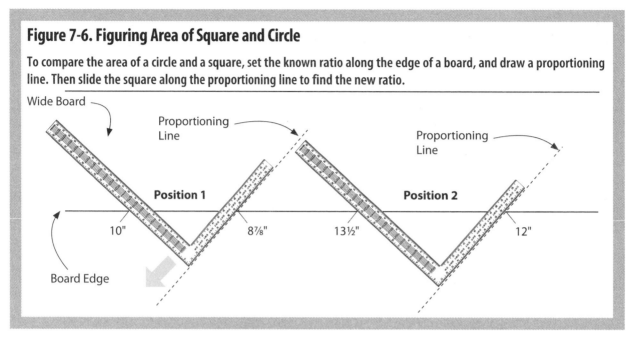

Using the Proportioning Line

Some carpenters prefer to use the edge of a wide board and a proportioning line to do their figuring. In **Figure 7-6**, a proportioning line is drawn on the board to record a special ratio, and then the square is slid along the proportioning line to find a similar ratio. The proportioning line functions the same as the adjustable-arm fence.

Problem 7-3. Comparing Circles and Squares

The goal is to join a round heating pipe to a 12-inch square duct. The area of the round pipe and the area of the square duct should be the same. What diameter should the pipe be?

Solution 7-3

Set the square on a wide board with a straight edge. (See **Figure 7-6**.) Align the square, as shown in **Position 1**, with the ratio 1:0.885 (or 10 and 8⅞) on the edge of the board. Draw a line along the blade of the square and extend it to create a "proportioning line." Slide the blade along the proportioning line until the 12 is on the board edge. Read 13½ on the body. Thus, a round pipe with a diameter of 13½ inches, or radius of 6.75 inches, equals the area of a 12-inch-by-12-inch square.

Math

The area of the square is:

$$12 \times 12 = 144 \text{ square inches}$$

The radius of the round duct is $13.5 \div 2 = 6.75$ inches. Its area is:

$$\pi r^2 = 3.14(13.5/2)^2$$

$$\pi r^2 = 3.14 \times 45.6$$
$$= 143.2 \approx 144 \text{ square inches}$$

Why It Works

In **Position 1,** 10 and 8⅞ were set as the ratio (actually 10 and 8.86) between the diameter of a circle and the side of a square when the areas are equal. The ratio was used in **Position 2** to find the required data.

Using the Diagonal

As discussed in Chapter 3 "A Close Look at the Steel Square," in any right triangle the square of the long side equals the sum of the squares of the other two sides. The relationship allows you to use the lengths of the sides to combine two smaller areas into one larger area, by finding the two smaller lengths on the arms of the square and measuring the diagonal distance (hypotenuse) between them. The maneuver is especially useful when you are joining two pipes or ducts in a Y shape, such as in forced-air heating systems and workshop dust-collection systems.

Problem 7-4. Combining Two Circles

Furnace ducting is being installed and a 6-inch-diameter round pipe must be joined with a 9-inch-diameter round pipe. The area of the common duct should equal the sum of the areas of the two smaller pipes. What size should the common duct be?

Solution 7-4

Use the steel square as in **Figure** 7-7. Place the diameter of one pipe (9 inches) on the body, and the diameter of the other pipe (6 inches) on the tongue. Measure the diagonal to find the diameter of the combined area, in this case 10¾ inches.

Math

Area of 6-inch circular duct:

$$Ac = \pi r^2 = 3.14 \times 3^2 = 3.14 \times 9$$
$$= 28.26 \text{ square inches}$$

Area of 9-inch circular duct:

$$Ac = \pi r^2 = 3.14 \times 4.5^2 = 3.14 \times 20.25$$
$$= 63.58 \text{ square inches}$$

Combined area:

$$\text{Area} = 28.26 + 63.58$$
$$= 91.85 \text{ square inches}$$

Area of 10¾-inch circular duct:

$$Ac = \pi r^2 = 3.14 \times 5.38^2$$
$$= 3.14 \times 28.9 = 90.75 \text{ square inches}$$

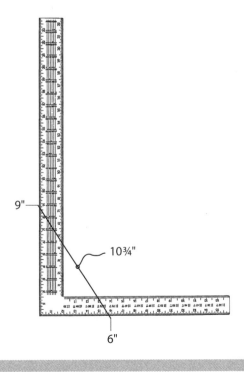

Figure 7-7. Combining Two Circles

The diameter of pipe 1 is marked on one arm (9 inches) and the diameter of pipe 2 (6 inches) on the other. The length of the diagonal (10¾ inches) is the diameter of the combined area.

9"

10¾"

6"

Square Attachments

In addition to shop-made fences, manufactured gauge sets and bubble levels can be useful add-ons to a steel square.

Gauge Set

A gauge set is a pair of small metal stops that clamp onto a square to make repetitive angle marking easy. (See **Figure 7-8**.) The stops are useful for laying out different rises and runs on stair stringers, roof framing, rafter angles, and other challenging cuts. They are about 1-inch high by ¾-inch wide with brass knobs. They are available at most home centers

Figure 7-8. Steel Square Gauges

Metal gauges, often called "stops," are fastened to the edges of the square as an assist for making repetitive marks. The stops are usually made of brass and the knurled knobs are tightened by hand.

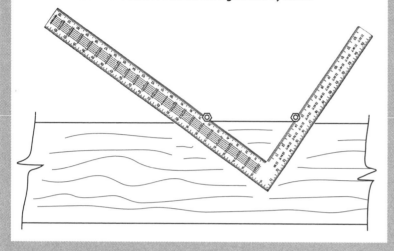

Figure 7-9. Bubble Levels

Levels can be attached to the steel square with magnets, as at (a), or by drilling and tapping holes for screws, (b).

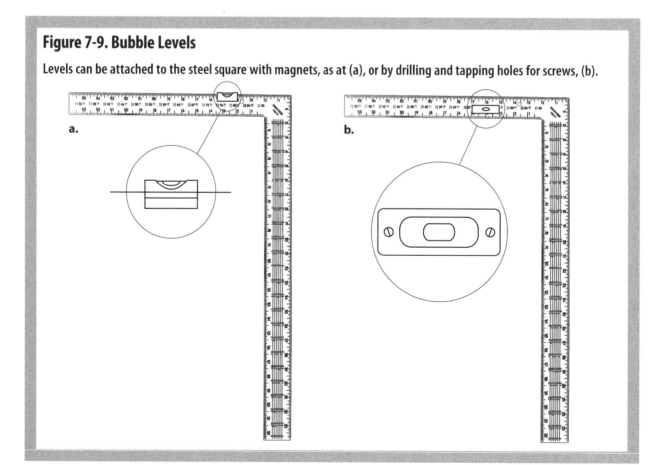

a.

b.

and come one pair to a package. In use, the gauge set is exactly the same as the adjustable fence shown in **Figure 7-3**.

Levels

Bubble levels can be purchased and attached to the blade or the body of the square with screws or magnets, as shown in **Figure 7-9a**. The levels are available from numerous suppliers and in the tools aisles of serious hardware stores and home centers.

(Years ago, I watched an old-timer use a framing square to check for plumb and level. He had drilled and tapped small screw holes in his steel square so he could attach small bubble levels, both vertically and horizontally. (See **Figure 7-9b**.) It seemed to do no harm to the square, and he found it very handy.)

A Makeshift Level

In the absence of a true bubble level, a serviceable level can be constructed with an ordinary steel square, a plumb bob, and a notched stake, as follows:

1. Take a sharpened stake and cut a notch in the top.

2. Drive the stake into the ground.

3. Place a steel square in the notch (see **Figure 7-10**).

4. Adjust the body of the square until its tongue is vertical according to the plumb bob. This means its body is level.

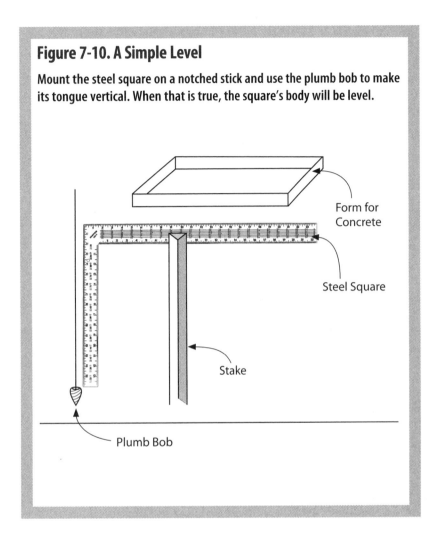

Figure 7-10. A Simple Level

Mount the steel square on a notched stick and use the plumb bob to make its tongue vertical. When that is true, the square's body will be level.

Form for Concrete

Steel Square

Stake

Plumb Bob

5. Once this makeshift device is level, any object sighted over the body of the square will also be level.

6. In an emergency, a stone and a piece of string will be adequate for the plumb bob.

Construct a Protractor

When framing a house, some carpenters prefer to use unit rise reckoned in degrees instead of slope (rise in inches per foot of run). The rules for cutting rafter angles (see Chapter 11, "Laying Out the Rafters") remain the same, but degree framing requires trigonometric formulas or a large protractor to determine the rise.

A large protractor is also useful in furniture and cabinet making, drywall work, sheet-metal work, and fabric layout. Here is how to construct such a protractor.

1. Lay out 90° with the steel square in **Position 1** of **Figure 7-11** and extend the tongue line.

2. Flip the square to **Position 2**.

3. Mark 23 inches on the body line.

4. Mark 23 inches on the tongue line and draw an arc.

5. Set trammels or dividers to 4 inches and step around the arc to set out 10° divisions.

6. Set dividers to ¼ inch to subdivide the 10° divisions into degrees.

Why It Works

Set the diameter of the circle at 46 inches.

$$\text{Circumference} = \pi\, d$$

$$C = 3.14 \times 46 = 144.44 \text{ inches}$$

There are 360° in a circle and there are 36 ten-degree sections in a circle.

$$144.44 \div 36 = 4.01$$

That means 4 inches = 10° around the circumference.

Figure 7-11. Construct a Protractor

Draw a quarter circle with a 23-inch radius. With trammels or dividers set at 4 inches, step around the circle to set out 10° divisions, then re-set the dividers to ¼ inch to mark single degrees.

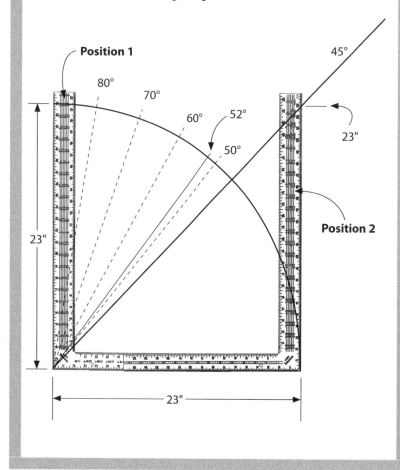

Chapter 8: Using the Scales on a Square

CHAPTER 8
Using the Scales on a Square

The scales and marks on the modern framing square all originated in the United States. The squares that came over on the Mayflower in 1640 were simple and often crude affairs like those used by masons and carpenters for thousands of years. Most were made of wood; some were all metal but again they were pretty basic, the arms being riveted or hammer-welded together by the town blacksmith. A few squares had inch and fraction marks added by the carpenter—a few marks suitable for his craft.

Then in 1817 Silas Hawes of southern Vermont, a blacksmith and inventor, started making precision squares that were a standard size and incised with inch and fractional-inch marks. Hawes received a patent in 1819 for an improved square, all steel and tapered in thickness from the heel toward each end. The patent probably also covered the **Essex scale** for figuring board feet and the **brace scale** to find the diagonal length of braces. (See Chapter 2, "History of the Steel Square" for more.)

Other blacksmiths in the area joined with Hawes and formed Eagle Square Company. They added refinements like the **octagon scale** for turning square timbers into eight-sided pieces, and the **hundredths scale** for converting decimals to fractions. During the next 50 years, Eagle Square Co. dominated the industry with their patented scales and tables, which became indispensable to the craftsman. They also became extremely efficient in making squares, first by installing a water powered drop hammer to forge the metal arms together under great pressure, then by introducing inventions such as grinders to remove oxides and scale, automatic rollers to taper the arms, jointers to make the edges parallel, and a graduating machine to incise nearly 200 marks at a time. Thus, a small area of southern Vermont became the steel square capital of the world.

Essex Board Feet Measure

A series of figures known as the **Essex Board Measure** appears on the back of the blade of the framing square (see **Figure 8-1**). The inch graduations on the outer edge are used in combination with the values along the incised parallel lines to provide a means for the rapid calculation of board feet, the unit of measure for lumber.

A board foot is defined as a volume of lumber equal to 1 inch in thickness

Figure 8-1. The Essex Scale

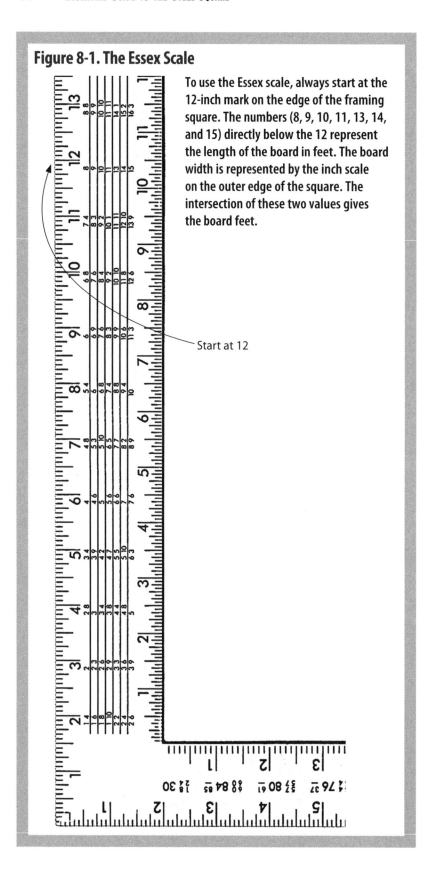

To use the Essex scale, always start at the 12-inch mark on the edge of the framing square. The numbers (8, 9, 10, 11, 13, 14, and 15) directly below the 12 represent the length of the board in feet. The board width is represented by the inch scale on the outer edge of the square. The intersection of these two values gives the board feet.

Start at 12

by 12 inches in width by 1 foot in length, that is, 1 inch x 12 inches x 12 inches. Calculating board feet requires all three dimensions– thickness, width, and length. When using the Essex scale, it is assumed the board is 1-inch thick (one dimension). Enter the scale at the 12 mark and the numbers directly below (8, 9, 10, 11, 13, 14 and 15) are the board length in feet (the second dimension). To find board feet, you now need only the board width in inches (the third dimension), which is found by moving left or right along the appropriate row to the width column represented by the inch numbers on the edge of the square's blade. The results are in board feet and twelfths.

Example

Find the board feet (Bf) in a plank that is 1-inch-thick, 10-feet-long, and 4-inches-wide.

Under the 12 on **Figure 8-1,** find 10 (10-feet-long) and follow the row left to the 4-inch mark (4-inches-wide) and read 3|4, which is interpreted as 3⁴⁄₁₂ Bf or 3⅓ Bf.

Problem 8-1. Finding Board Feet

Find the board feet in a 1-inch board that is 8 feet long and 4 inches wide.

Solution 8-1

1. Start at the 12-inch mark on the edge of the square.

2. Drop down to 8 on the Essex scale, which represents an eight-foot length.

3. Follow the row to the left until the 4-inch mark (4-inch-width) on the outer edge of the square is reached.

4. Read 2|8, which translates to 2 and $^8/_{12}$ board feet or $2^2/_3$ Bf.

Problem 8-2. Board Feet in Thick Plank

Find the number of board feet in a plank 2 inches thick, 10 feet long, and 5 inches wide.

Solution 8-2

Because the Essex scale assumes all boards are 1 inch thick, find the board feet in a 1-inch board, then double it.

1. Start at the 12-inch mark on the outside edge of the square.

2. Drop down to the 10-feet row on the Essex scale.

3. Follow along the horizontal line to the left until you come to the column of figures under the 5-inch mark (5-inches-wide) at the edge of the blade.

4. Read 4|2, that is, a 1-inch board has $4^2/_{12}$ Bf.

5. A 2-inch board will have double $4^2/_{12}$ Bf.

$2 \times 4^1/_6 = 8^2/_6 = 8.33$ Bf.

Math Proof 8-2

$Bf = (T \times W \times L) \div 144$

Note: All dimensions are in inches.

Where T = 2, W = 5 and L = 120

$Bf = (2 \times 5 \times 120) \div 144$

$Bf = 1200 \div 144 = 8.33$

Problem 8-3. Board Feet in Long Plank

Find the number of board feet in a board 1-inch-thick, 9-inches-wide, and 22-feet-long.

Solution 8-3

To find the board feet of a piece of lumber longer than 15 feet, find the board feet in two or more shorter lengths. Doubling the length of the lumber doubles the number of board feet. So, because the board is 22-feet-long, find the number of board feet in an 11-foot board and double the result.

1. Under the 12-inch mark, find the number 11 in the fourth row down.

2. Follow along to the left to 9 on the edge of the square's blade.

3. Read 8|3.

4. Thus an 11-foot board has $8^3/_{12}$ Bf, which is one-half of the board feet in the 22-foot board:

$2 \times 8^3/_{12} = 16^6/_{12} = 16^1/_2$ Bf.

Rule of Thumb: Fractional Board Length

For fractions of a foot in length, change the fraction to the nearest whole number and find the board feet. Almost always, this will be close enough.

Rule of Thumb: Fractional Board Width

To find Bf for fractional board width, use averages.

What is the Bf for a 1-inch x 6½-inch board that is 10 feet long?

Under the 12, read left in the third row (10-feet-long) to the 6 (6-inches-wide) and read 5 Bf. Next to the 6 under the 7 (7-inches-wide) read $5^{10}/_{12}$ Bf. The average is $5^5/_{12}$ Bf or 5.42 Bf.

Rule of Thumb: Brace Miter

To cut a wooden 2x4 at 45°, scribe a square line across the width of the board. Transfer the line down the thickness of the board. Measure along the bottom edge to a distance equal to the thickness (1½ inches) and make a mark. Draw a line from the mark back to the starting point.

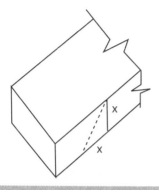

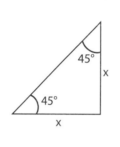

Brace Measure

The brace measure scale (see **Figure 8-2**) is located along the center of the back of the square's tongue. The brace scale gives the diagonal length of a brace for different rises and runs. The process is the same as finding the hypotenuse (brace length) of a right-angled triangle whose sides (the rise and run) are known. (See **Figure 8-3**.) In all sets except one (the rightmost on the square tongue), the long points of the brace will be cut at 45° because the rise and run are equal. The measurement given by the brace scale is from the long points of the miters. The brace will fit between legs that measure 24, 27, 30, 33, 36, 39, 42, 45, 48, 51, 54, 57, or 60 inches.

Figure 8-2. Brace Scale

The brace scale gives the length of diagonal braces, between 24-and 60-inches-long for various lengths of rise and run in post-and-beam construction. In the example, a run of 36 inches and a rise of 36 inches give a brace length of 50.91 inches.

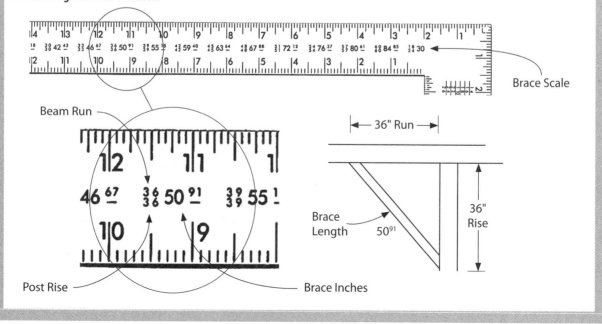

Problem 8-4. Brace Length

Find the length of a brace when both the rise and run are 48 inches.

Solution 8-4

1. Find the brace figures 48, 48, and 67.88, following the method shown in **Figure 8-2**.

2. Interpret the figures to mean a post with a rise of 48 inches and a beam with a run of 48 inches will need a brace 67.88-inches-long.

$0.88 \times 16 = 14.08/16 = 14/16$
$= \frac{7}{8}$ inches

$67.88 = 67\frac{7}{8}$ inches

3. Because the rise and run are the same, cut the end miters at 45°.

The only set of figures on the brace scale that is not at 45° is 18, 24, and 30, the rightmost set nearest the square's heel, which means that when the run is 18 inches and the rise is 24 inches (or the other way around), the length of the brace is 30 inches. Note the end cuts will not be 45°.

Problem 8-5. Brace Length

What is the diagonal (brace length) when the post length and the beam length are 27¾ inches?

Solution 8-5

$1.414 \times 27.75 = 39.24 \approx 39\frac{1}{4}$ inches

Problem 8-6. Brace Length

What is the length of a brace that has a rise of 31½ inches and a run also of 31½ inches?

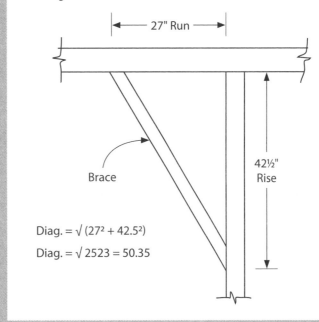

Figure 8-3. Figuring Brace Length

If the rise and the run are not equal, use the Pythagorean Theorem to find the diagonal length. With a run of 27 inches and a rise of 42½ inches, the brace length is 50.35 inches.

27" Run

42½" Rise

Brace

Diag. $= \sqrt{(27^2 + 42.5^2)}$
Diag. $= \sqrt{2523} = 50.35$

Solution 8-6

The rise and run are not given on the square. To find the brace for 31½ inches, find 30 inches and 33 inches and take the average.

1. A 30-inch rise and 30-inch run give a brace length of 42.43 inches.

2. A rise of 33 inches and run of 33 inches show a length of 46.67 inches.

3. The length 31½ inches is halfway between 30 inches and 33 inches, and because the brace table is linear, you can extrapolate between values.

4. Find the midpoint by adding $42.43 + 46.67 = 89.10$, and divide by 2 = 44.55 ≈ 44½ inches.

Rule of Thumb: Equal Rise and Run

To find the length of a diagonal when the run and rise are equal, multiply the length of the run (or rise) by 1.414. The rule applies only when both runs are equal.

Example: Rise and Run = 37½ inches.

$37.5 \times 1.414 = 53$ inches

Figure 8-4. Hundredths Scale

Use this scale to convert decimal values to fractions. In Figure 8-3, we calculated a brace length of 50.35 inches. To find the fractional equivalent, on the top scale find $^{35}/_{100}$ and directly below read a little over $^{5.5}/_{16}$. This can be used as $^3/_8$ ($^6/_{16}$) inch, or more accurately as $^{11}/_{32}$ inches.

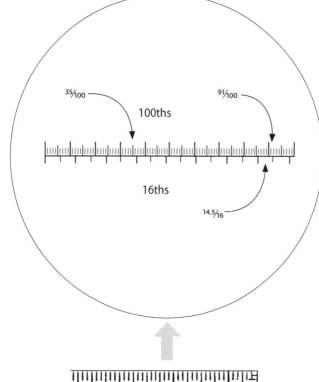

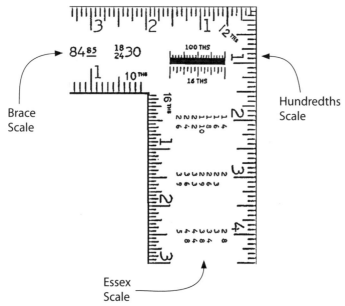

Brace Scale

Hundredths Scale

Essex Scale

Problem 8-7. Long Brace Length

Find the length of a brace with a rise and run of 75 inches.

Solution 8-7

1. Because the table is linear, all of the brace length values are additive. For 75 inches, use 36 inches and 39 inches.

2. The brace length of a brace with a rise and run of 36 inches is 50.91 inches.

3. The length of a similar brace with a rise and run of 39 inches is 55.16 inches.

4. Because the combined rise of the two braces is equal to 75 inches, the combined values of the brace lengths will equal the new brace length.

   50.91 + 55.16 = 106.07 inches

Hundredths Scale

Some of the more expensive squares have a **hundredths scale** located on the back of the tongue near the heel of the square. (See **Figure 8-4.**) The scale shows an inch graduated into 100 parts, making it possible to set dividers to hundredths of an inch and transfer the measurement. Under the scale are 16 graduations so hundredths can be converted to sixteenths.

1. The brace tables give results in hundredths of an inch, and the hundredths scale is used to set a pair of dividers to the correct

length and transfer measures to the workpiece. The subdivisions of the scale are necessarily very small, but with careful inspection, you will be able to pick up and transfer any required number or read the nearest ¹⁄₁₆ inch.

2. The scale also can be used as a decimal-to-fraction conversion table. The brace table gives results in hundredths. By using the ¹⁄₁₆ scale, you can convert hundredths to sixteenths.

Problem 8-8. Decimal to Fraction

On the brace table, a 36-inch run and a 36-inch rise give a brace length of 50.91 inches. What is 0.91 as a fraction (see **Figure 8-4**)?

Solution 8-8

1. On the hundredths scale, find 91.

2. Directly below on the 16th scale is a value halfway between ¹⁴⁄₁₆ and ¹⁵⁄₁₆.

3. Use either of these fractions, or, for more precision, use ²⁹⁄₃₂ inches.

Math

0.91 x 16 = 14.6/16 ≈ ¹⁵⁄₁₆ inch

0.91 x 32 = 29.1/32 ≈ ²⁹⁄₃₂ inch

Diagonal Scale

The diagonal scale is found on some squares near the heel (see **Figure 8-5**) and is used for transferring hundredths of an inch to dividers. The line a-b, shown here, is 1-inch-long and is divided into ten equal parts; the line c-d is also divided

into ten equal parts. Diagonal lines are then drawn connecting the points, as shown in the figure.

Problem 8-9. Hundredths of an Inch

Suppose we wish to find ⁷⁶⁄₁₀₀ of an inch and transfer this to a set of dividers.

Solution 8-9

1. Count off seven spaces from c on line c-d in **Figure 8-5**.

2. This position (point e) equals ⁷⁰⁄₁₀₀ of an inch.

3. Count up the diagonal line until the sixth horizontal line is reached (point g).

4. Set the dividers to distance fg. This is ⁷⁶⁄₁₀₀ inch.

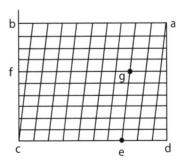

Figure 8-5. Enlarged Diagonal Scale

The diagonal scale is used to find hundredths of an inch. Dividers are set to the distance, which is then transferred to the workpiece.

Octagonal Table or Eight-Square Scale

The octagon scale (see **Figure 8-6**) is on the face of the tongue and is used to lay out octagons (objects with eight sides) from square beams. The scale consists of multiples of a slash followed by four dots. The indented slashes denote multiples of five, and the dots represent increments of one. The dots start under the 2-inch mark and continue to the 16-inch mark where the number 65 appears. To use the scale, place one point of a divider on the 0 mark and the other point on the length of one side of the square. Transfer the measurement to the square, as shown in **Figure 8-6**. The method is very accurate.

Problem 8-10. Square to Octagon

Suppose the square in **Figure 8-6** is the end of a large beam 6 inches by 6 inches, which we want to turn into an octagon.

Solution 8-10

1. Draw lines AB and CD through the center of the beam so they are both parallel to the sides. (See **Figure 8-6b**.)

2. With dividers, mark off as many spaces (6) from the octagon scale as there are inches in the width of the beam. (See **Figure 8-6a**.)

3. Mark off the distance on both sides of the points A, B, C, and D. (See **Figure 8-6c**.)

4. Call the new points a and a', b and b', and so on.

5. Draw lines a'd, d'b', and so on. (See **Figure 8-6d**.)

6. Cut off the shaded corner areas to leave an octagon or "eight-square" beam.

Figure 8-6. Octagonal Table

If the beam is 6 inches on a side, use dividers to transfer the distance of 6 dots to the end of the square beam.

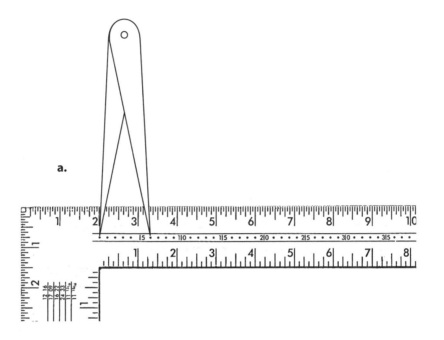

a.

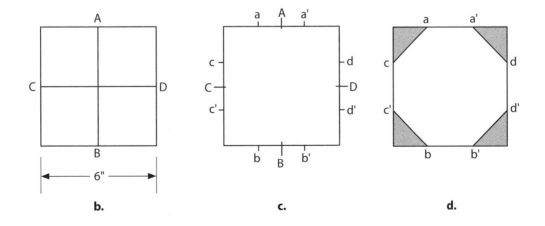

b.

c.

d.

Chapter 9

Stairs

A staircase, when carefully designed and constructed, adds to the beauty and character of the entire house. Stair work is considered a special field of carpentry, and the general carpenter who tackles the job must be careful the design is safe. There is no other home project fraught with so much danger as a poorly designed staircase. In a stairway, every step must be the same height and every tread the same depth. Imagine walking down the stairs carrying a laundry basket or a baby in your arms. Once into the rhythm, you find each step without looking until . . . one step isn't there or it comes too soon. You're surprised, you falter, and you fall.

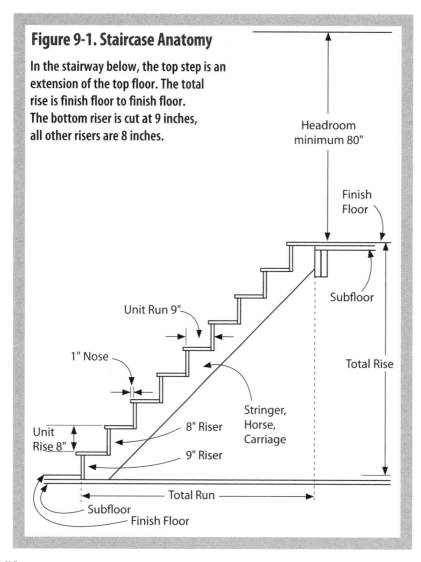

Figure 9-1. Staircase Anatomy

In the stairway below, the top step is an extension of the top floor. The total rise is finish floor to finish floor. The bottom riser is cut at 9 inches, all other risers are 8 inches.

Headroom minimum 80"

Finish Floor

Subfloor

Unit Run 9"

1" Nose

Total Rise

Stringer, Horse, Carriage

8" Riser

Unit Rise 8"

9" Riser

Total Run

Subfloor

Finish Floor

Data from the National Safety Council show stairways are the largest single cause of accidents in the home; some mishaps are human (trip, stumble, or slip), but too many are the result of faulty stair design.

The usual culprit is either the top or bottom step. It's easy to cut the stringer so all of the risers are the same height and all of the treads are the same depth. The problem comes when finish flooring is added after the stairs have been installed—a 1-inch floor at the bottom reduces the first riser by one inch. A new finish floor at the top makes the top step one inch higher. If the total rise of the staircase is figured from subfloor to subfloor, then the top and bottom risers will have to be cut to accommodate it. Steps next to a landing also will require special treatment if the landing has carpeting or other flooring that makes the unit rise differently from the other steps.

Stairway Design Considerations

A stairway is designed according to its intended use. Exterior steps leading from the sidewalk to the front porch are wide, made of durable material such as concrete or stone, and have an outward slope to drain melting snow and ice. Stairs used daily to move traffic inside a house, from one floor to another, are wide and comfortable to use. Service stairs to the basement or the attic, which get only occasional use, can be more narrow and steep.

The most important considerations in designing a stairway are safety and ease of travel. To meet those goals, consider the importance of riser height, tread depth, stairway width, headroom, and the handrail. Every step must be the same size; all risers must be identical in height, and all treads the same depth. That includes the steps to a landing and the steps from the landing. Variations in riser height, even differences as small as ¼ inch, can cause accidents. The potential for accidents is why most building codes allow a maximum variation of only ³⁄₁₆ inch in riser heights for two adjacent steps, and a maximum difference of only ⅜ inch between any two nonadjoining risers in the stairway. **Figure 9-1** shows a staircase anatomy.

General Stair Rules (Residential)

The rules for residential stairs vary widely throughout the country. Consult an architect or a local code official before you finalize your design. The following standards are general rules, but might not be approved in your area.

Landings and Maximum Total Rise

Limit the total rise, that is, the floor-to-floor height, in any straight run of stairs to 12 feet. If the total rise is more than 12 feet, provide a landing. Landings interrupt a fall, provide a rest stop, and should be at least as long as the stair is wide, up to 48 inches and not less than 44 inches. Some building codes do allow 36-inch landings in homes.

Width

Width of staircases is determined by the need for two people to pass. Primary stairs in a home should be at least 36 inches wide. Some codes allow 32 inches, but that is the minimum. Service stairs, such as for the porch, basement, and attic, should be at least 30 inches wide.

Headroom

The headroom on primary stairs should be at least 80 inches, measured vertically from one tread nosing to the nearest ceiling. The psychological sense of clearance can be as important as the physical clearance. Accordingly, the headroom should be such that a

Rule of Thumb: Residential Rise and Run

- The step rise should not exceed 8¼ inches.

- The step run should not be less than 9 inches.

- Variations in the height of risers and the depth of treads in any two adjacent steps should not exceed ³⁄₁₆ inch.

- Variations in the height of risers and the depth of treads in any flight should not exceed ⅜ inch.

Figure 9-2. Ratio of Riser Height to Tread Depth

If the unit rise is 7⅞ inch, then use a tread depth of 9⅛ inch to 10⅛ inch. Values in the shaded area are in the preferred zone (30° and 35° slope). The other values have slopes between 35° and 42°; the steeper inclines can be used for shorter total runs.

Unit Rise (Decimal)	Unit Rise (Inches)	Minimum Tread (Inches)	Maximum Tread (Inches)
6.50	6½	10½	11½
6.56	6⁹⁄₁₆	10⁷⁄₁₆	11⁷⁄₁₆
6.63	6⅝	10⅜	11⅜
6.69	6¹¹⁄₁₆	10⁵⁄₁₆	11⁵⁄₁₆
6.75	6¾	10¼	11¼
6.81	6¹³⁄₁₆	10³⁄₁₆	11³⁄₁₆
6.88	6⅞	10⅛	11⅛
6.94	6¹⁵⁄₁₆	10¹⁄₁₆	11¹⁄₁₆
7.00	7.00	10.00	11.00
7.06	7¹⁄₁₆	9¹⁵⁄₁₆	10¹⁵⁄₁₆
7.13	7⅛	9⅞	10⅞
7.19	7³⁄₁₆	9¹³⁄₁₆	10¹³⁄₁₆
7.25	7¼	9¾	10¾
7.31	7⁵⁄₁₆	9¹¹⁄₁₆	10¹¹⁄₁₆
7.38	7⅜	9⅝	10⅝
7.44	7⁷⁄₁₆	9⁹⁄₁₆	10⁹⁄₁₆
7.50	7½	9½	10½
7.56	7⁹⁄₁₆	9⁷⁄₁₆	10⁷⁄₁₆
7.63	7⅝	9⅜	10⅜
7.69	7¹¹⁄₁₆	9⁵⁄₁₆	10⁵⁄₁₆
7.75	7¾	9¼	10¼
7.81	7¹³⁄₁₆	9³⁄₁₆	10³⁄₁₆
7.88	7⅞	9⅛	10⅛
7.94	7¹⁵⁄₁₆	9¹⁄₁₆	10¹⁄₁₆
8.00	8.00	9.00	10.00

Unit Rise + Unit Run = 17 to 18

person cannot reach up and touch the ceiling from any step. Some architects set headroom at 84 inches. Basement stairs and other nonprimary stairs may have a headroom of 78 inches.

Handrails

Provide at least one handrail placed not less than 34 inches nor more than 38 inches above, and parallel to, the nosing of the treads. The handrail should accompany all steps and have no interruption at newel posts. A person's hand should be able to slide along the rail without interruption, and the ends of the handrail should be returned to, or end at, a post. The easiest handrail to grasp is a round profile between 1½ inches and 2 inches in diameter. Handrails may not be required for stairways with fewer than three risers.

Risers and Treads

Ideally, risers should be 7 to 8 inches high; treads should be 9 to 11 inches deep exclusive of the nosing. The tread thickness should be 1¼ inch minimum, and the tread nosing should be 1-inch maximum. Closed risers are preferred, but stairs may have open risers in some areas and applications.

Builders consider the 7-11 staircase ideal—a 7-inch rise with an 11-inch tread—because it is universally approved and is a safe design. If the combination of rise and run is too great, the steps are tiring. If the combination is too small, the foot may kick the riser at each step.

Narrow treads are more dangerous when coming down the stairs than when going up.

Stair Ratio

The stair ratio is the relationship between the tread depth (unit run) and the riser height (unit rise). In a properly designed staircase, as one increases, the other decreases, and vice versa. **Figure 9-2** gives values for safe rises and runs; in the shaded area, the slope is between 30° and 35°. After finding the total rise and unit rise, use the chart to find the unit run. The chart is based on the formula:

Tread depth + Riser height = 17 inches minimum to 18 inches maximum

A minimum tread depth and a maximum riser height keep the stairs from exceeding the critical angle (slope) of the staircase. **Figure 9-3** shows the critical angles for a staircase are a 20° minimum slope and 50° maximum slope. The preferred slope is between 30° and 35°; this is both the safest and the easiest to use. The common 7-11 ratio of rise-to-run is 32.5°, right in the middle of the preferred zone.

Stringers

The stringer, also called the horse or carriage, is the backbone and most important part of the staircase strength. The stringer is the cutout support for the risers and treads. If it is cut correctly, the stairs will be perfect when installed. Stringers usually are sawn from a 2x10 or

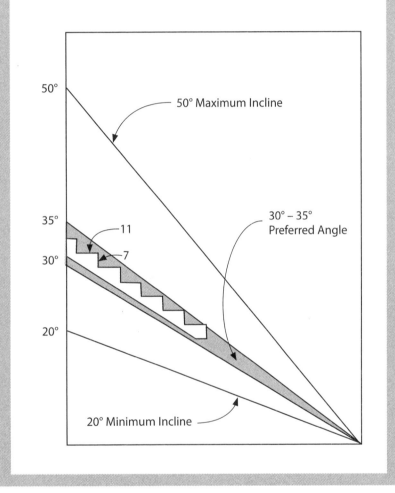

Figure 9-3. Preferred and Critical Angles for a Staircase

The best staircase is designed so the incline is between 30° and 35°. The ideal 7-11 rise-to-run falls in the preferred 30° to 35° area.

50° Maximum Incline

30° – 35° Preferred Angle

20° Minimum Incline

2x12 beam, so a minimum of 3 to 4 inches of material are left to carry the load. (See **Figure 9-1**.) Adjustments must be made at the top and bottom of the stringer to accommodate finish flooring. The thickness of the bottom flooring will make the bottom rise larger, while the top riser must be cut smaller to accommodate the top flooring.

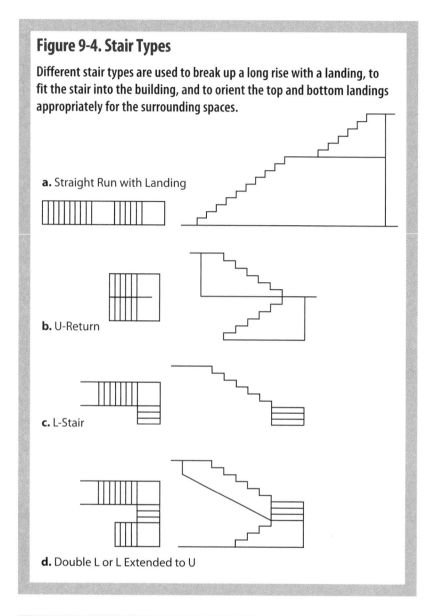

Figure 9-4. Stair Types

Different stair types are used to break up a long rise with a landing, to fit the stair into the building, and to orient the top and bottom landings appropriately for the surrounding spaces.

a. Straight Run with Landing

b. U-Return

c. L-Stair

d. Double L or L Extended to U

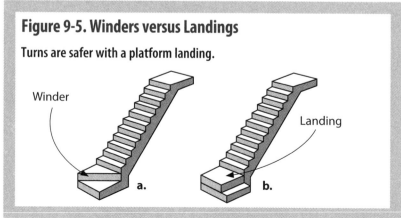

Figure 9-5. Winders versus Landings

Turns are safer with a platform landing.

Winder

Landing

a.

b.

Stairway Types

Builders install different types of stairs to accommodate the space in the building, as well as for the aesthetic benefit of such features as landings and turns.

Straight Run

A straight stairway is limited to 12 feet of total rise, at which point a landing should be provided. (See **Figure 9-4**.)

U-Return

A stairway with a U-shaped return may occupy a square or rectangular area. Flights may be equal or unequal in total rise and run, but the best design is when the risers and treads are of equal size on both runs. The landing depth should be at least 44 inches.

L-Stair

An L-shaped stair may have equal legs or one short and one long leg separated by a landing at the turn. The landing depth should equal the stair width but should be no less than 44 inches.

Double L or Extended U Stair

The L-shaped stair may be extended to a U shape with a short flight between the two corner landings.

Winders

A turn can be made with radiating treads called winders, as in **Figure 9-5a**. Winders are not safe for new construction and will not pass building codes although still found in older homes. At the inner corner where all winders meet, there is very little tread to support the foot, making the design dangerous. Turns can be made safely with a landing, as in **Figure 9-5b**.

Many codes do allow, under special circumstances, the winding staircase in residential uses. In such cases, winding staircases should be designed so the tread width of all steps at the line of travel is the same. The winder design must provide the minimum allowable tread depth at a point 12 inches from the side of the stairs where the tread is narrowest, but in no case should any tread depth be less than 6 inches (see **Figure 9-6**).

Designing a Staircase

To design a staircase, first measure the distance from finished floor to finished floor. The number is the total rise, and using it, the number of risers and the exact unit rise can be calculated. The appropriate relationship between rise and run will determine the unit run, and from that, the total run can be calculated. The total run–the length of the staircase–also will be governed by the available space in the building. The design sequence may need to be repeated until it all works out.

Run and Rise

On any flight of stairs, there is always one less tread than riser. The total run can be determined once the unit rise, the unit run, and the number of risers are known.

Rule of Thumb: The 7-11 Standard

Ratio or Unit Rise to Unit Run
Builders use the following guidelines to figure a safe riser-to-tread ratio:

Rise = 7 inches, tread = 11 inches, the so-called 7-11 standard

Rise plus tread = 17 to 18 inches
For example: 7-inch rise plus 11-inch tread = 18 inches

Rise doubled plus tread = 24 to 25 inches
For example: (7-inch rise x 2) = 14 inches + 11 inches = 25 inches

Rise times tread = 73 to 78
For example: 7 inches x 11 inches = 77 inches

Figure 9-6. Winders

Winding stairways are not as safe as those with a landing because there is less tread at the inner circle. If allowed, building codes require a minimum tread depth of 6 inches and at least 10 inches of tread at a point 12 inches from the side of the stairs.

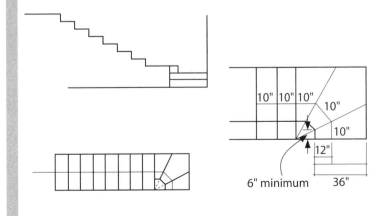

Total Rise

Measure the distance from the bottom finish floor to the top finish floor. Adjust the distance if the measurement is to a subfloor and a finish floor is to be added later: add ¾ inch for wood and ⅜ inch for carpeting.

Number of Risers

To determine the number of risers, divide the total rise by an average unit rise; use 7 inches for the average ascent, 8 inches for a steeper ascent. Disregard fractions and use this number to find the number of risers.

Unit Rise

Unit rise is the height of each step. The best unit rise will be between 7 inches and 8 inches. Use 8 as the starting point in your calculations.

Unit Run

Unit run is the depth of each tread. The standard is 9½ inches to 11 inches. The best combination of unit rise and unit run is 7-11. Use 9 inches as a minimum for service stairs, 10 inches for others. The unit run does not include nosing.

Total Run

The total run is the distance the stairs will occupy (floor space) on the bottom floor. It is calculated by multiplying the number of treads times the unit run.

The Steel Square in Stair Design

In 1881, several correspondents, in letters to the editor of a trade paper, asked for more articles on stair-building subjects. A woodworker lamented, "Is it that the initiated are too jealous of their craft to care to enlighten the uninformed?" Four months later, an expert stairbuilder from Cleveland answered in the same trade paper (*Carpentry and Building*, April 1882, p. 78). He stated that, indeed, "We are jealous of our craft, and I believe justly so." The specialist listed the reasons: "Stairbuilding is worked as a separate trade; only competent men can design and build stairs; stairbuilders are few in number, and lastly, all competent stairbuilders command at least a dollar a day more than for ordinary joinery." The same trade paper gave the following data for salaries in 1882: carpenters were paid $2.75 per day, laborers $1.00 to $1.50 per day, and stairbuilders about $4.00 per day. The master craftsman from Cleveland noted that learning to design and build stairs required considerable cost in time and study and went on to ask, "After an outlay of this kind, would a stairbuilder be doing justice to himself . . . to give away the secrets of his trade without compensation?" He wrote, "most of the craft are so afraid of their art they will not make a drawing or a pattern . . . for fear something may be given away." He further wrote, "Few competent stairbuilders will give instruction, even for pay."

The way master stairbuilders designed and built a staircase was without math—just using a folding rule, a square, a pencil, and the straight edge of a board. To the nail pounders and the common laborers, it probably looked like magic—certainly sleight of hand. The master stairbuilder would whip out his rule and jot down the floor-to-floor height; then he would grab a wide board and put it across two sawhorses. He would lay his steel square on the board, wiggle it back and forth a little, all the time making marks and jotting numbers in his little notepad or on the board itself. After doing it a few times, he would set a couple of gauges on the body and the tongue of the square, grab a 2x12, and start marking out the stair carriages. How did he do it?

To most woodworkers, the framing square, with all of its scales and tables and complicated markings, was magic. The difference between the fellow who knew how to make the marks and the guy who merely cut to the mark, was the difference between a master craftsman and an ordinary drudge. And as the stairbuilder from Cleveland admitted, the master craftsmen could be very jealous and protective of their craft.

Staircase Layout

In **Figure 9-7**, the distance from floor to floor (total rise) is 9 feet, 6 inches (9½ feet) or 114 inches. Find the size of the risers (unit rise), the tread depth (unit run), and finally, the total run. Use a tread depth of 11 inches and start with a unit rise of 8 inches. The exact unit rise will be determined. Here's an overview of the layout sequence:

1. Measure the total rise from finished floor to finished floor.

2. Determine the number of steps needed, as in **Figure 9-8**, using an approximate unit rise of 8 inches.

3. Find the exact unit rise, as in **Figure 9-9**.

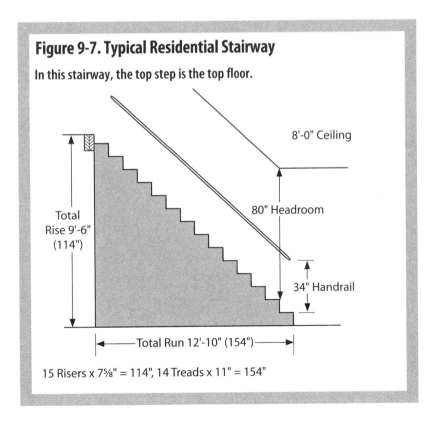

Figure 9-7. Typical Residential Stairway

In this stairway, the top step is the top floor.

8'-0" Ceiling

80" Headroom

Total Rise 9'-6" (114")

34" Handrail

←——Total Run 12'-10" (154")——→

15 Risers x 7⅝" = 114", 14 Treads x 11" = 154"

4. Find the number of treads needed. Remember the number of treads is always one less than the number of risers.

5. Set the tread depth at 11 inches and determine the total run, as in **Figure 9-10**.

That process will give you total rise, total run, unit rise, unit run, number of treads, and number of risers—and that's all the info you need to design a set of stairs. Here's the detail:

Figure 9-8. Finding the Number of Risers

With the square on the face of a straight board, use 8 inches (the maximum unit rise) on the blade and 12 inches on the body to draw a proportioning line, Position 1. Slide the square along the line until the total rise of 9.5 feet on the blade falls on the board's edge, Position 2. Read the number of 8-inch risers (14.25) on the square's body, and round up to 15.

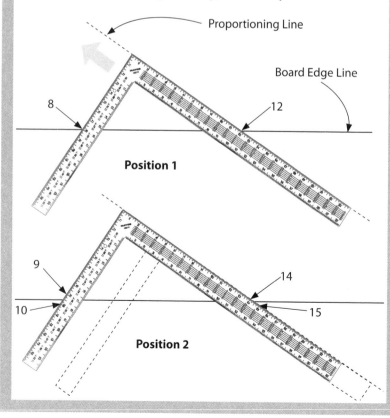

Proportioning Line

Board Edge Line

8

12

Position 1

9

10

14

15

Position 2

Find the Number of Risers

1. Using a board with a straight edge, position the square so that 12 on the body and 8 (the maximum unit rise) on the blade both fall on the board's edge line.

2. Draw a proportioning line along the square's body, as in **Figure 9-8, Position 1**, and extend it.

3. Slide the body of the square up the proportioning line until the total rise (9.5 on the blade) lies on the board's edge line (see **Figure 9-8, Position 2**).

4. Read 14¼ (the number of risers) on the body.

5. Round the number of risers up to the next whole number (15).

You now know:

- Total rise = 114 inches
- Total number of risers = 15

Math

Total rise 9½ feet = 114 inches

Divide total rise by the approximate riser height (8 inches).

114 inches ÷ 8 inches = 14¼

You can't have a fractional riser, so round the number of risers up to 15. This means the actual unit rise will be a bit less than 8 inches—quite safe according to **Figure 9-2**.

Find the Unit Rise

1. Using a board with a straight edge once more, position the square so 15 (the number of risers) on the body and 9.5 (the total rise) on the blade are on the edge line.

2. Draw the proportioning line along the body of the square, as in **Figure 9-9**, **Position 1**, and extend it.

3. Slide the body of the square down the proportioning line until 12 on the body lies on the edge line, as in **Figure 9-9**, **Position 2**.

4. Read 7⅝ inches (the actual unit rise) on the blade.

You now know:
- Total rise = 114 inches
- Total number of risers = 15
- Unit rise = 7⅝ inches

Math

Total rise of 9½ feet = 114 inches

Find the unit rise by dividing the total rise by the actual number of risers.

$$114 \div 15 = 7.6 \approx 7⅝ \text{ inches}$$

Find the Number of Treads

The number of treads is always one less than the number of risers, so there will be 14 treads.

You now know:
- Total rise = 114 inches
- Total number of risers = 15
- Unit rise = 7⅝ inches
- Total number of treads = 14

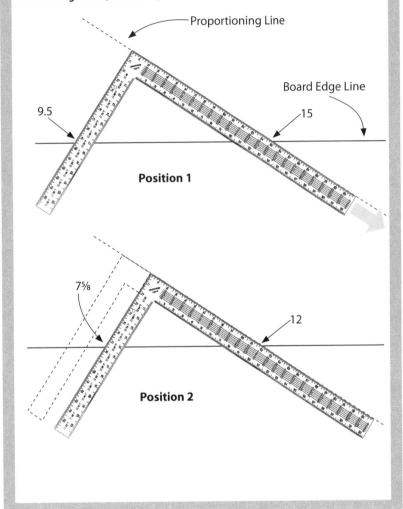

Figure 9-9. Find Unit Rise

Position the square on the board so 15 (the number or risers) and 9½ (the total rise) lie on the edge line. Draw a proportioning line (Position 1) and slide the square until 12 on the body lies on the board's edge line. Read the exact unit rise, 7 ⅝ inches, where the square's tongue crosses the board's edge line (Position 2).

Proportioning Line

Board Edge Line

9.5   15

Position 1

7⅝

12

Position 2

Find the Tread Depth

You want the stairs to be easy to ascend, so use 11 inches as the tread depth.

You now know:

- Total rise = 114 inches
- Total number of risers = 15
- Unit rise = 7⅝ inches
- Total number of treads = 14
- Tread depth (unit run) = 11 inches

Figure 9-10. Find Total Run

Place the square on the board so 11 (the tread depth) on the tongue and 12 on the body both lie on the edge line, and draw a proportioning line (Position 1). Slide the square along the proportioning line until 14 (the number of treads) on the body lies on the board's edge line, and read 12⅞ (the total run) where the square's tongue crosses the board's edge line (Position 2).

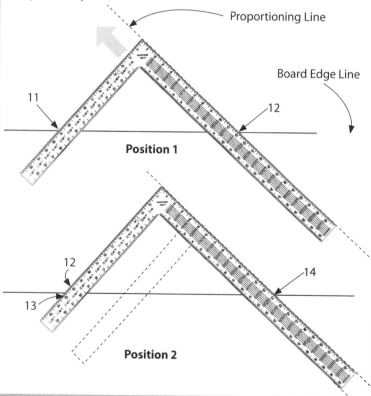

Proportioning Line

Board Edge Line

11

12

Position 1

12

13

14

Position 2

Find the Total Run

The remaining unknown dimension is the total run.

1. Using the straight-edge board, position the square so 12 on the body and 11 (the unit run) on the blade are on the edge line.

2. Draw the proportioning line along the body of the square, as in **Figure 9-10**, **Position 1**, and extend it.

3. Slide the body of the square up the proportioning line until 14 (the number of treads) on the body is on the edge-line as in **Figure 9-10**, Position 2.

4. Read 12⅞ (the total run in feet) on the blade.

> 12⅞ feet = 12 feet 10½ inches.

Math

> Number of risers − 1
> = number of treads
>
> 15 − 1 = 14
>
> 14 x 11 inches (unit run)
> = 154 inches (total run)
>
> 154 inches = 12.83 feet
> = 12 feet 10 inches

Final Staircase Dimensions

- Total run = 12 feet 10 inches
- Total rise = 9 feet 6 inches
- Unit rise = 7⅝ inches
- Unit run = 11 inches
- Number of treads = 14
- Number of risers = 15

Marking the Stringer

Use the steel square to lay out the stringer, as shown in **Figure 9-11**. To hold the correct setting, use a pair of metal stair gauges (page 40), or an adjustable shop-made fence (page 35). See Chapter 7, "Problem-Solving Techniques," for more on making and using an adjustable fence.

1. Set the unit run, 11 inches, on one arm of the square.

2. Set the unit rise, 7⅝ inches, on the other arm of the square.

3. Fasten a fence or a pair of gauges across these points.

4. Step the square along the stringer plank, drawing around it at each position. This marks the wood to be cut away.

5. You might have to adjust the ends of the stringer, as shown in **Figures 9-1** and **9-12**, to compensate for the finished floors at the top and bottom.

Stair and Baluster Problems

Problem 9-1. Building a Ladder Stair

Sometimes steep stairs are needed for access to an attic or cellar. A ship's ladder stair fits the bill. It is made with treads but without risers and, with handrails, is quite safe.

For example, there is a floor-to-floor distance of 7 feet 6 inches and the well hole is 5 feet long. To allow easy passage up and down the ladder

Rule of Thumb: Stairs Fence

Make a fence for the framing square (see **Figure 9-11**).

1. Fasten two short pieces of straight wood together using short bolts and wing nuts.

2. Clamp the fence onto the framing square and adjust to the proper rise and run.

3. Slide the square along the edge of the carriage and mark the steps.

Figure 9-11. Fence for Run and Rise

Slide the fence along the board edge and mark rise and run.

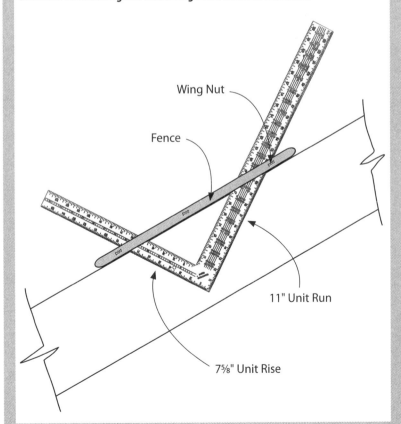

Wing Nut

Fence

11" Unit Run

7⅝" Unit Rise

Rule of Thumb: Stringer Layout

Use a framing square to mark the stair stringer (see **Figure 9-12**).

1. Set unit run on the tongue of the square.

2. Set unit rise on the body of the square.

3. Draw line AB, the tread depth.

4. Draw line BC, the unit rise.

Figure 9-12. Use a Framing Square to Lay Out a Stringer

Use the shop-made fence or a pair of stair gauges as stops on the square's tongue and body. Step the square along the stringer, drawing along its outer edge at each position.

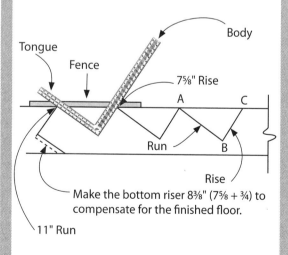

Rule of Thumb: Pitch Board and Stair Gauge

The pitch board is a handy template that can be used with or without the stair gauge, see **Figure 9-13**.

1. Cut the pitch board from ½-inch or ¾-inch plywood.

2. Make one edge equal to the unit rise.

3. Make one edge equal to the unit run.

4. Use the pitch board with or without the stair gauge.

Figure 9-13. Pitch Board and Stair Gauge

The pitch board and stair gauge are handy templates for laying out stair stringers.

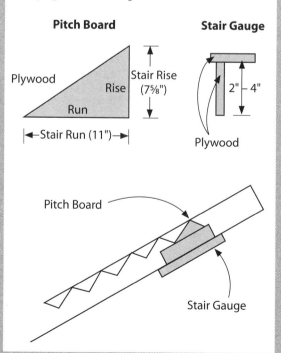

stair, make the total run 4 feet 9 inches, just a little smaller than the well hole. There are no risers, so the toe of the shoe resting on any tread will project under the tread above.

What will be the unit rise for the treads, and how is the stringer marked?

Solution 9-1

The unit rise for such a ladder stair can be 9 or 10 inches, more than regular stairs, because the stair is almost a ladder. At 10 inches, there'll be nine risers.

1. Lay out a story pole 7 feet 6 inches long (90 inches) and mark off nine equal 10-inch divisions, as shown in **Figure 9-14**.

2. Set a fence on the steel square with a rise of 18 (2 x 9) and run of 11.4 (2 x 5.7) (see **Figure 9-14a**). Doubling both values makes the fence setting more precise; the slope and ratio remain the same.

3. Find the length of the stringer by measuring the distance across the square from 11⅜ to 18, as in **Figure 9-14b**. That is 21¼ inches, and because of the doubling in Step 2 above, it is twice the stringer length of one step.

   21.25 ÷ 2 = 10.625 x 10
   = 106.25 inches

That is the total length of the stringer.

4. Trim the top and bottom of the stringer and nail it in place.

5. Stand the story pole upright against the stringer, and mark off the positions of the center of each tread on the front of the stringer.

6. Move the square along from one mark to the next and mark off the positions of the treads.

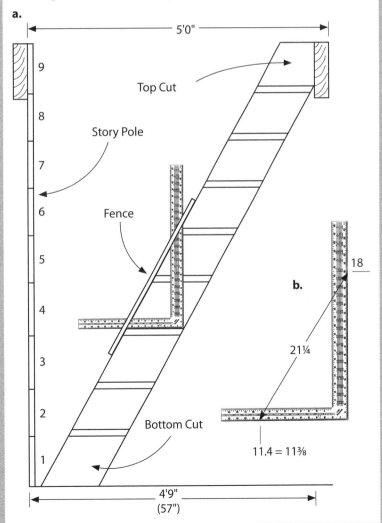

Figure 9-14. Building a Ladder Stair

Set a fence on the steel square corresponding to the rise and run of the ladder stair, as at (a), and use it to lay out the top and bottom cuts. Use a story pole to locate each tread on the stringer, and then use the square to lay it out. Measure the distance between 11⅜ and 18 to find the length of the stringer (b). Ladder stairs require a handrail.

Figure 9-15. Baluster Spacing

The square is used as a proportioning tool to find equal spacing of balusters, (a). Position the square so the distance (8 feet) and the number of spaces (22) are on the edge line, (b). Draw a proportioning line and slide the square on it until 12 is on the line. Read 4⅜, as at (c). Space the balusters 4⅜ inches on center.

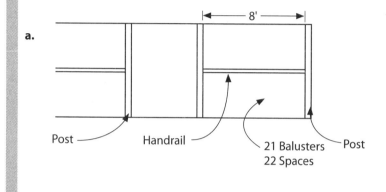

a.

Post   Handrail   21 Balusters   Post
                                22 Spaces

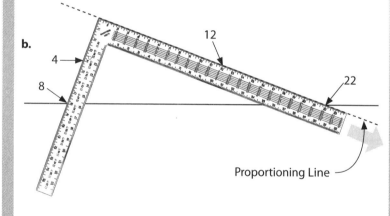

b.

12

4

8

22

Proportioning Line

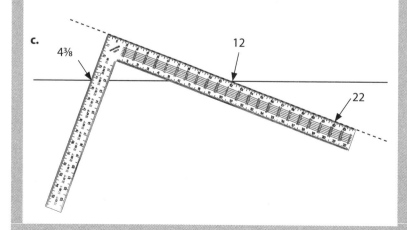

c.

4⅜

12

22

Problem 9-2. Baluster Spacing

When you are installing balusters between posts in a railing, the spacing must be uniform or the error is easily noticeable. We have 8 feet between the posts, and you want to install 21 balusters. What is the spacing? The problem arises any time you want to divide a space—in making the sides of a child's crib or a cradle, or when working on a deck with a railing.

Solution 9-2

1. Because there always is one more space than balusters, you need to find 22 equal spaces. (See **Figure 9-15a**.)

2. On the edge of a board, place the tongue of the steel square at 8 (the post-to-post distance) and the body at 22 (the number of spaces). (See **Figure 9-15b**.)

3. Draw a proportioning line along the long edge of the square (see Chapter 7, "Problem-Solving Techniques" for more on the proportioning line).

4. Slide the square down the proportioning line until 12 on the body is at the edge of the board.

5. Read 4⅜ (the unit spacing) on the tongue. (See **Figure 9-15c**.) That is the spacing for the balusters from center to center, not the spacing in between.

Why It Works

The proportions of 22 spaces in 8 feet are translated into inches thus:

22 spaces is to 8 as 12 inches is to X inches

$X = (8 \times 12) \div 22 = 4\frac{3}{8}$ inches

Problem 9-3. Spacing Staircase Balusters

When staircase balusters are to be installed, there is always one more space than balusters. By measuring the distance between newel posts and using the steel square, equal spacing can be found.

For example, consider a staircase with a distance of 11 feet 5½ inches newel to newel. You want to install 21 balusters. What is the spacing (see **Figure 9-16**)?

Solution 9-3

1. Remember, when there are 21 balusters, there will be 22 spaces.

2. Place the steel square on a board and draw a proportioning line with the body at 22 (the number of spaces) and the tongue at 11.5 (the post-to-post distance), as shown in **Figure 9-16a**.

3. Move the square down the proportioning line until the mark 12 is on the bottom edge of the board. (See **Figure 9-16b**.)

4. Read 6¼ where the bottom edge crosses the tongue.

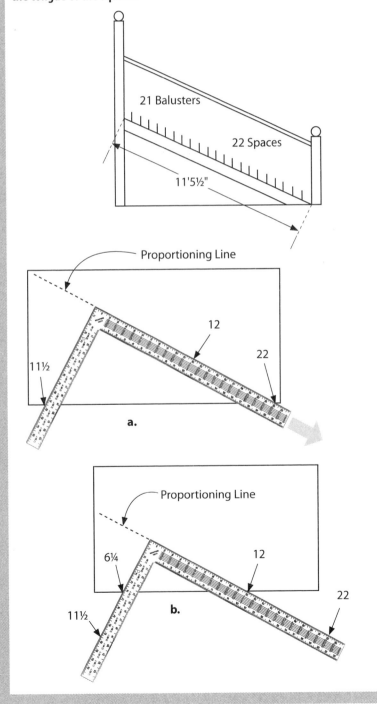

Figure 9-16. Spacing Staircase Balusters

Use the proportions of 11½ (stringer length) and 22 (spaces) to draw a proportioning line, as at (a). Slide the square down the proportioning line until 12 is on the bottom line, as at (b). Read the spacing of 6¼ inches on the tongue of the square.

21 Balusters

22 Spaces

11'5½"

Proportioning Line

11½

12

22

a.

Proportioning Line

6¼

11½

12

22

b.

5. The spacing will give the midmark for 21 balusters and 22 spaces.

6. The width of the balusters is not needed using this on-center method.

Why It Works

Here is another proportioning problem.

22 spaces is to 11.5 feet as 12 inches is to X inches

X = (11.5 x 12) ÷ 22 = 6.25 inches

Problem 9-4. Spacing Balusters with a Story Pole

You want to put railing balusters on the front porch between two posts. Without measuring, you can use a steel square and a story pole to space them evenly. Assume for example that the two porch posts are about 10 feet apart. The exact measurement isn't needed. The balusters are each 2 inches wide, so about 4 inches of space in between ought to look good. What won't look good are uneven spaces.

Solution 9-4

1. Cut a length of 1x2 pine a little longer than the post-to-post distance, say 12 feet. It will be the story pole.

2. Make marks on the story pole using this logic:

Marks = Slat Width + Space Distance

Marks = 2 inches + 4 inches = 6 inches

3. Start at one end of the pole and make a mark every 6 inches. Do it the entire length of the pole.

4. Make a mark 1 inch from the left end of the pole. Also make a mark 1 inch from the last mark on the right end, as shown in **Figure 9-17**. The 1-inch marks are one-half the width of a slat. If the slats had been 4 inches wide, then the end marks would have been 2 inches.

5. Drive a small nail near the left end of the story pole and attach it to the left post at the 1 inch mark.

6. Tilt the pole up and nail it to the other post so the 1-inch mark is even with the inside edge of the post.

7. Use a steel square to transfer the marks on the pole down to the porch floor.

8. Center the slats on these marks.

Why It Works

Woodworkers use proportional division on a diagonal line to divide boards, roofers use the method to lay shingles, and carpenters use it to equally space siding on a house. Here it's used to space balusters.

Figure 9-17. Spacing Balusters with a Story Pole

Make a story pole that is longer than the distance between posts and mark uniform spaces on it. Mark one-half the baluster width at each end. Tilt the pole to align the end marks with the posts, and then use the steel square to drop the marks to the floor. These marks represent the centers of the balusters.

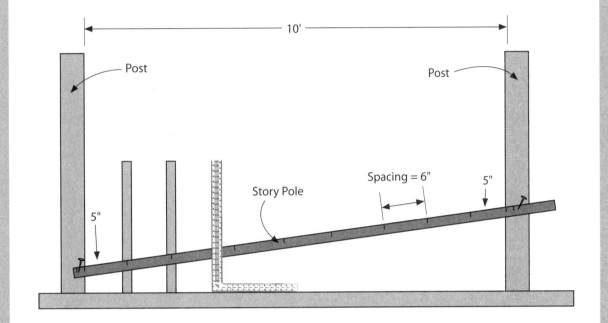

Chapter 10

Roofs

A roof protects a building and its contents from the elements and enhances the building's appearance. It should be strong enough to carry loads of snow and ice, and rigid enough to withstand wind and the occasional earth tremor. It must also support the weight of the roofing and of the workmen who apply it.

Rafters are the ribs of the roof. They are arranged at equal intervals and extend up from the top of the wall to the ridge, or the backbone. The framing square is the traditional tool for laying out and marking the rafters—to find the length of each rafter and to mark the complex cuts at each end so the rafters will have solid bearings on top of the wall plate and fit snugly at the ridge.

The size and spacing of rafters depend on the span of the building, the slope of the roof, the type and grade of lumber used, and the load that will be carried. Regional variations are important. Provisions should be made in some localities for heavy snow loads and in others, for earthquakes. High winds require special anchoring of the roof to the building.

Rule of Thumb

Flat roofs leak. And it is incredibly hard to find the source.

Roof Types

Roofs can be simple, like a flat roof, or complex with hips and valleys and dormers, but in all roofs, the rafter length and end cuts depend on the span and the slope. Working drawings rarely include a roof plan. Carpenters must learn how to frame a roof using the floor plans, which give the shape of the building, and the elevation views, which show the contour of the roof.

If carefully designed, the roof adds greatly to the beauty of a building. Contemporary houses feature a number of roof styles. The shape of the house plan and requirements of the climate are some of the limiting factors. Some owners may want the building to have the flavor of a particular architectural period or style, such as Dutch Colonial or Cape Cod. The roof is very important in bringing out these special effects. Common types of roofs used in construction of houses are flat, shed, gable, hip, mansard, gambrel, and combinations of two or more—as shown in **Figure 10-1**.

Flat Roof

In a flat roof, the joists are laid level or at a slight angle for drainage. Sheathing and roofing are applied to the top of the rafters, and ceiling material is applied to the underside. Flat roofs supported with large poles are common in the American southwest where snow and rain are rare.

Lean-To or Shed Roof

The lean-to roof is the simplest roof having a slope. The lean-to roof was once used only for farm buildings—chicken coops, garages, and granaries and for simple additions to existing homes. In recent years, it has become common in contemporary home design. When the shed roof is used as an addition, the roof is attached to the side of the existing structure or to the existing roof.

Gable or Pitch Roof

The gable roof has two slopes which meet at the center of the ridge, forming triangular gables at each end. It is simple in its design and easy to construct. The slope can vary from almost flat in warm climates to very steep when snow load is a factor.

Hip Roof

The hip roof consists of at least three sides, all of which slope from the center of the building outward. The line where two adjacent sloping sides meet is called a hip. The common rafters rise to meet the ridge, and jack rafters rise to hips. The hip roof has an even overhang all around the building and is a popular home choice.

Gable Roof with Dormer

The gable roof may include dormers which add space, light, and ventilation to attic and second-floor rooms.

Gable and Valley Roof

The gable and valley roof design combines two gable roofs. The valley is the meeting place of two slopes of the roof, which run in different directions.

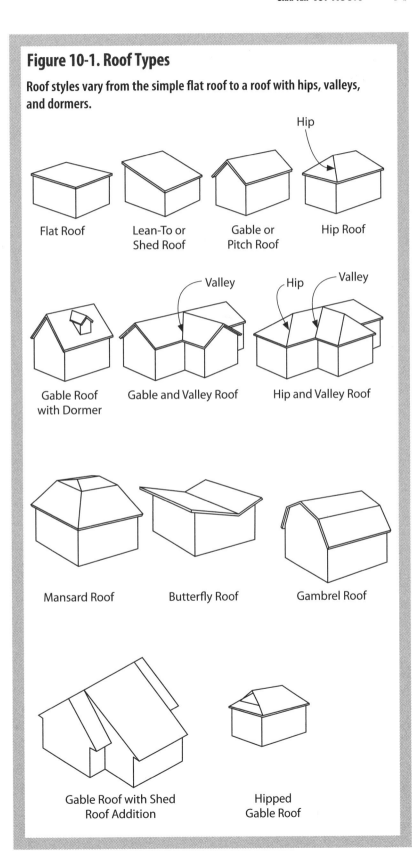

Figure 10-1. Roof Types

Roof styles vary from the simple flat roof to a roof with hips, valleys, and dormers.

Hip

Flat Roof

Lean-To or Shed Roof

Gable or Pitch Roof

Hip Roof

Valley

Hip   Valley

Gable Roof with Dormer

Gable and Valley Roof

Hip and Valley Roof

Mansard Roof

Butterfly Roof

Gambrel Roof

Gable Roof with Shed Roof Addition

Hipped Gable Roof

Rule of Thumb: Draw the Rafters

If you are confused about rafter layout, draw it out. Make a simple freehand sketch showing the building with the rafters in place. Then, superimpose a square and you can see how to make the angles and cuts.

Hip and Valley Roof

The hip and valley roof design is a combination of two hip roofs with the valley as the meeting place of the two slopes, each running in different directions.

Mansard Roof

The mansard is a variation of the hip roof. It has steep slopes on all four sides, but they do not meet at the center as in the hip roof. Partway up each side, a second slope begins—it is almost flat and continues toward the center of the building where it meets with the slopes from the other sides. The mansard roof was brought to America by French settlers in Quebec. In the United States, it is used for apartment buildings and commercial buildings, mainly to provide an architecturally decorative effect. The mansard design is used on houses throughout the country.

Butterfly Roof

The butterfly roof is usually seen in multiples, especially in commercial buildings such as libraries and museums. The sloping roofs allow windows and lighting from above. The valley must slope for easy drainage.

Gambrel Roof

The gambrel roof is a variation of the simple gable roof, with two different slopes on each side. Partway up the lower slope, a second slope begins and continues toward the center of the building where it meets with the roof from the other side. The gambrel roof provides a large underspace and is used for barns, providing enclosed space for hay. It was first brought to the United States by German settlers in New York and Pennsylvania. The Dutch Colonial with its gambrel roof provides more attic space than either hip or gable roofs.

Gable Roof with Shed Roof Addition

The usual shed roof addition ties to the main building at or under the eaves. In such a design, the shed roof rises to meet the main gable at the peak.

Hipped Gable Roof

The hipped gable roof is often used in garages and outbuildings because it provides a place to install windows and vents just under the roof line.

The Theory of Roof Framing

The most complicated part of house framing is the roof. The carpenter must find the length of the various rafters, scribe the top and seat lines, mark the bird's mouth, settle on the length of the tail, and then mark the bottom plumb line. Over the years, carpenters have relied on the framing square to work out such tricky problems—using the principles of the right triangle, whether they knew it or not.

Rafter Measurement

The rise, the run, and the rafter length in a roof correspond to the three sides of a right triangle. In the simplest roof (see **Figure 10-2a**), the total rafter length is the diagonal plus the thickness of the wall. In the more complex case (see **Figure 10-2b**), the rafter is shortened at the top to accommodate the ridge beam, a notch, or bird's mouth, is cut to fit the top of the wall, and it extends outward for the overhang—all figured and marked with the framing square. In each case, the shaded area is the right triangle we'll use to figure lengths and angles.

Over the years, roof framers and carpenters have come up with many ways to determine rise, run, and rafter length. **Figure 10-3** shows the three methods most often used.

The textbook method of finding rafter length is in **Figure 10-3a**, where a measuring line is first scribed down the center of the rafter. The base of the triangle is measured horizontally beginning at the outside of the wall to the middle of the ridge, the rise is from wall height to this measuring line at the top, and rafter length is measured along the measuring line down the middle of the rafter. Using the method in **Figure 10-3b**, the rise is to the bottom of the ridge, diagonal length is measured along the bottom of the rafter, and the run is to the inside of the wall. In the method shown in **Figure 10-3c**, the rise is to the top of the ridge, the run is to a spot above the outside wall at the top of the rafter, and the rafter length is measured along the top.

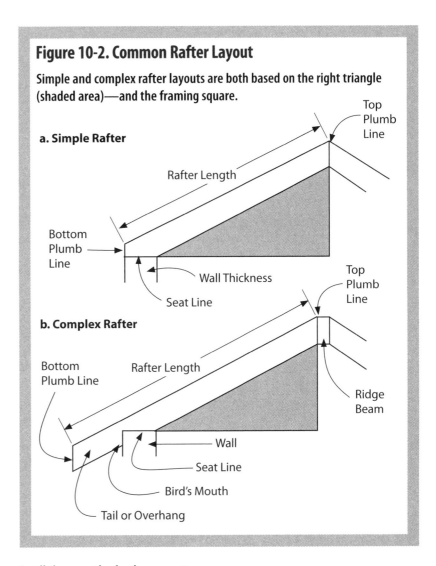

Figure 10-2. Common Rafter Layout

Simple and complex rafter layouts are both based on the right triangle (shaded area)—and the framing square.

a. Simple Rafter

Rafter Length

Top Plumb Line

Bottom Plumb Line

Wall Thickness

Seat Line

b. Complex Rafter

Bottom Plumb Line

Rafter Length

Top Plumb Line

Ridge Beam

Wall

Seat Line

Bird's Mouth

Tail or Overhang

In all three methods, the correct rafter length can be found. All three methods rely on the same logic and the same math. At times, all three methods have been used on one house. One instruction book says, "On rafters made by 2x4s, make the measuring mark 2 inches from the top; for rafters made from 2x6s or larger, make the mark 2 inches from the bottom; on rafters without an eave, measure along the top." That naturally leads to confusion.

Figure 10-3. Three Ways to Determine Rafter Length

The "textbook" method of finding rafter length is (a), where a measuring line is first scribed down the rafter. The base of the triangle is measured horizontally beginning at the outside of the wall, the rise is from wall height to the measuring line at the top and rafter length is measured along the line down the interior of the rafter. Using method (b), the rise is to the bottom of the rafter, and diagonal length is measured along the bottom of the rafter and the run is to the inside of the wall. In method (c), the rise is measured to the top of the rafter, and the run to a spot above the outside wall at the top of the rafter and rafter length along the top. In all three cases, the correct rafter length can be found.

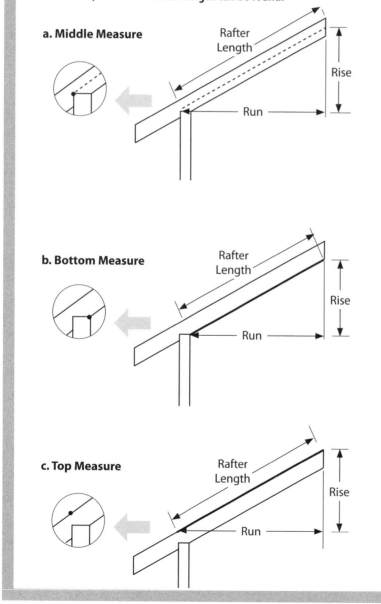

a. Middle Measure

Rafter Length

Rise

Run

b. Bottom Measure

Rafter Length

Rise

Run

c. Top Measure

Rafter Length

Rise

Run

Middle Measure

Over the years, middle measure has been the procedure most commonly used. When purchasing a new framing square, the instruction booklet will probably use this method. A line is drawn down the rafter board parallel to the edges, and the rise and run begin at the ends of this measuring line. (See **Figure 10-3a**.) The rise is measured from the top of the wall to the measuring line at the ridge. The run is measured from the line at the ridge to the point where the measuring line touches the outside wall. The rafter length is then measured along that line. If the roof is symmetrical, the run is one-half of the distance from the outside of one bearing wall to the outside of the other.

The middle measure method is confusing for two reasons. First, it's hard to determine just where to draw the measuring line. The instructions say it should be parallel to the rafter edges near the middle, but that will vary depending on the size of the rafter, the thickness of the wall, and the slope of the roof. (See **Figure 10-4**.) Second, the measuring line hits the ridge board at some undetermined spot. That makes it hard to figure how high to set the ridge. Using middle measure, all measurements are made on the measuring line, and there'll be a lot of trial and error before the final rafter pattern is set.

Top Measure

Using the top measure method, the rise is measured from an unspecified spot directly above the outside wall to the top of the ridge. The run is measured horizontally from the same spot, and rafter length is measured along the top of the rafter. (See **Figure 10-3c.**) Top measure is confusing because measurements are made from an unknown spot above the outside wall at the top of the rafter. The spot varies with the size of the rafter.

Bottom Measure

Architects and engineers prefer bottom measure, and it is the easiest to learn and to visualize. The rise is measured from the top of the wall to the bottom of the ridge. The run is measured from the inside of the wall, and rafter length along the bottom of the rafter, as in **Figure 10-3b**. The ridge beam will be positioned above the rise. In this book, I will use bottom measure to show how to use the framing square in roof framing.

Figure 10-4. The Measuring Line

The textbook method of determining rafter length uses a measuring line. Usually instructions say to "draw this line parallel to both edges extending to the outside of the wall," but as shown here, the placement will vary according to wall thickness and rafter size.

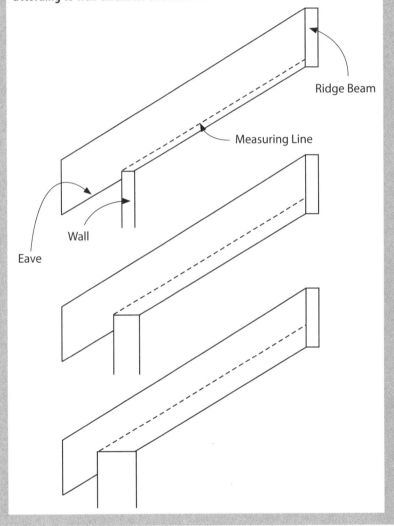

Definition of Terms

There are three Rs to consider in the problem of roof framing—run, rise, and rafter length. The following terms are important when considering roof framing (see **Figure 10-5**):

The Measuring Triangle

The measuring triangle is a theoretical area with a base, altitude, and hypotenuse. (See the shaded area in **Figure 10-5**.) It is the same whether the rafters are made of 2x4, 2x6, or 2x10 materials. The altitude is always the distance between the top of the wall and the bottom of the ridge. The hypotenuse is always the bottom of the rafter (any size rafter) from the bottom edge of the ridge beam to the top inside edge of the wall.

Top Plate

The top plate is usually a double set of 2x4s or 2x6s at the top of the wall. The rafter sits on this plate, and the run and rise are measured from here. It is sometimes called the double plate. (See **Figure 10-5**.)

Span

The span of a roof is the distance from the outside of one wall to the outside of the opposite wall. (See **Figure 10-5**.) The span can be found from the working drawings by studying the floor plans for the area directly below the roof. When a building is under construction, the span can be measured. If siding extends to the top of the wall, include it in this measurement.

Run

The run of a roof is the distance from the inside of the wall to a plumb line dropped below the highest point of the roof. (See **Figure 10-5**.) If there is a ridge beam, the horizontal dimension is plumbed from the side of the beam. **Figure 10-6** shows different rafter rises and runs.

Figure 10-5. Terms Used in Roof Framing

The various terms used in roof framing are interrelated. Note that the run is measured to the inside of the wall and the rise to one side of and beneath the ridge board. The shaded area is the measuring triangle used to calculate the rise, the run, and the rafter length.

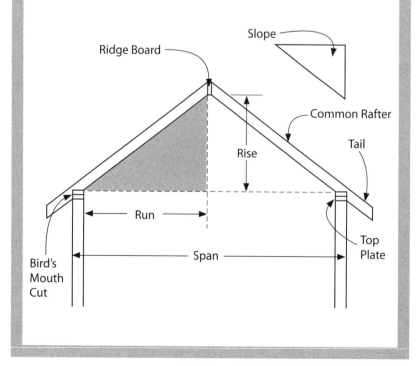

Rise

The rise of a roof is the vertical distance, measured in feet, from the top of the wall to the bottom of the ridge. (See **Figure 10-5**.)

Ridge Board

The ridge board (see **Figure 10-5**) is the highest framing member of a roof. It connects the upper ends of the rafters on one side to the rafters on the opposite side. In some framing, the ridge board is not used, and the opposing rafters are joined directly together, as in **Figure 10-2a**. In construction, the ridge board is held in position by a post at each end of the building until the rafters have been erected.

Ridge Board Length

The ridge should be drawn in the plans so the hip rafters extend from the ridge to the corner top plates at a 45° angle. All of the rafter figures on the framing square assume that distance (x) and distance (y) in **Figure 10-7b** are equal and that distance (x) and distance (z) are equal in **Figure 10-7c**.

Gable Roof

Finding the length of the ridge of a gable roof is a simple process—the ridge length is the same as the building length.

Figure 10-6. Rafter Rise and Run

A shed roof, (a), has a run the width of the building. In a symmetrical gable roof, (b), the two runs are equal. In roof (c), Run A and Run B are not equal and Rafter A will be longer and have different angles than Rafter B. In the complex roof (d), the lengths and cut angles of each set of rafters are determined using the corresponding rise and run.

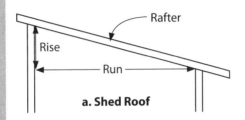

a. Shed Roof

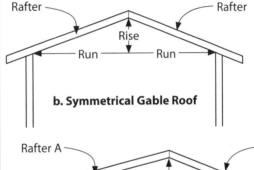

b. Symmetrical Gable Roof

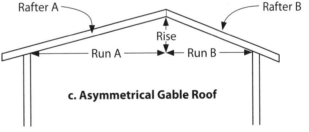

c. Asymmetrical Gable Roof

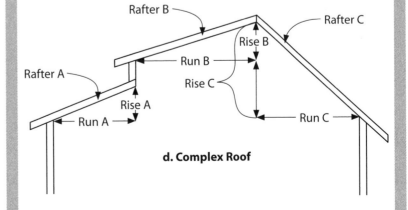

d. Complex Roof

Figure 10-7. Finding the Length of the Ridge

In a double hip roof as in (a) and (b), the length of the ridge is equal to the length of the building minus the width. In a single hip roof (c), the length of the ridge is the length of the building minus half the building width. Note that in all cases, the hips are constructed so the length of one common rafter (x) is equal to the other common rafter (y), and they are equal to half of the building width (z).

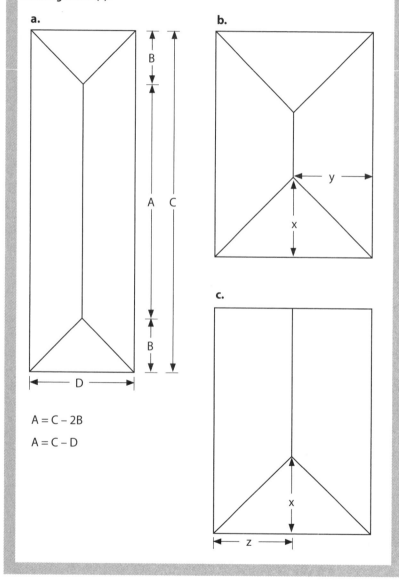

$A = C - 2B$

$A = C - D$

Single Hip Roof

The length of the ridge in a single hip roof (see **Figure 10-7c**) is the length of the building minus half the building width.

Double Hip Roof

The length of the ridge in a double hip roof (see **Figure 10-7a** and **10-7b**) is the length of the building minus the width of the building.

Roof Pitch

The pitch is the angle the roof makes with a horizontal plane. It is the ratio of the rise to the span. (See **Figure 10-8**.) A roof with a 6-foot rise and a 24-foot span is said to have a ¼ pitch or one-quarter pitch.

Pitch = Rafter Rise ÷ Building Span

Pitch = 6 feet ÷ 24 feet = ¼

A roof with ½ pitch (one half-pitch) rises one-half the distance of the span. Thus, for a 24-foot span, the rise of a ½ pitch roof would be 12 feet. (See **Figure 10-8**.)

Slope

The slope is the incline of a roof measured as inches of vertical rise per 12 inches of horizontal run. It is expressed as a fraction, for example 6-in-12 or $^6/_{12}$. A roof that rises at the rate of 4 inches for each foot of run is said to have a 4-in-12 slope or $^4/_{12}$. The triangular symbols above the roofs in **Figure 10-8** convey this information.

Figure 10-8. Roof Pitch and Slope

Pitch is rise divided by span. Slope is rise per foot of run. A roof with a 6-foot rise and 24-foot span, (a), is said to have a one-quarter pitch (6 ÷ 24) and a 6-in-12 slope. Similarly, a roof with a 12-foot rise and a 24-foot span, (b), has a pitch of one-half (12 ÷ 24) and a slope of 12-in-12.

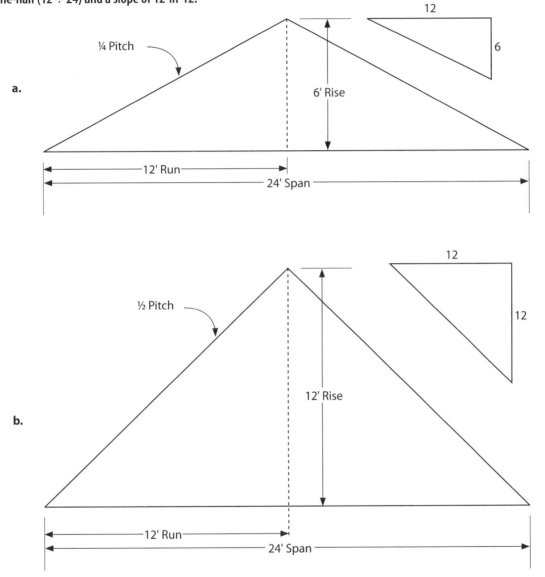

Figure 10-9. Plumb Lines and Level Lines

The framing square is used to lay out the plumb line and the level line on a rafter for a roof with $^6/_{12}$ slope. The plumb line is drawn along the tongue of the square and the level line is drawn along the body. The plumb line is for the ridge cut, and the level line is for the top plate cut.

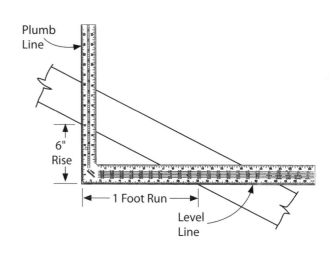

Plumb Line

6" Rise

◄— 1 Foot Run —►

Level Line

Figure 10-10. The Parts of a Roof Frame

The main rafters—common, hip, valley—all fit together to frame a roof. The jacks are shortened and extend from ridge to valley and from plate to hip.

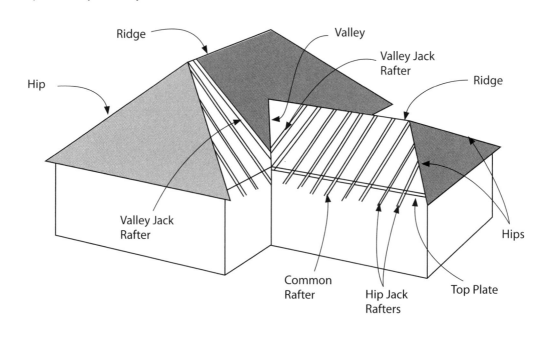

Ridge

Valley

Valley Jack Rafter

Ridge

Hip

Valley Jack Rafter

Hips

Common Rafter

Hip Jack Rafters

Top Plate

Plumb and Level Lines

Plumb and level lines refer to the direction of a line drawn on a rafter to be used later for cuts. Any line that is vertical when the rafter is in its proper position is called a plumb line. If the rafter were in place, the line could be drawn using a plumb bob and line. Any line that is horizontal when the rafter is in its proper position is called a level line. If the rafter were in place, the line could be drawn using a bubble level. (See **Figure 10-9**.)

Rafters

The rafters are the inclined members of the roof framework. They form the backbone and ribs of a house and serve the same purpose in the roof as joists do in the floor and studs in the wall. Rafters usually are spaced 16 inches or 24 inches on center. They vary in size (2x4 to 2x12) depending on their length, spacing, slope, and the kind of roof covering that will be used. Rafters usually extend beyond the wall to form eaves to protect the sides of the building. (See **Figure 10-4**.)

Common Rafters

Common rafters extend from the top plate to the ridge board at 90° to both. (See **Figure 10-10**.)

Rafter Tail

The rafter tail (eave or overhang) is the portion of the rafter that extends beyond the outside of the wall. The length of the tail is figured separately and is not included in the rafter length. (See **Figure 11-8**.)

Hip Rafters

Hip rafters run diagonally from the ridge to an outside corner of the plate. (See **Figure 10-10**.)

Valley Rafters

Valley rafters run diagonally from the ridge to an inside corner of the plate. (See **Figure 10-10**.)

Jack Rafters

Jack rafters (sometimes called cripples) are shortened and never extend the full distance from plate to ridge board. (See **Figure 10-10**.)

There are three kinds of short rafters:

• Hip jacks extend up from the plate at 90° to a hip rafter.

• Valley jacks extend down from the ridge at 90° to a valley rafter.

• Hip valley jacks extend from a hip to a valley rafter or between two valley rafters. The valley rafter (sometimes called a cripple jack rafter) touches neither the ridge of the roof nor the rafter plate, and both ends have miter cuts. They are used when dormers or additions meet sloped roofs (not shown).

Chapter 11

Laying Out the Rafters

Rafters are the skeleton of a roof and must be carefully cut and fitted to support the covering and the weight of anticipated snow, and to resist wind and tremors. The top end of the rafter rests against the ridge board and is cut with a plumb cut; the bottom end rests on the top plate and is cut with a level cut (see **Figure 11-1**). Both the length and the angles of these cuts must be exact if the rafter is to fit properly.

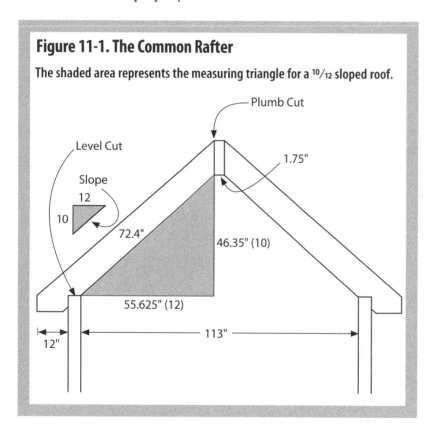

Figure 11-1. The Common Rafter

The shaded area represents the measuring triangle for a ¹⁰/₁₂ sloped roof.

Plumb Cut

Level Cut

Slope
12
10

1.75"

72.4"

46.35" (10)

55.625" (12)

113"

12"

Rafter Length

The important dimensions of a rafter are its length, the top cut and the bottom cuts. The angles are easy and can be set on a square once you know the slope of the roof. (See Chapter 10, "Roofs," **Figure 10-8**.) The length is more difficult but it can be found in any of five ways:

1. Mathematically by using the Pythagorean Theorem.

2. By using the rafter tables on the framing square.

3. By stepping off the length with a steel square.

4. By using the square as a proportioning tool.

5. By measuring and laying out directly on a rafter.

The Building Dimensions

To demonstrate how to find the length of a rafter using these five methods, the example is of a small storage shed constructed in snow country above Angel's Camp, California. The walls (2x6s) and the rafters (2x10s) were substantial to accommodate lots of insulation. A steep (10-in-12) gable roof was used to shed snow. (See **Figure 11-1**.) Of the five methods for finding rafter length, the easiest (No. 2, using the rafter tables) was utilized for length and then stepped off the eaves. *I taught my helpers, grandkids Wyatt (12) and Collin (10), how to use the framing square the first day, and from then on they were setting the fence and marking rafters like old hands.*

Certain data are needed before a roof can be designed. Some can be found on building plans, the rest by measuring:

1. Gable roof with equal runs on each side. (See Chapter 10, "Roofs".)

2. Inner wall-to-wall measurement (span) of 9 feet 5 inches (113 inches).

3. Roof slope of 10-in-12 (ten inches rise for each foot of run).

4. Ridge beam 1.75 inches thick.

5. Walls 6 inches thick (actual 5.5 inches).

6. 2x10 rafters (actual 1.75 inches x 9.5 inches).

7. Eaves 12 inches from wall.

1. Finding Rafter Length with Math

The bottom measure technique requires a measuring triangle, as explained in Chapter 10, "Roofs," **Figure 10-5**. The rise will be from the top of the wall to the bottom of the ridge board; the run is from the inner wall to a plumb line on the side of the ridge, and the rafter length is measured along the bottom of the rafter, as in **Figure 11-1**.

Using this method:

1. Find the run of the measuring triangle. (See **Figure 11-1**.)

2. Calculate the rise of the measuring triangle.

3. Use the rise and run to find the rafter (hypotenuse) length.

Finding the Base (Run) of the Measuring Triangle

The base or run of the measuring triangle is the room width minus the width of the ridge board, divided by 2.

1. Measure the inside distance between the walls. (See **Figure 11-1**.) The distance is 9 feet, 5 inches or 113 inches.

2. Subtract the thickness of the ridge board (1.75 inches).

    113 − 1.75 = 111.25 inches

3. Divide this number by 2.

    111.25 ÷ 2 = 55.625 inches.

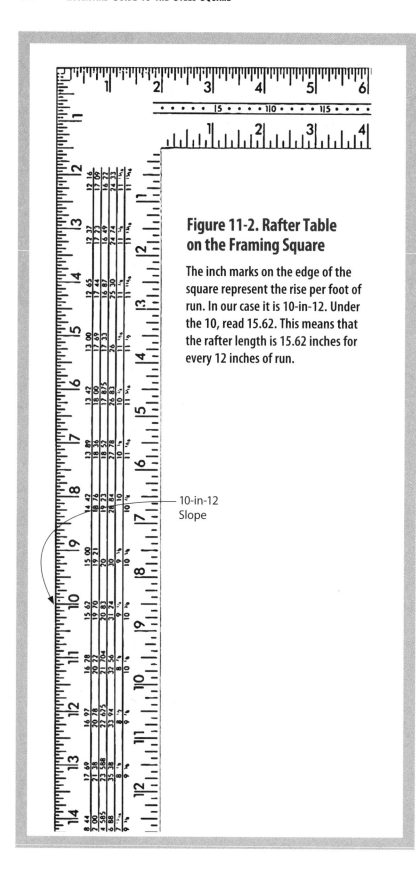

Figure 11-2. Rafter Table on the Framing Square

The inch marks on the edge of the square represent the rise per foot of run. In our case it is 10-in-12. Under the 10, read 15.62. This means that the rafter length is 15.62 inches for every 12 inches of run.

10-in-12 Slope

This is the length of the base of the measuring triangle (the run) used in the formula for calculating the rafter length (see **Figure 11-1**).

Finding the Rise of the Measuring Triangle

Unlike the base (run), the rise of the measuring triangle can't be measured because it does not physically exist yet. However, we do know both the slope of the roof ($^{10}/_{12}$) and the run (55.625 inches).

1. The roof will have a 10-in-12 slope; therefore, it will rise 10 inches for every 12 inches along the base.

2. Divide the run (55.625 inches) by 12 to find how many 12-inch increments there are in the base.

   55.625 ÷ 12 = 4.635

3. Multiply these increments by 10 to get the rise.

   4.635 x 10 = 46.35 inches

This is the altitude (rise) of the measuring triangle and the height from the top of the wall to the bottom of the ridge board.

Finding the Rafter Length

The rafter length can now be found because we know the run and rise of the measuring triangle (see **Figure 11-1**).

1. The rafter length is the hypotenuse of the measuring triangle.

Figure 11-3. Proportions with a Framing Square

Set the square at 10 and 12 along a straight line (Position 1). This represents the slope of 10-in-12. Move the square downward along the proportioning line to 11⅛; this represents the run of 55.625 divided by 5. Read 9¼ on the blade (Position 2). This is a rise of 46¼ inches (9.25 x 5 = 46.25).

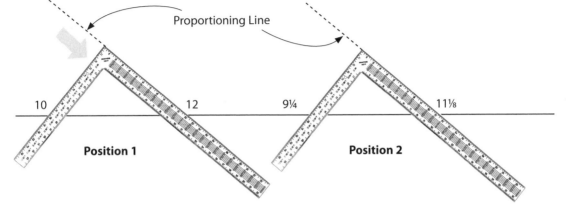

Proportioning Line

| 10 | 12 | 9¼ | 11⅛ |

Position 1 **Position 2**

2. The hypotenuse is the square root of the sum of the rise squared and the run squared.

$$H = \sqrt{(\text{Rise}^2 + \text{Run}^2)}$$

Where rise = 46.35 and run = 55.625

$$H = \sqrt{(46.35^2 + 55.625^2)}$$

$$H = \sqrt{(2148.3 + 3094.1)}$$

$$H = 72.4 \text{ inches}$$

The rafter length is 72.4 inches ≈ 72⅜ inches. We now know the rise (46⅜ inches) and the rafter length (72⅜ inches), and we can lay out the rafters.

2. Finding Rafter Length Using the Rafter Tables

Finding rafter lengths using the rafter tables on the framing square is incredibly easy. Each of the numbers in the top row, which is labeled Length of Common Rafters per Foot of Run (see **Figure 11-2**), is the square root of a slope. We merely locate the slope we want and multiply the given value by our run. In our case, the slope is 10-in-12. The number under the 10 mark is 15.62. This means on a roof with a ¹⁰⁄₁₂ slope, the common rafter is 15.62 inches long for each foot of run.

> Rafter Length = Table Value x Run (in feet)

Where Table Value = 15.62 and run = 55.625 inches (4.64 feet)

> 15.62 x 4.64 = 72.48 inches

> Rafter Length ≈ 72½ inches

Now wasn't that easy?

Finding the Rise

You know the run and the rafter length but still need to find the rise.

Rule of Thumb: How the Rafter Table Values are Derived

The rafter table value for slope ¹⁰⁄₁₂ is 15.62. How was this number found?

Hypotenuse (Rafter Length) = $\sqrt{(\text{rise}^2 + \text{run}^2)}$

Where rise = 10 and run = 12

$H = \sqrt{(10^2 + 12^2)}$

$H = \sqrt{(100 + 144)}$

$H = \sqrt{(244)} = 15.62$

Thus the rafter length for all ¹⁰⁄₁₂ roofs is 15.62 inches per foot of run.

Figure 11-4. Stepping Off the Length of a Common Rafter

Use the framing square to step off the total length of the rafter, in the example, 4 feet 7⅝ inches. Set the fence at the slope (¹⁰⁄₁₂). Measure 7⅝" from the top plumb line along a level line (see inset) and make a new plumb line. Step off as many times down the board as there are feet in the total run. In this case, it will be four times. The step-off ends at the level cut for the top of the wall.

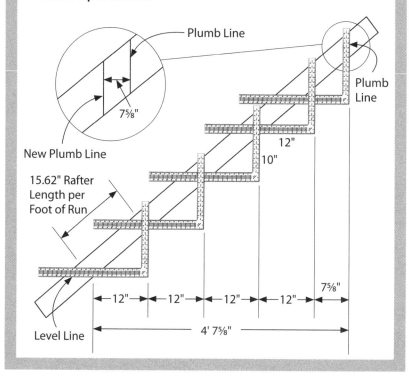

The slope of the roof is ¹⁰⁄₁₂ and the run is 55⅝ inches (see **Figure 11-1**). You can use the framing square as a proportioning tool to find the rise. For more on proportioning, see Chapter 15, "Proportioning Problems," **Figure 15-3**. We will set the slope on the square (10-in-12) and then use the run (55⅝) to find the rise.

1. Lay the framing square along a straight edge so 10 on the blade and 12 on the body touch the line (see **Figure 11-3**, **Position 1**).

2. Draw a proportion line along the body extending from the edge of the board out a few inches beyond the heel of the square.

Note: The number 55.625 cannot be set on the square, so we divide it by 5, for convenience, to get a smaller number.

3. Move the square downward along the proportion line until 11⅛ (55.625 ÷ 5 = 11.125) on the body touches the line (see **Figure 11-3**, **Position 2**).

4. Read 9¼ on the blade (this number is ⅕ the total rise).

5. The rise is 9.25 x 5 = 46¼ inches.

Using the rafter tables, we know the rafter length is 72½ inches and, using the steel square as a proportioning tool, we know the rise is 46¼ inches.

3. Finding Rafter Length Using the Step-Off Method

The third method for finding rafter length is by using the framing square to step off the length on the wood itself. (See **Figure 11-4**.) Again, the given data is:

1. Slope of roof = 10-in-12

2. Run = 55⅝ inches
   (4 feet 7⅝ inches)

The theory of the framing square method and the practice are simple. When you set a fence on the square equal to the slope (10-in-12), then for every foot of run you measure (step off) down the board, an equivalent length of rafter also is marked off. To set the square for the slope of 10-in-12, make a simple wooden fence, as shown in **Figure 11-5**.

The Run Is Not Even

In this case, the run is 4 feet 7⅝ inches.

1. The extra 7⅝ inches is taken care of first.

2. Measure 7⅝ inches over from the top plumb cut on a level line.

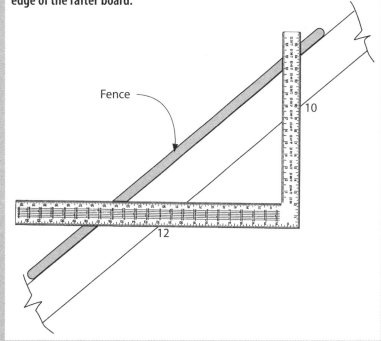

Figure 11-5. A Fence

Fasten a fence to the square so the run is 12 and the rise is 10 (the roof slope is ¹⁰/₁₂). Use it to mark the correct angles for the plumb line (ridge) and the level line (wall top). A fence also makes it easy to step off the rafter length. The fence can be attached so it rides along the top or underneath the board—as long as the 10 and 12 marks are on the bottom edge of the rafter board.

Fence

10

12

3. Mark a new plumb line here along the tongue. (See **Figure 11-4**, inset.)

4. Mark a level line on the rafter along the outside of the body.

5. Step off four times down the rafter; at each step, place the tongue of the square on the new level line.

6. The last level mark will be the rafter length to the inside of the wall. The level line also will be the seat level line.

4. Finding Rafter Length by Proportioning

The square was used as a proportioning tool in Method 2 (see **Figure 11-3**) to find the rise of 46¼ inches. Using this value and a run of 4 feet 7⅝ inches, you can find the rafter length, as in **Figure 11-6**.

1. Use the side of the square that has inches divided into twelfths on both arms. Using the twelfths scale allows direct measurement of feet and inches without conversions.

2. The run is 4 feet 7⅝ inches, so lay a 12-inch rule at 4 and $^{7.5}\!/_{12}$

(between the $^{7}\!/_{12}$ and the $^{8}\!/_{12}$ mark) inches on the body.

Note: Approximate 7⅝ inches as $^{7.5}\!/_{12}$ on the square.

3. The rise is 3 feet and 10¼ inches so set the rule at $3^{10}\!/_{12}$ inches on the tongue.

Note: You can ignore the extra ¼ inch.

4. Measure the distance across the square and read 6 inches.

5. The rafter length is 6 feet (72 inches).

5. Finding Rafter Length by Direct Layout

The layout method (see **Figure 11-7**), does not actually give you the length of the rafter, it's not needed. The layout method produces an accurate pattern you can use for all the other rafters.

1. Lay a 4x8 sheet of plywood on the subfloor.

2. Use a tape to mark the rise (46⅜ inches) along the short edge. Drive a nail here.

3. Measure the run (55⅝ inches) along the long edge. Drive a nail here.

4. Lay a straight board (a 1x4 works fine) across the diagonal just touching the two nails–it will be your pattern.

Figure 11-6. Finding Rafter Length by Proportioning

Use the back of the blade where inches are divided into twelfths. Lay a ruler between the rise (3¹⁰/₁₂) and the run (between 4⁷/₁₂ and 4⁸/₁₂) and measure a distance of 6 inches. The rafter length is 6 feet.

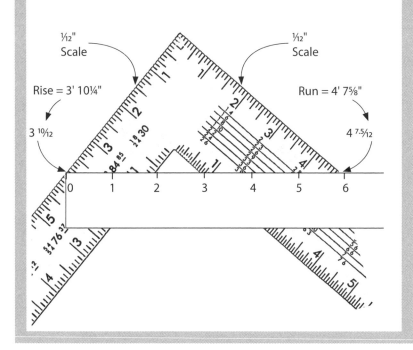

5. Use a straight edge and mark the top plumb line as an extension of the edge of the plywood. (See **Figure 11-7**.)

6. Mark the seat level line on the rafter.

7. Mark the wall thickness on the level line. (See **Figure 11-7**, inset.)

8. Mark the seat plumb line for the bird's mouth.

9. Measure for the overhang and draw the bottom plumb cut.

Cut at these marks and use the board as a pattern.

Summary of Methods to Find Rafter Length

The results of the five different methods are:

1. With Math: Rafter length = 72⅜ inches, Rise = 46⅜ inches.

2. Using Framing Square Rafter Tables: Rafter length = 72½ inches, Rise = 46¼ inches.

3. With Framing Square Step Off: Rafter length = A pattern only, No rise found.

4. Using Proportions with a Framing Square: Rafter length = 72 inches, No rise.

5. Using Direct Layout: Rafter length = A pattern only, No rise.

All of these methods give a good pattern for marking and cutting

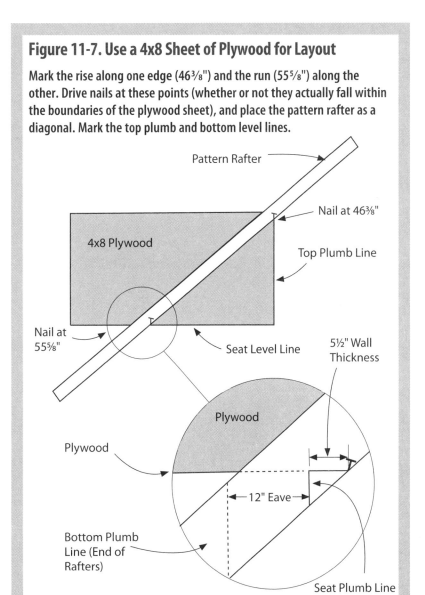

Figure 11-7. Use a 4x8 Sheet of Plywood for Layout

Mark the rise along one edge (46⅜") and the run (55⅝") along the other. Drive nails at these points (whether or not they actually fall within the boundaries of the plywood sheet), and place the pattern rafter as a diagonal. Mark the top plumb and bottom level lines.

Pattern Rafter

Nail at 46⅜"

Top Plumb Line

4x8 Plywood

Nail at 55⅝"

Seat Level Line

5½" Wall Thickness

Plywood

Plywood

12" Eave

Bottom Plumb Line (End of Rafters)

Seat Plumb Line

the common rafters. Even the Proportioning Method (Number 4), which gave a rafter length of 72 inches (instead of 72⅜ inch by the math method), will give a good pattern. A 72-inch rafter will give a rise of 45¾ inches instead of 46¼ inches; the ½-inch difference won't be noticeable.

Rule of Thumb: Test the Pattern

Snap chalk lines on the subfloor representing the run and rise, and then test the pattern for fit.

Figure 11-8. Rafter Cut for Bird's Mouth and Overhang

Measure 6 inches along the seat level-line for the wall thickness. The length of the rafter overhang may be found by using the rafter tables on the framing square. It is measured from the seat plumb line (the outside of the wall). The end can be cut square or plumb.

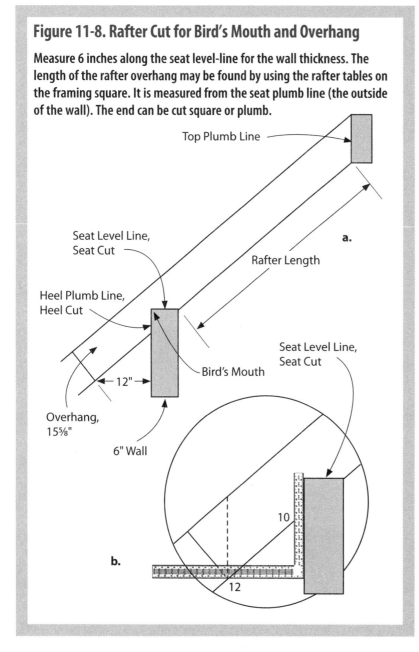

Top Plumb Line

Seat Level Line, Seat Cut

Rafter Length

a.

Heel Plumb Line, Heel Cut

Seat Level Line, Seat Cut

Bird's Mouth

← 12" →

Overhang, 15⅝"

6" Wall

10

b.

12

Laying Out Common Rafters

Now that rafter length has been found using one of the above five methods, the cut angles can be marked using the framing square, as in **Figure 10-9**.

Bird's Mouth

A rafter with an overhang has a notch in it called a bird's mouth. (See **Figure 11-8a**.) The part which bears against the outside of the rafter plate is called the heel plumb cut; the part which bears on the top of the rafter plate is called the seat level line cut. The bird's mouth is laid out much the same way as the seat on a rafter without an overhang. Measure off the length of the seat on a level line, set the square, and draw the heel plumb cut along the blade. (See **Figure 11-8b**.)

Rule of Thumb: Plumb and Level

To lay out plumb cuts and seat level cuts:

Common Rafter—Use the rise over 12.

Hip/Valley Rafter—Use the rise over 17.

Common Rafter Overhang

Most roofs have an overhang for aesthetics and for protection of the walls from rain and sun. The overhanging part of the rafter for the eave is called the tail and must be added to the length of the rafter. The length of the tail is calculated as if it were a separate small rafter using any of the five methods. Here are my two favorites.

1. Using the Rafter Scale

In this case, you want the eave to be 12 inches from the wall (horizontal), and the roof has a slope of 10-in-12. The rafter table (see **Figure 11-2**) shows the rafter should be 15.62 inches per foot of run (15⅝ inches). (See **Figure 11-8**.)

2. Using the Step-Off Method

Place the square so the tongue is on the heel plumb line (outer side of the wall), and set the tongue at 10 and the body at 12. Remember, the slope is 10-in-12. Make a mark to give a 12-inch eave. Cut the end square or with a plumb cut. (See **Figure 11-8**, inset.)

Many carpenters do not cut the tail to finished length until after the rafters have been nailed in place. The length of the tail is calculated, and more than enough material is left beyond the bird's mouth for the overhang. All other cuts except the tail plumb cut are made. After the rafters have been nailed in place, the exact length of the tail is marked on the two end rafters. A chalk line is snapped on the top edge of all the rafters. A tail plumb line is then drawn down from the chalk line on each rafter, and the tails are cut.

Common Rafter Pattern

Find the rafter length by any of the five methods. Mark the dimensions on a piece of stock. When laying out rafters, if there is any crook in the board material, remember to use the crown of the board for the top edge. Carefully cut the top and bottom angles.

Use this as a pattern and cut a second rafter. Try the two rafters on the building with the ridge board in place to see how the heel and the top cuts fit. If they are correct, label one rafter on both sides "Common Rafter Pattern" and use it to cut all others needed. Distribute the rafters to their locations around the building; lean them with the ridge cut up. The carpenters on the building can then pull them up as needed and nail them in position.

Figure 11-9. Hip and Valley Rafters

The rise of a common rafter and the rise of a hip/valley rafter are the same—from the top of the wall to the ridge beam. The run of a common rafter is along one side of an imaginary square (light shaded area). The run of a hip/valley rafter is the diagonal of the imaginary square (dark shaded area).

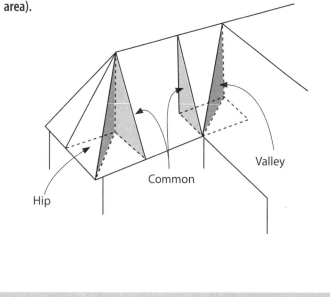

Hip   Common   Valley

Hip and Valley Rafters

Hip and valley rafters can be treated the same; both extend from the ridge to the plate—the hip to an outside corner, and the valley to an inside corner. Hip and valley rafters are the same length, and the top plumb cuts and the bottom level cuts are the same angles. They both represent the hypotenuse (diagonal) of a right triangle where one side is a common rafter and the other side is the top plate or the ridge.

Finding Top Plumb Cuts and Seat Level Cuts

When a roof has a slope of 4-in-12, the rise is 4 inches for every 12 inches of run; therefore, the unit run of the common rafter is 12 inches. See **Figure 11-9** where the run of the common rafter is the side of a square. The run of a hip/valley rafter is the diagonal of that same square.

The length of the diagonal of a 12-inch square is:

$$\text{Diagonal} = \sqrt{(12^2 + 12^2)}$$
$$= \sqrt{288} = 16.97 \approx 17$$

Therefore, the run of a hip/valley rafter is always $^{17}/_{12}$ longer than the run of a common rafter.

Figure 11-10a shows the position of the framing square to mark the top and seat cuts on a common rafter with roof slope of 6-in-12. On the same roof, the square is set at 6 and 17. See **Figure 11-10b** for the plumb and seat cuts for a hip/valley rafter.

Finding Hip/Valley Rafter Length

There are four methods for finding the length of a hip/valley rafter— using math and the Pythagorean Theorem, using the tables on the framing square, stepping off, and direct measurement.

1. Finding the Hip/Valley Rafter Length by Math

To figure the length of the hip (or valley) rafter consider:

1. The rise of a hip rafter and the rise of a common rafter are the same.

2. The run of a hip rafter is $^{17}/_{12}$

longer than the run of a common rafter—no matter what the slope is.

That means that with a 6-in-12 slope:

Common Rafter:

Rise = 6, Run = 12.

Hip (or Valley) Rafter:

Rise = 6, Run = 17.

Problem 11-1. Length of Hip Rafter

What is the hip rafter length for a 6-in-12 slope and a run of 10 feet?

Solution 11-1

Once the run of the common rafter–10 feet–is known, then the hip run can be found:

Hip Run = Common Run x $^{17}/_{12}$

Hip Run = (10 x 17) ÷ 12

= 170 ÷ 12 = 14.17 feet

= 14 feet, 2 inches

Knowing the slope is $^{6}/_{12}$ and the run of a common rafter is 10 feet, you can figure the rise.

Rise = Slope x Run

Rise = $^{6}/_{12}$ x 10 feet = 60 ÷ 12

= 5 feet

Then, using the Pythagorean Theorem:

Hypotenuse = $\sqrt{(Run^2 + Rise^2)}$

Where Run = 14.17 feet and Rise = 5 feet

Hypotenuse = $\sqrt{(14.17^2 + 5^2)}$
= $\sqrt{(200.8 + 25)}$

Hypotenuse = $\sqrt{(225.8)}$
= 15.03 ≈ 15 feet

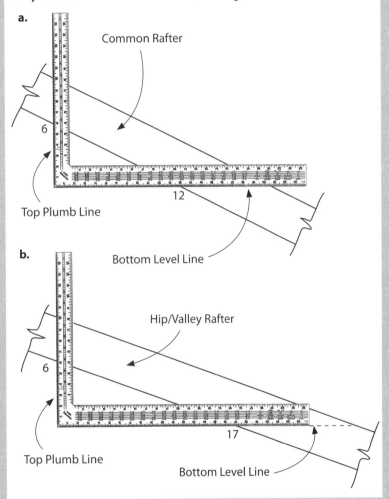

Figure 11-10. Stepping off for Hip Rafter Length

To find the length of the common rafter (a), the fence is set at 6 and 12. To find the length of the hip rafter (b), set the fence at 6 and 17 and step off as many times as there are feet in the run, as in Figure 11-4.

a.

Common Rafter

6

12

Top Plumb Line

Bottom Level Line

b.

Hip/Valley Rafter

6

17

Top Plumb Line

Bottom Level Line

The hip rafter is 15 feet long and the rise is 5 feet.

The common rafter is 134.2 inches = 11.18 feet = 11 feet, 2⅛ inches

Figure 11-11. Measuring for Hip Rafter Length

Measure from the outside corner of the top plate to the top end of the ridge beam once three common rafters are in place (b). When the length is transferred to the hip rafter, make sure it is along a diagonal (c).

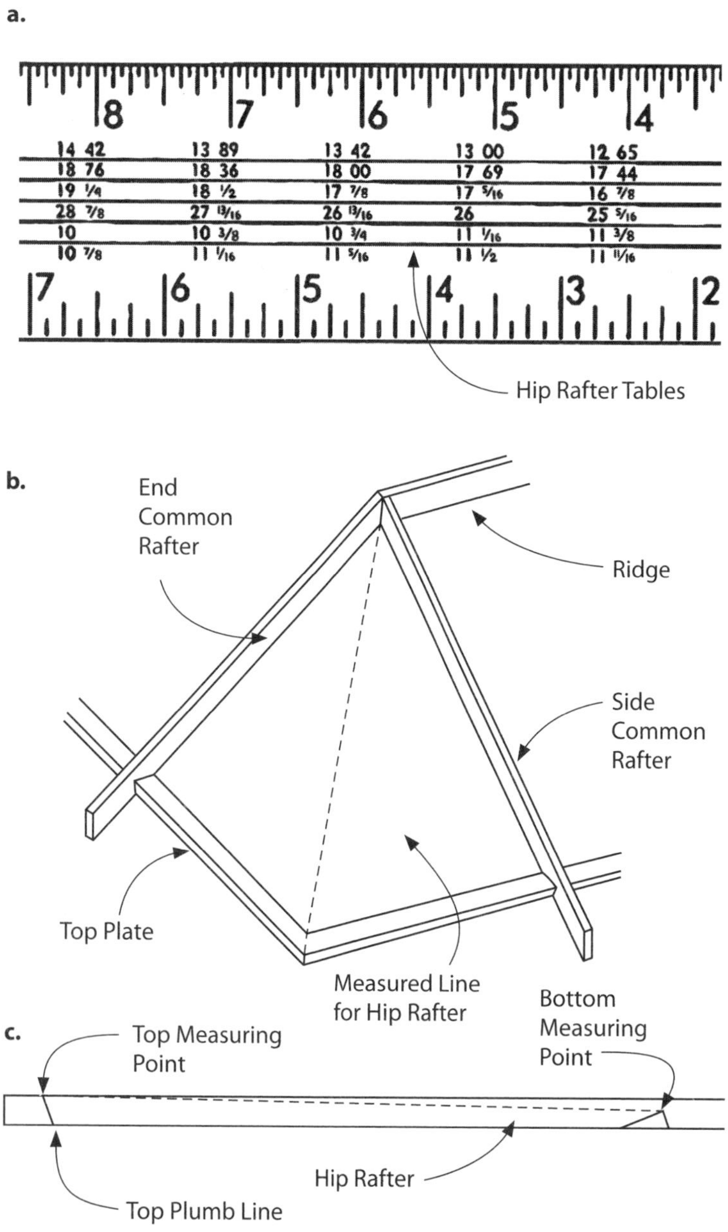

a.

14 42	13 89	13 42	13 00	12 65
18 76	18 36	18 00	17 69	17 44
19 1/4	18 1/2	17 7/8	17 5/16	16 7/8
28 7/8	27 13/16	26 13/16	26	25 5/16
10	10 3/8	10 3/4	11 1/16	11 3/8
10 7/8	11 1/16	11 5/16	11 1/2	11 11/16

Hip Rafter Tables

b.

End Common Rafter

Ridge

Side Common Rafter

Top Plate

Measured Line for Hip Rafter

Bottom Measuring Point

c.

Top Measuring Point

Hip Rafter

Top Plumb Line

2. Finding the Length of a Hip Rafter Using Tables

The rafter tables on the framing square can be used to find the length of the hip and valley rafters. Consider the case where the slope is 6 in 12 and the run of the common rafter is 10 feet.

In **Figure 11-11a**, look under the 6 (the slope is 6/12) on the scale and read 13.42 (the length in inches of the common rafter per foot of run) and 18 (the length in inches of the hip/valley rafter per foot of run of the common rafter). Note that 18 is the hip/valley rafter length per foot of run of the common rafter, NOT the run of the hip/valley rafter.

In this case, the run of the common rafter is 10 feet, therefore:

> Hip Rafter Length = 10 x 18
> = 180 inches ÷ 12 = 15 feet

Using the rafter tables is a lot simpler than the math method.

3. Finding the Length of a Hip Rafter by Stepping Off

The slope of a roof is 6-in-12. To step off a common rafter, set the fence at 6 and 12. (See **Figure 11-10a**.) Because the run of the hip rafter is 6-in-17, the fence is set differently.

1. Set the fence on the square at 6 & 17.

2. Lay the framing square on the board, as shown in **Figure 11-10b**, and mark the top plumb line.

3. Step off ten times in the manner described in **Figure 11-4**.

4. Mark the bottom level line—it is the length of the hip rafter.

4. Finding the Length of a Hip Rafter by Measuring

The measuring method is almost foolproof. The roof must be partially completed (see **Figure 11-11b**) with the ridge board and the end and side common rafters in place. The measuring method provides for variations in construction and can be used for roofs with unusual features.

1. Hold a tape at the outside corner of the top plate.

2. Measure to the top end of the ridge beam.

3. Use a long 1x4 and mark the distance from the top plumb line to the center of the board at the seat. (See **Figure 11-11c**.)

Cutting Side Angles on the Hip Rafter

The V-cuts at the ridge are made using data in the rafter tables on the framing square. (See **Figure 11-2**.) Look in the column under the 6 (6-in-12 slope), the sixth row down is labeled "Side Cut Hip or Valley Use," and read 11⁵⁄₁₆. Position the square on the hip rafter, as in **Figure 11-12a**, with the body at 11⁵⁄₁₆ and the tongue at 12, and make a mark on the outside edge of the tongue.

Reverse the square and mark from the other side of the board to make a V. That is the top cut.

Mark the seat level cuts in a similar manner. (See **Figure 11-12b**.)

Figure 11-12. Marking the Ridge and Seat Cuts on a Hip Rafter

Use the framing square to draw the side cut lines for the ridge, (a). The number 11⁵⁄₁₆ is found on the rafter square table "Side Cut Hip or Valley Use." The hip rafter must be shortened by half of the 45° thickness of the ridge, (b).

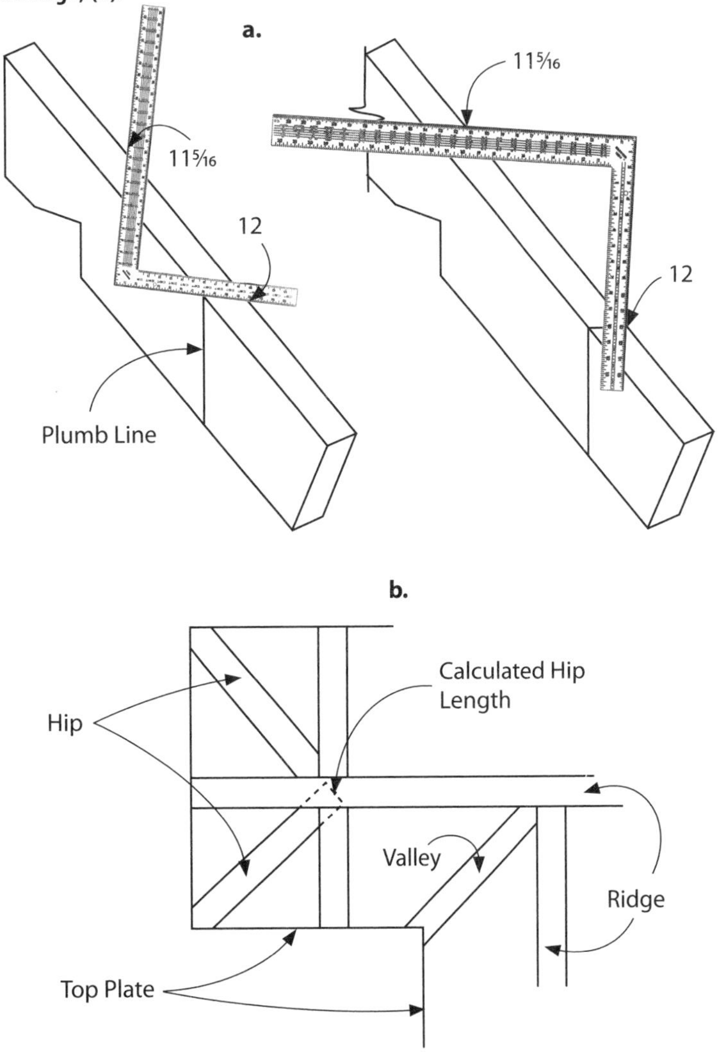

a.

11⁵⁄₁₆

12

Plumb Line

11⁵⁄₁₆

12

b.

Hip

Calculated Hip Length

Valley

Ridge

Top Plate

Jack Rafters

Jack rafters are common rafters with either the lower or upper end cut diagonally to fit against a hip or valley rafter. (See **Figure 11-13**.) The unit rise and roof slope are the same for jacks as for common rafters, and the common difference between the lengths of evenly spaced jack rafters is a constant. Data for the length is found in rows three and four on the framing square. (See **Figure 11-2**.) Row three is for jacks spaced 16 inches on-center, and row four is for jacks spaced 24 inches on center.

Problem 11-2. Jack Rafter Length

Your roof has ⁶⁄₁₂ slope and you are spacing the rafters 16 inches on-center (OC). Find the length of the first jack rafter and the common difference. Use the scales on the framing square.

Solution 11-2

1. Row three under the 6 (slope = ⁶⁄₁₂) is labeled "Diff in Length of Jacks 16 Inches Centers."

2. Read 17.875 or 17⅞ inches. That is the length of the first jack rafter spaced 16 inches OC from the hip.

3. The second jack is also spaced 16 inches OC and will be twice the common difference in length:

$$2 \times 17.875 = 35.75 \text{ inches long}$$

4. The third jack will be three times the common difference, and so on. (See **Figure 11-14**.)

$$3 \times 17.875 = 53.625$$
$$= 53⅝ \text{ inches long}$$

Angle Cuts for Jack Rafters

After the length is found, a common rafter is used to lay out the jacks so the cuts are marked and ready for transfer to individual rafters. Draw out the first jack with the tail, bird's mouth, and length, according to the common difference found on the square. (See **Figure 11-14**.) Measure from the point and mark jack two and so on. Finally, draw plumb lines at the end of each jack.

Side Cuts for Jack Rafters

On the framing square under 6, read "Side Cuts of Jacks use . . ." and read 10¾. The side cuts are made by setting gauges on the square at 10¾ and 12. (See **Figure 11-13**.) Hold the square on the top of the rafter and scribe along the 12-inch side.

Figure 11-13. Jack Rafter Layout

The slope is ⁶/₁₂. When the jacks are spaced 16 inches on-center (OC), the length of the first jack will be 17⅞ inches. That is also the common difference in length for all the jacks measured long point to long point. The side cuts are made with the square at 10¾ and 12—these numbers are found on the rafter table (see Figure 11-2).

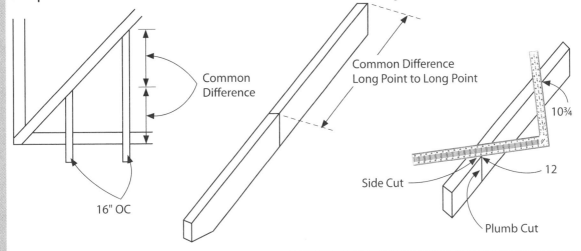

Figure 11-14. Laying Out a Jack Rafter

Use a common rafter to lay out all the jacks. Each will have a tail, bird's mouth, and length equal to a multiple of the common difference found in the rafter table on the framing square. The plumb lines and the level lines are the same as used for the common rafters. The common difference lengths are measured point to point.

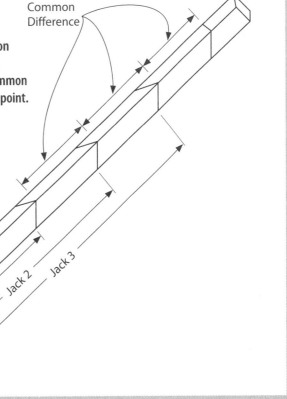

CHAPTER 12

The Speed Square

The speed square is more properly called the triangular framing square. It is shaped like a 45° right triangle (see **Figure 12-1**) and has various marks specific to roof framing. The double fence along one edge and the pivot point make it handy for marking degrees and rafter angles. It's small enough (anywhere from 5 inches to 12 inches on a side) to be tossed into a tool box, and because of the design, it's quite sturdy. Speed squares typically are made of lightweight aluminum or plastic so they don't rust.

Figure 12-1. Triangular Framing Square

The speed square has a fence along one edge, making it especially easy to hold against a rafter to either mark or cut. The numbers (1-30) on the Common Top Cuts row represent roof slopes (1-in-12 through 30-in-12). The Hip-Val Top Cut scale is also listed by slope from 1-30. The degree scale is used as a protractor or for marking angles based on degree rise. A small booklet that comes with the square shows rafter lengths.

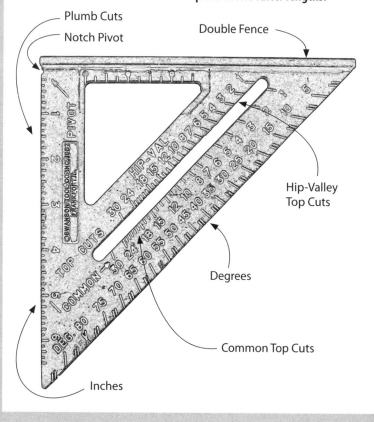

Plumb Cuts
Notch Pivot
Double Fence
Hip-Valley Top Cuts
Degrees
Common Top Cuts
Inches

In use, the speed square is positioned so the roof slope number is aligned with the edge of the board—the number 6 means a slope of 6-in-12. Both the plumb lines and the level lines can be marked from this position. Unlike a framing square, there are no scales for rafter length, but a little book of charts takes care of it. Both sides of the square have the same figures, which makes it easy to mark from either side of a rafter, useful for right-handed framers and for southpaws. The speed square does have limitations, but, all in all, it's quite handy for its intended use—marking rafter angles. It's also extremely handy as a fence for steering a portable circular saw through 45° miters and square crosscuts.

History

Triangular squares are not new; in fact, they predate the L-type square. Triangular squares were used by the Egyptians and Romans thousands of years ago. In the United States, an 1850 Stanley catalog listed a triangular miter square—but with no graduations. Twenty years later Stanley was selling an improved model having an iron frame with a lacquered boxwood rule inlay. The beveled wood base had a scale graduated in eighth-inches. (See **Figure 12-2**.)

The speed square as we use it today, with all of its markings, first appeared in the United States in the early 1930s. It has been sold under various names—speed square, quick square, rafter square, pocket square, layout square, angle square, mini-square, and poly square. It was initially advertised as a combination rafter square, miter square, try square, scribing guide, protractor, and saw guide. When it was first introduced, older carpenters treated it as a novelty—they were used to their L-shaped framing squares with rafter length tables and all the familiar scales. Soon younger framers began to use the speed square—partially to be different (rebellious youth) but also because its compact size allowed it to be easily hung from a utility belt. By 1950, the extras on the steel framing square such as the octagon, board feet, brace, and hundredths scales weren't used as much—especially by the roof framers—and the speed square became quite popular.

Figure 12-2. 1870 Stanley Triangular Miter Square

The 45°-90°-45° square was made of iron with a boxwood inlay for the rule. The 9-inch wood base was graduated in eighth-inches and could be used as a fence.

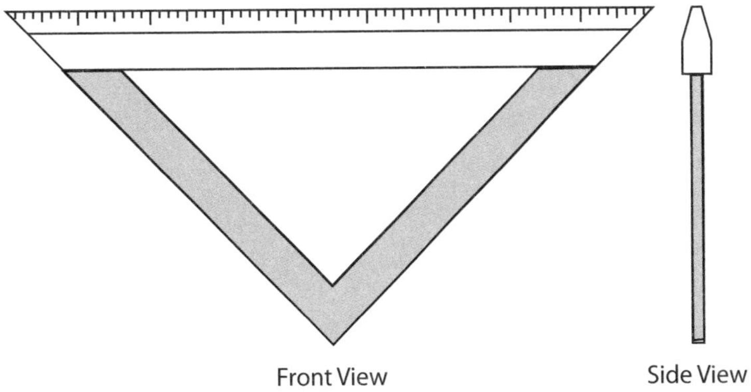

Front View   Side View

Description

The 1930 version of the triangular miter square had improvements over the old Stanley model: a double fence with a pivot point, a degree scale, and scribe lines for roof slopes. The fence made it easy to hold the tool against the edge of a board for 45° and right-angle cuts. The slope lines were used to mark common and hip/valley rafter angles, and the degree scale could be used as an adjustable protractor or to mark rafter angles using degree rise instead of slope.

Rule of Thumb: Rise and Run

Run x Slope = Rise

10-foot Run x $\frac{6}{12}$ Slope = 10 x $\frac{6}{12}$ = 5-foot Rise

Rise ÷ Slope = Run

5-foot Rise ÷ $\frac{6}{12}$ Slope = 5 ÷ $\frac{6}{12}$ = (5 x 12) ÷ 6 = 10 feet

Figure 12-3. Rafter Rise and Rafter Run

The run is measured horizontally from the inner wall to a plumb line beneath the side of the ridge. The rise is measured vertically from the bottom of the ridge to the top of the plate.

Slope = Rise (inches) ÷ Run (inches)

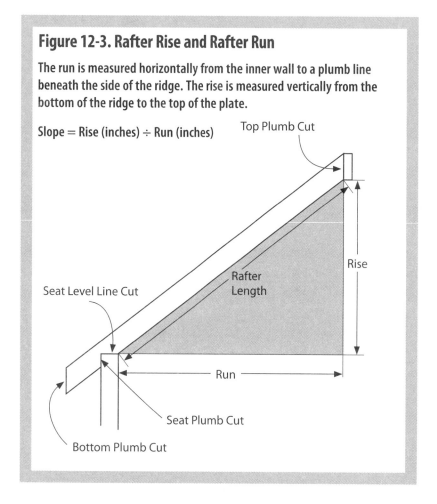

Figure 12-4. Marking the Top Plumb Line

Set the fence of the square against the edge of the rafter and pivot it until the 4 of Common Top Cuts is lined up with the edge. Mark the top plumb line.

Using the Speed Square to Cut Common Rafters

The use of the speed square to mark angles on a rafter is based on the right triangle. (See **Figure 12-3**, shaded area.) The steps to lay out a rafter are:

1. Mark the top plumb line (using the known slope).

2. Find the rafter length (by using a table).

3. Mark the bird's mouth (seat level line and plumb line).

4. Find the length of the eave (from the table).

5. Mark the tail (end plumb line).

1. Mark the Top Plumb Line

To show how to use the speed square to lay out a rafter, use the example of a roof with a 4-in-12 slope. Lay the square flat on the board, as in **Figure 12-4**. Hold the fence firmly against the board and find 4 on the Common Top Cuts scale. Pivot the square so the 4 (the slope is 4-in-12) is lined up with the edge of the board. Hold the pivot point of the square firmly against the board and mark the top plumb line. Note in **Figure 12-4**, the bottom of the rafter is at the top of the figure; rafter length will be measured along the bottom.

2. Find the Rafter Length

To compensate for the lack of rafter length scales on the square itself (as on the steel framing square), the

Figure 12-5. Speed Square Rafter Length Table

This is one of 48 Building Width tables used to find rafter lengths. The common rafter length of a 10-foot run with 4-in-12 slope is 10 feet 6½ inches.

Building Run: 10 Feet

Rise in Inches Per Foot of Run	Common (Feet-Inches)	Hip-Val (Feet-Inches)
1	10' 7⁄16"	14' 2"
2	10' 1⅝"	14' 2⅞"
3	10' 3¹¹⁄16"	14' 4¹⁵⁄16"
4	10' 6½"	14' 6⅜"
5	10' 10"	14' 8¹⁵⁄16"
6	11' 2³⁄16"	15' 0"
7	11' 6¹⁵⁄16"	15' 3⁹⁄16"
8	12' ¼"	15' 7⅝"
9	12' 6"	16' ⅛"
10	13' ³⁄16"	16' 5"
11	13' 6³⁄16"	16' 10¼"
12	14' 1¹¹⁄16"	17' 3⅞"

Figure 12-6. Speed Square Rafter Length Table

A rafter length table is sorted by slope (4-in-12) instead of span. To find the rafter length of a 10-foot run, read 10'6½".

4-Inch Rise (4/12 Slope)

Run (in Feet)	Common Rafter Length
1	1' ⅝"
2	2' 1¼"
3	3' 2"
4	4' 2⅝"
5	5' 3¼"
6	6' 3⅞"
7	7' 4½"
8	8' 5¼"
9	9' 5⅞"
10	10' 6½"
11	11' 7⅛"
12	12' 7¼"

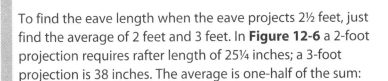

Rule of Thumb: Rafter with Eave

To find the eave length when the eave projects 2½ feet, just find the average of 2 feet and 3 feet. In **Figure 12-6** a 2-foot projection requires rafter length of 25¼ inches; a 3-foot projection is 38 inches. The average is one-half of the sum:

25.25 + 38 = 63.25 ÷ 2 = 31.625 = 31⅝ inches

speed square comes with a small booklet containing multiple tables of rafter lengths. **Figure 12-5** shows a table for a building with a run of 10 feet. For a slope of ⁴⁄₁₂, the common rafter length is 10 feet 6½ inches.

Other manufacturers of the speed square have different tables. **Figure 12-6** shows a table of rafter lengths sorted by slope (4-in-12). The table gives a similar rafter length (10 feet 6½ inches) for a 10-foot run.

Figure 12-7. Marking the Common Rafter

Measure the rafter length from the top plumb line along the bottom of the rafter to the inside of the wall, (a). Mark a seat level line for the top of the wall and another plumb line for the bird's mouth, (b). Measure the eave rafter length from the outside of the wall, (c). Mark the bottom plumb line last.

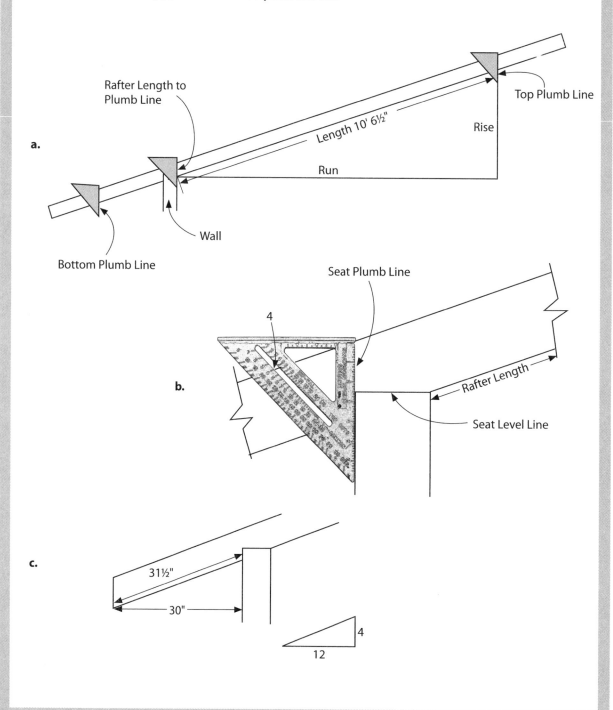

3. Mark the Bird's Mouth

Start at the top plumb mark and measure 10 feet 6½ inches along the bottom edge of the rafter.

Draw a plumb line at the bottom mark–it is the distance to the inside wall of the building. To mark the wall thickness, hold the square on the plumb mark and make a line at 90°, as shown in **Figure 12-7**, inset. The bird's mouth should not be cut more than halfway through the rafter.

4. Find the Length of the Eave

For a 2-foot-6-inch eave on the roof, use the table in **Figure 12-6** to find the rafter length.

> 2-foot Run = Rafter Length of 2 feet 1¼ inches = 25.25 inches
>
> 6-inch Run = Rafter Length of 25.25 ÷ 4 = 6.3 inches
>
> Total Eave Length = 25.25 + 6.3 = 31.55 inches
>
> Rafter Eave Length ≈ 31½ inches

5. Mark the Tail

Add the tail length (31½ inches in the example) and measure from the seat plumb line at the outside of the wall. Make the bottom plumb line the same as in **Figure 12-7**.

If the mark is too close to the end of the rafter, turn the speed square 180° and pivot from its lower edge, as shown in **Figure 12-8**.

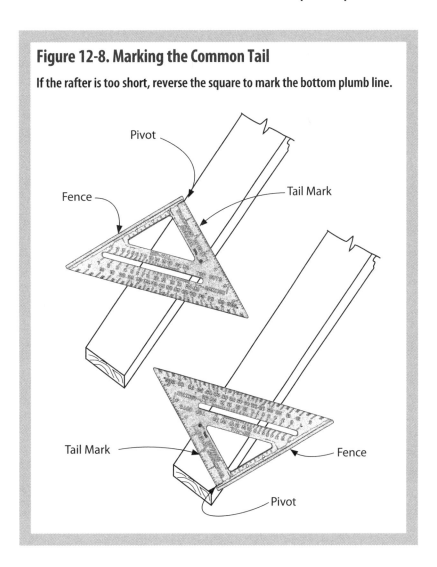

Figure 12-8. Marking the Common Tail

If the rafter is too short, reverse the square to mark the bottom plumb line.

Pivot

Fence

Tail Mark

Tail Mark

Fence

Pivot

Figure 12-9. Marking the Hip/Valley Rafters

The common rafter is marked using the Common Top Cuts scale for $^4/_{12}$ slope, (a). The hip/valley rafters are marked with the Hip-Val Top Cuts scale for $^4/_{12}$ slope, (b). Both rafter lengths are measured along the bottom of the beam. The seat level line (the width of the wall) at the bird's mouth is drawn at 90° to the bottom plumb line. The outside plumb line is 90° to the level line. The run of a hip/valley rafter is 1.4 times ($^{17}/_{12}$) longer than the run of a common rafter.

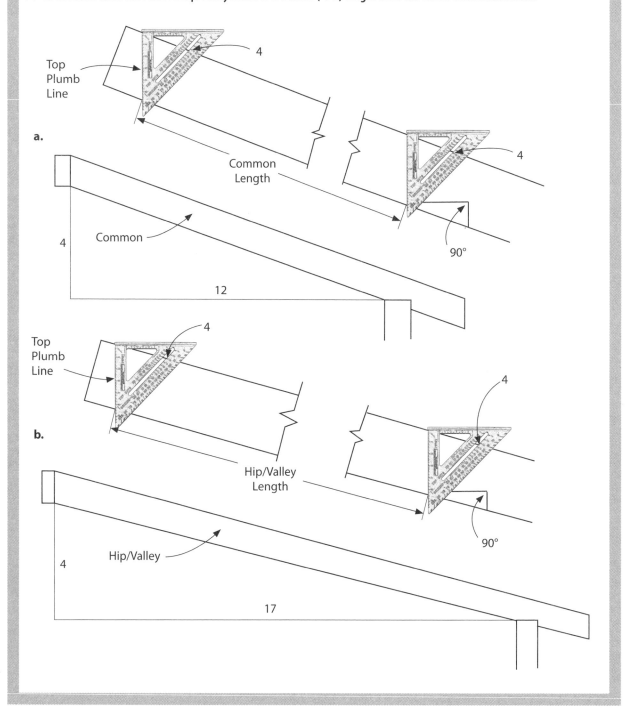

Hip and Valley Rafters
Length of Hip and Valley Rafters

The lengths of hip and valley rafters are found in the same tables as the common rafters. (See **Figure 12-5**.) For a roof where the run of the common rafter is 10 feet and the slope is ⁴⁄₁₂, the length of a hip or valley rafter is 14 feet 6⅜ inches.

Marking the Top Plumb Cut

Use the square in the same manner as in **Figure 12-4** for the common rafter layout, except reading the Hip-Val Top Cuts scale. (See **Figure 12-9**.)

Marking the Bottom Plumb Cut

The bottom plumb cut is made in the same manner as the top cut. The level line at the bird's mouth is made at 90° to the plumb line. The outside wall plumb line is at 90° to the level line. (See **Figure 12-9**.)

Degree Scale

The degree scale on the speed square can be used to mark any angle across a board.

1. Mark on the edge the point where the cut is to be made.

2. Put the pivot point on the mark.

3. Swivel the speed square until the desired degree reading is found.

4. Scribe across the board, as in **Figure 12-10**.

Figure 12-10. Using the Degree Scale

Use the degree scale to mark angles on the rafter. The degree scale is on the long side of the triangle; the angle is marked along the adjacent short side.

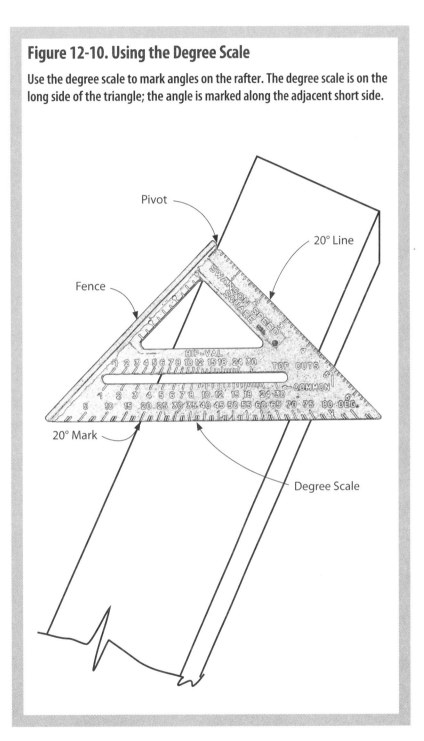

Chapter 13

Circles and Square Problems

The relationship between a polygon and a circle is sometimes difficult to master using regular math, and frequently is counter-intuitive. However, the steel square affords straightforward solutions to otherwise difficult problems.

In Chapter 13, the square (in its role as a right triangle) is used to find a circle whose area is equal to that of a square, to find a larger circle that is equal in area to two smaller circles, to convert a square to an octagon, and starting with a polygon, to find the diameter of a circumscribing circle.

Problem 13-1. Find the Center of a Circle

It often is necessary to find the center of a circle, for example when attaching a faceplate to a rough disk for mounting on the lathe, or when making dowel wheels for a toy car.

Solution 13-1

1. Place the steel square anywhere on the circle so its heel (A) is on the circumference. (See **Figure 13-1a**.)

2. Mark points B and C where the outside edges of the tongue and body touch the circumference.

3. Draw a line from B to C. The line is the diameter of the circle.

4. Shift the square to any other position and mark points D and E (see **Figure 13-1b**).

5. Draw a line from D to E. The line is another diameter.

6. The point where the two diameters cross is the center of the circle.

Why It Works

According to classical geometry, if you place the right angle of a triangle on the circumference of a circle, the hypotenuse will cut the circumference at the extremities of a diameter. Two diameters of the same circle always cross at the center.

Figure 13-1. Find the Center of a Circle

Place the heel of the square on the circumference and draw a diameter. Then move the square to draw a second diameter. The center of the circle lies where the two diameters intersect.

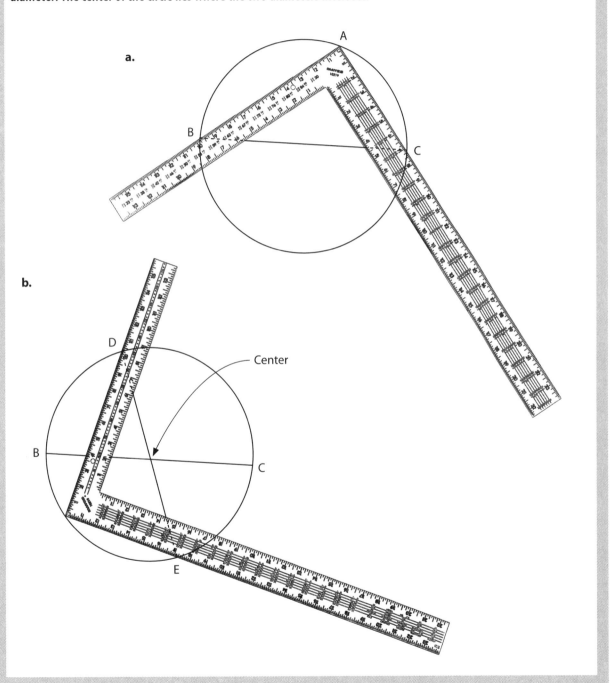

Problem 13-2. Lay Out a Semicircle of Given Diameter

The project is to construct a semicircular arch above a door of known width. To do so, draw a semicircle, knowing only the end points (A and B) of the circle's diameter. **Note:** If the width is too great for a framing square, construct a large L-type square.

Solution 13-2

1. Drive nails at points A and B, the ends of the given diameter (see **Figure 13-2**).

2. With a pencil held at the inner corner of the heel C, slide the square around with its sides in contact with A and B to draw the semicircle.

Math

According to classical geometry, from any points A and B where the diameter of a circle intersects with the circumference, draw lines to any point (for example, C) on the circumference. The resulting triangle will have a right angle at point C. This will be true for any diameter and any point on the circumference.

Why It Works

Instead of finding a diameter by placing A and B on the circumference (as in **Problem 13-1**), the diameter is known and the half-circumference is unknown.

Figure 13-2. Lay Out a Semicircle of Given Diameter

Use the steel square to draw a semicircle. Place nails at A and B and with a pencil at the inner heel, slide the square against the nails to draw the semicircle.

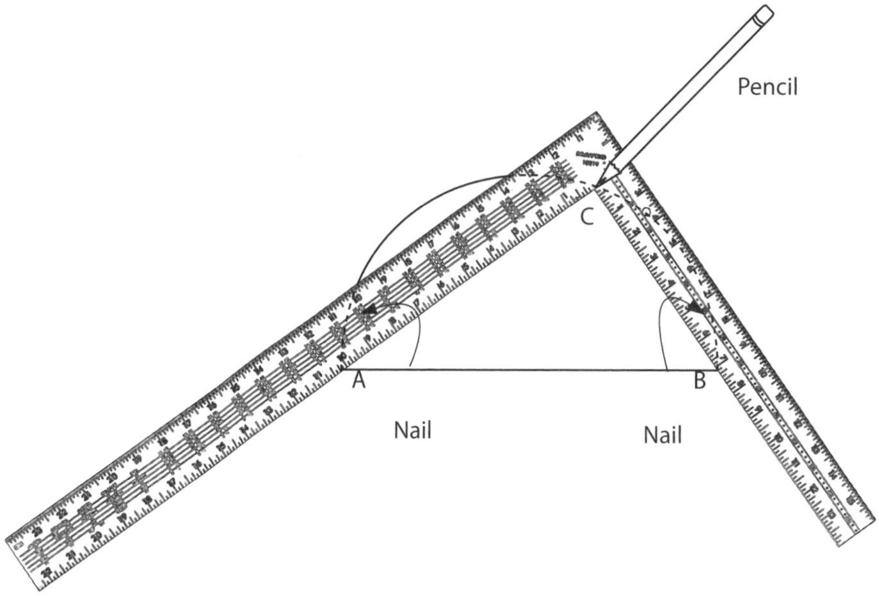

Problem 13-3. Draw a Circle through Three Points

Draw a circle through three points not in a straight line. You would encounter the problem in furniture design if you were designing a molding or a curved bracket that had to connect a table or cabinet top, an apron, and a base. It's not possible to lay out a single circle that cuts through three points on a straight line; it can only cut two of them.

Solution 13-3

1. Let A, B, and C be the three points (see **Figure 13-3a**).

2. Join these points with lines AB and BC.

3. Bisect each line at 1 and 2.

4. Use the square to draw perpendicular lines from points 1 and 2.

5. The intersection of the perpendiculars (D) is the center of the circle.

6. Use a compass and draw a circle with D as the center.

Figure 13-3. Lay Out a Circle through Three Points

To draw a circle through three points (A, B, C) not in a straight line, bisect lines AB and BC, to give point D. Draw the required circle using D as the center.

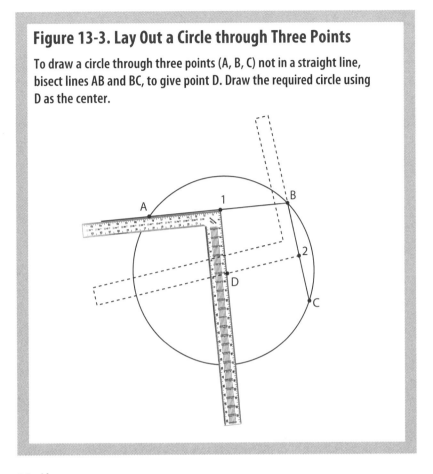

Math

By classical geometry, if you bisect any chord of a circle with a perpendicular line, the two points where the line crosses the circumference will be the end points of a diameter. Two such perpendiculars/diameters will cross at the center point (D).

Figure 13-4. Draw a Circle around a Polygon

Consult the table (c) to find the tongue and body values for the required polygon and set the diagonal fence on the steel square (a). Slide the fence along the tongue until the arm reaches the side length on the body, and read the answer on the tongue (b).

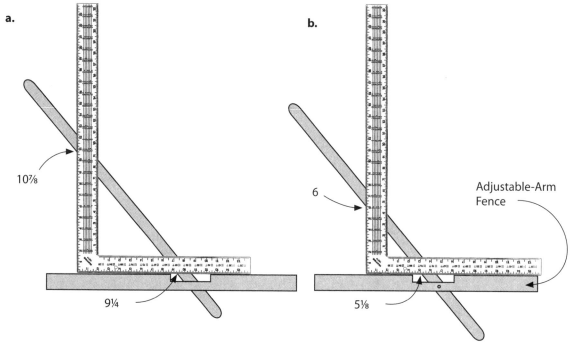

a.

10⅞

9¼

b.

6

Adjustable-Arm Fence

5⅛

c.

Table for Inscribed Polygons

Number of sides	Tongue	Body
3	7	12⅛
4	8¾	12⅜
5	9¼	10⅞
6	7½	7½
7	7½	6½
8	12¼	9⅜
9	2¾	1⅞
10	11⅛	11⅞
11	10	5⅝
12	10⅝	5½

d.

Sides	Radius constant
3	0.5774
4	0.7071
5	0.8507
6	1.0000
7	1.1524
8	1.3066
9	1.4619
10	1.6180
12	1.9319
16	2.5629
20	3.1962

Radius Constant x side length = circle radius

Problem 13-4. Draw a Circle around a Polygon

The project is to construct a redwood stand for a five-sided (pentagonal) plant bucket. The bucket measures 6 inches on a side and is to fit inside a ring cut into the stand. For a pentagon with sides equal to 6 inches, find the diameter of the circle that will just fit around it.

Solution 13-4

1. Use the adjustable-arm fence (see **Figure 7-4**) on the steel square. Set the diagonal arm of the fence to the appropriate pair of numbers in the table in **Figure 13-4c**. In this case, for a five-sided figure, set the diagonal arm to 9¼ inches on the tongue and 10⅞ inches on the body of the square. (See **Figure 13-4a**.)

2. Lock the diagonal.

3. Slide the fence along the tongue to 6 (the side length) on the body. (See **Figure 13-4b**.)

4. Read 5⅛ (the radius of the desired circle) on the tongue.

5. The diameter is double the radius:

    5⅛ x 2 = 10¼ inches

You would cut a hole with a diameter of 10¼ inches in the redwood stand.

Math

In math, when working with polygons and wanting to find the diameter of the circumscribing circle, we use a mathematical table of constants. Such a table is shown in **Figure 13-4d**. Note the constant for a five-sided polygon is 0.8507. The constant, multiplied by the length of a side, provides the circle radius.

Why It Works

To find the radius of the circumscribing circle for a five-sided polygon with sides 6 inches long, multiply the length of a side (6 inches) by a constant (0.8507).

    0.8507 x 6 = 5.10 inches radius

    5.10 x 2 = 10.2 inches diameter

That is the same diameter as found by the steel square method. The reason:

    9.25 (on the tongue) ÷ 10.875 (on the body) = 0.8505.

That is the radius constant for all five-sided figures. All of the ratios in **Figure 13-4c** are the same as the constants in **Figure 13-4d**.

Problem 13-5. Make an Octagon from a Square

The project is to convert a square table top into an eight-sided (octagonal) table. The square top is 25½ inches on a side, which is too large for the Octagon Scale on a framing square (see Chapter 9, "Using the Scales on a Square").

Solution 13-5

1. Draw square A, B, C, and D to scale (see **Figure 13-5a**).

2. Draw diagonal lines AC and BD.

3. Locate center O.

4. Mark distance AO on line AB starting at corner A. This is point E.

5. Lay the body of the square on diagonal line BD with the tongue at E and mark the octagon half-side line.

6. Flip the square and mark the other half-side line.

7. Mark the other three corners in a similar manner.

8. The required octagon is shown in **Figure 13-5b**.

Why It Works

Distance AO is 0.70 of AB. Distance AO is also 0.70 of BC.

That means that in **Figure 13-5a**, distance BE is 0.3. Mathematically, the actual value is 0.293. Some very clever person back in 1890 discovered the relationship between the length of the side of an octagon and the length of the half-diagonal of a square and applied it in the same manner.

Figure 13-5. Make an Octagon from a Square

Use the steel square to locate the vertices of the octagon by transferring the square's diagonal to its side, (a). Flip the square to extend the line, (b), and repeat on the other three sides.

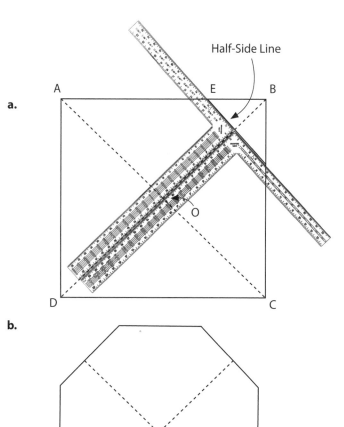

Half-Side Line

a.

A   E   B

O

D   C

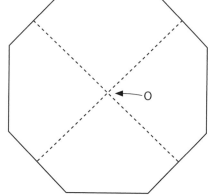

b.

O

Problem 13-6. Make an Eight-Sided Column from a Square Post

The project is to make an eight-sided column from a square post. Use a steel square to mark the post so it can be cut.

Solution 13-6

1. Lay the steel square diagonally across one face of the square post so as to measure 24 inches on it, with the end of the body and the heel both touching the edges of the post. (See **Figure 13-6**.)

2. Make marks at 7 inches and 17 inches.

3. Do this at each end.

4. Snap a line through these points to show what material is to be cut off to make the post octagonal.

5. Repeat on all four faces of the square post.

Note: If your framing square has the octagon scale, the post also can be marked that way (see Chapter 8, "Using the Scales on a Square").

Figure 13-6. Make an Eight-Sided Column from a Square Post

Extend the steel square across the face of the post with its heel on one edge and the end of the body on the other. Since the corners of a 24-inch octagon would be at 7 and 17 on the square, mark these points on the post. Snap lines through the points.

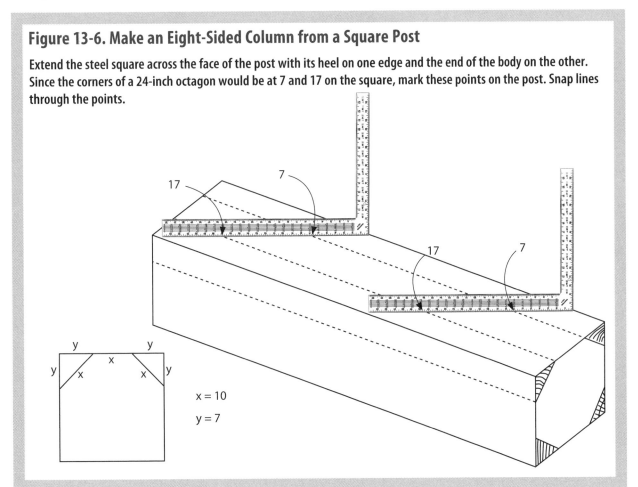

x = 10

y = 7

Why It Works

To change a square to an eight-sided figure, four corners must be cut away. In the final octagon, all sides must be equal in length (x) and the sides of the triangle (y) removed must be equal. (See **Figure 13-6**.) The two acute angles of the triangle are 45°.

Cos 45° = 0.70

We set x = 10 and y = 7 when we marked the post.

7 ÷ 10 = 0.70

In the example, the lengths x and y were proportional to the real distances. Using the square on the diagonal, as shown in **Figure 13-6**, is a good way to divide lengths and lay out proportions.

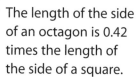

Rule of Thumb: Octagons

The length of the side of an octagon is 0.42 times the length of the side of a square.

To make an octagon from any square, multiply the length of the side by 0.42.

For example, to turn a 12-inch square into an octagon:

12 inches x 0.42 = 5

Make a mark on the middle of one side of the square, and measure over 2½ inches in each direction—that is one side of the octagon.

Problem 13-7. Convert a Square to an Octagon

The problem of laying out an octagon on a square blank occurs in building, as well as in furniture design. Here is another ingenious method for converting a square to an eight-sided figure using the steel square.

Solution 13-7

1. Start with square ABCD.

2. Extend lines AB and CD.

3. Place the body of a 24-inch square diagonally across the extended lines so that the end of the body and the heel touch opposite edges. (See **Figure 13-7a**.)

4. Make marks at 7 inches and 17 inches, as in the figure.

5. Draw line EF parallel to AB and draw line GH parallel to CD (see **Figure 13-7b**).

6. To lay out side A'E, place the square with the heel touching line AB and the tongue at E and the body touching G.

7. The remaining sides are laid out in a similar manner. (See **Figure 13-7c**.)

Math

The small triangle (A-E-A') is a 45° triangle. Cos 45° = 0.707.

Figure 13-7. Convert a Square to an Octagon

Extend the sides of the square, and then use the full length of the square diagonally to divide the side at 7 and 17. Extend these points across the original square, then mark off the sides of the octagon.

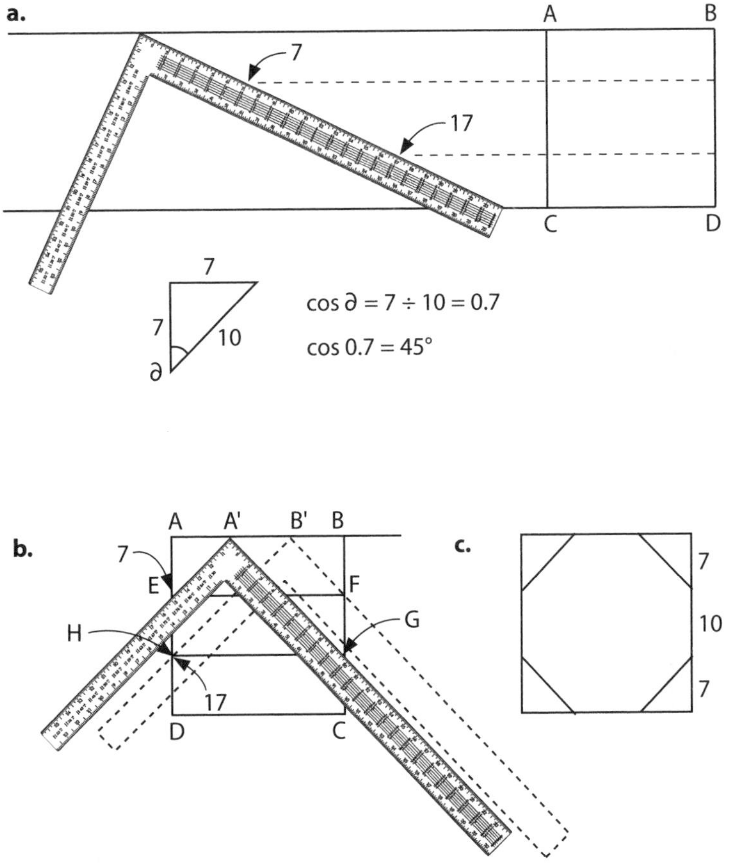

a.

$$\cos \partial = 7 \div 10 = 0.7$$
$$\cos 0.7 = 45°$$

b.

c.

Why It Works

The ratio was set at 7-10 initially or $7 \div 10 = 0.70$. By cutting the corners at the marks we made the cut-off diagonal = 10. All eight sides, therefore, are equal.

Problem 13-8. Testing a Semicircle

The project is to hog out a large 4-inch cove and have it be an exact half circle. The project is a classic pattern-making problem. In order to cast a cylindrical shaft or housing, the two parts of the mold must each contain precisely one-half of the cylinder. Otherwise, the casting won't emerge round, and one of its halves won't even come out of the mold.

Solution 13-8

Fit the heel of the steel square into the cove. Rotate the square and if the heel touches all parts of the cove while the two arms are resting on the edges, the cove is semicircular. In **Figure 13-8a**, it is obvious that it is not. In **Figure 13-8b**, the cove is semicircular.

Why It Works

It is well known in geometry that in a half-circle, when two lines cut a diameter and meet at the circumference, the angle of intersection is always 90°. Here we are using the same principle in reverse—a right-angled square (90°) to test whether the cove is a true half-circle.

Figure 13-8. Testing a Semicircle

Fit the heel of the square into the cove and see whether it can touch the bottom and the edges at the same time.

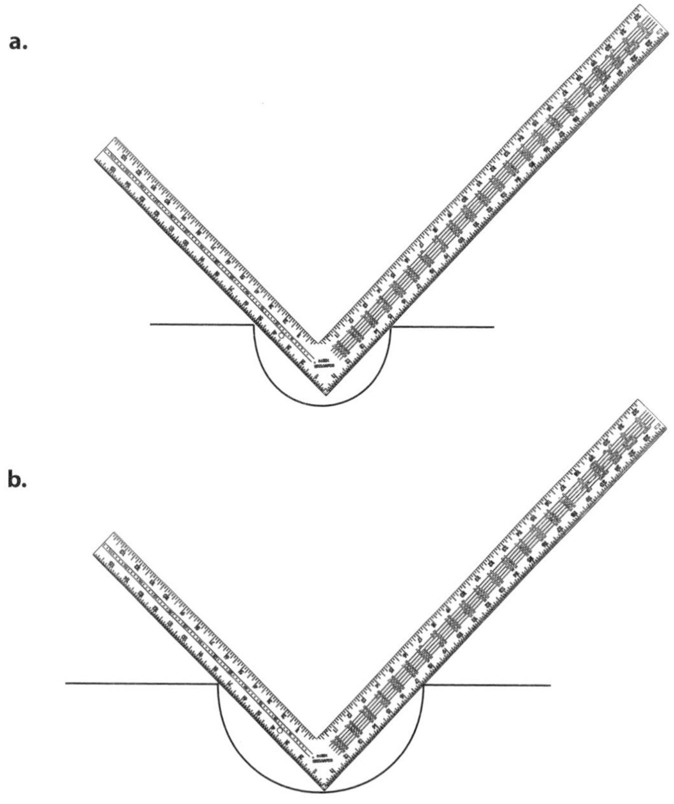

a.

b.

Problem 13-9. Find the Circumference of a Circle from Its Diameter

The project is to find the circumference of a circle with a diameter of 4½ inches. Such a problem might be encountered any time you need to wrap something around a pipe, or divide the circle into parts, for example. The solution is easy using the shop-made fence with adjustable arm. (See **Figure 7-4**.)

Solution 13-9

1. Set the diagonal arm of the fence (see **Figure 13-9a**) to 7 on the tongue of the square and 22 on the body. The Math block on page 118 explains why.

2. Lock the fence in place, as in **Figure 13-9a**.

3. Move the fence along the tongue of the square until the diagonal is against the 4½ mark on the tongue. (See **Figure 13-9b**.)

4. Read 14⅛ where the diagonal touches the body. This is the circumference of the circle.

A 24-inch square may only be used for circles with a diameter of less than 8 inches, unless the numbers are decreased equally.

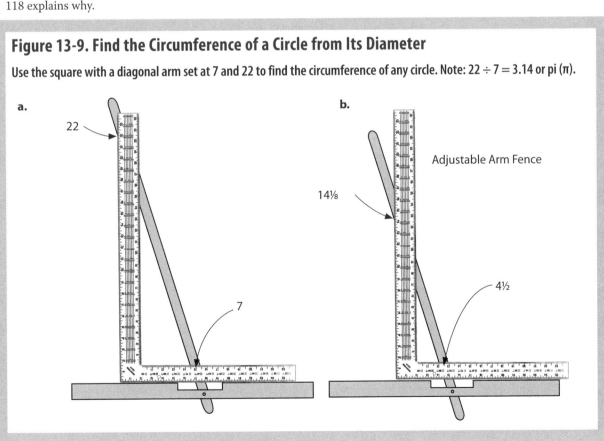

Figure 13-9. Find the Circumference of a Circle from Its Diameter

Use the square with a diagonal arm set at 7 and 22 to find the circumference of any circle. Note: 22 ÷ 7 = 3.14 or pi (π).

a.

22

7

b.

14⅛

Adjustable Arm Fence

4½

Math

The circumference of a circle is 3.14 (pi or π) times the diameter. When the diagonal of the steel square is set at 7 and 22, the ratio is 22 ÷ 7 = 3.14 or pi.

The math solution to the problem is:

C = πd or 3.14 x diameter

C = 3.14 x 4.5 = 14.13

≈ 14⅛ inches

Other pairs of numbers could be used in **Figure 13-9a**:

23½ and 7½: (23.5 ÷ 7.5 = 3.13)

18⅞ and 6: (18.875 ÷ 6 = 3.15)

15¾ and 5: (15.750 ÷ 5 = 3.15)

Why It Works

By setting the adjustable arm at 22 and 7, you are setting up a proportion, 22 is to 7 or 22 ÷ 7. By moving the arm to 4.5, you set up the equation:

7 : 22 = 4.5 : X

7X = 22 x 4.5

X = (22 x 4.5) ÷ 7 = 14.14 ≈ 14⅛

Problem 13-10. Find a Square with Area Equal to a Circle

A length of circular ducting has a diameter of 5¾ inches. The project is to join it with a square duct, and have the area of the two to be equal. What is the size of the square duct? Such an application often occurs in joining heating ducts. Solve it using the steel square with the adjustable-arm fence (see **Figure 7-4**).

Solution 13-10

1. Set the diagonal arm of the adjustable-arm fence to 10⅝ on the tongue of a steel square and to 12 on the body (see **Figure 13-10a**). The proportion 10⅝ : 12 is equivalent to 0.089 : 1, as demonstrated in Why It Works, on page 119.

2. Lock the bevel arm.

3. Move the bevel along the tongue of the square until point B on the body is at 5¾, the diameter of the circle.

4. Read 5⅛ where the bevel touches the tongue at A. (See **Figure 13-10b**.)

5. That is the required length of the sides of the square.

Math

Area of a circle:

Where diameter = 5.75,
radius = 2.87.

$$Ac = \pi\, r^2 = 3.14 \times 2.87^2$$
$$= 3.14 \times 8.24 = 25.86 \text{ sq. in.}$$

Area of a square:

Where sides = 5.125

$$As = 5.125^2 = 26.27 \text{ sq. in.}$$

Therefore, the method works.

Why It Works

When the area of a circle and the area of a square are equal, the ratio of the diameter of the circle to the side of the square is always 1 : 0.89.

In the problem, the ratio (10.625 and 12) was set on the square:

$$10.625 / 12 = 0.89$$

The ratio 10⅝ : 12 is chosen for convenience. Any pair of numbers will work on the square, as long as the ratio is 1 : 0.89.

Figure 13-10. Find a Square with Area Equal to a Circle

Working from the given diameter of the circle, use the square with an adjustable-arm fence to find the required side length of a square of equal area.

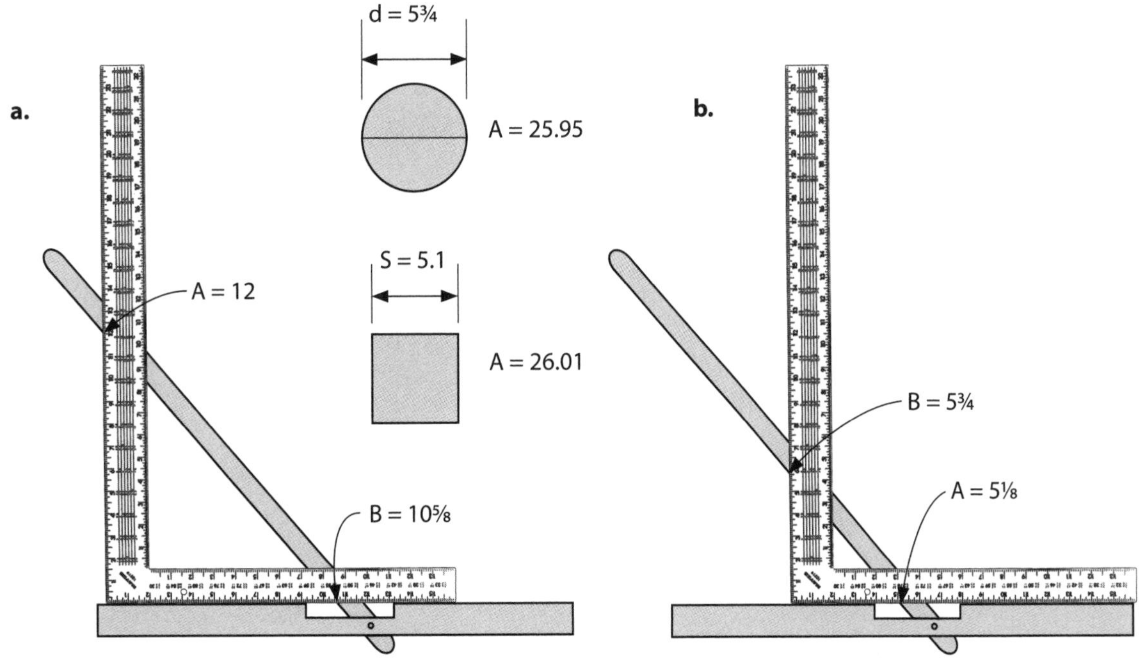

a.

d = 5¾

A = 25.95

A = 12

S = 5.1

A = 26.01

B = 10⅝

b.

B = 5¾

A = 5⅛

Problem 13-11. Find a Circle with Area Equal to a Square

The project is to join a round pipe to a square duct. Find the diameter of the pipe whose area is equal to a square with sides 7 inches long. Solve it using the steel square with the adjustable-arm fence. (See **Figure 7-4**.)

Solution 13-11

1. Set the diagonal arm to 10⅝ on the tongue of the square and to 12 on the body. The ratio is the same as 0.089 : 1, the relationship between the diameter of any circle and the side of an equal-area square. (See **Figure 13-11a**.)

2. Lock the angle in place.

3. Move the fence along the tongue until point A on the tongue of the square is at 7 (the length of the side of the square piece).

4. Read the required diameter (7⅞) off the body at point B. (See **Figure 13-11b**.)

Math

The problem uses the same logic and math as **Problem 13-10**.

Why It Works

When the area of a circle and a square are equal, the ratio of the diameter of the circle and the side of the square is 1 : 0.89. That is the ratio set out on the square using the convenient numbers 12 : 10⅝. Any pair of numbers will work as long as the ratio is 0.89.

Figure 13-11. Find a Circle with Area Equal to a Square

Working from the given side of a square, use the steel square with the adjustable-arm fence to find the diameter of a circle of equal area.

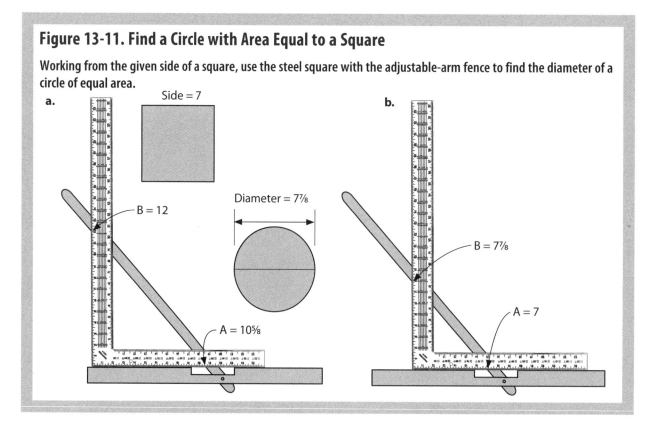

a. Side = 7

B = 12

Diameter = 7⅞

A = 10⅝

b.

B = 7⅞

A = 7

Problem 13-12. Doubling the Area of a Square

The project is to join two equal-sized square ducts to a third, larger duct. The large duct should have the same area as the two smaller ducts combined. Similar problems are encountered in furniture design when proportioning the drawer fronts and doors of a cabinet.

Solution 13-12

1. Construct the starting square ABCD full size. (See **Figure 13-12**.)

2. Draw another adjoining square of the same size ADFE.

3. Draw diagonals AC and AF.

4. Place the steel square on line AC with its heel at C and draw line CG.

6. Place the steel square on line AF with its heel at F and draw line FG.

7. The new square ACGF has sides equal to the diagonal of the original square, and it has twice the area of the original square.

Math

If the sides of square ABCD are 10 inches (area = 100 square inches), then the length of diagonal AC is:

$AB^2 + BC^2 = AC^2$

$10^2 + 10^2 = AC^2$

$AC = \sqrt{200} = 14.14$ inches long

The new square ACGF now has sides = 14.14 inches

Area ACGF = 14.14 x 14.14

= 200 square inches

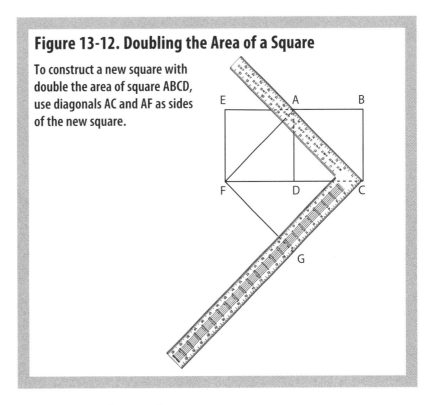

Figure 13-12. Doubling the Area of a Square

To construct a new square with double the area of square ABCD, use diagonals AC and AF as sides of the new square.

This is two times the area of square ABCD.

Why It Works

Triangle ACD is ½ of square ABCD.

Triangle ACD is ¼ of square ACGF.

Therefore, the area of square ACGF is twice that of square ABCD.

Figure 13-13. Halving the Area of a Square

Construct new square HIJC with sides equal to one-half the diagonal AC. This new square will have one-half the area of the original square.

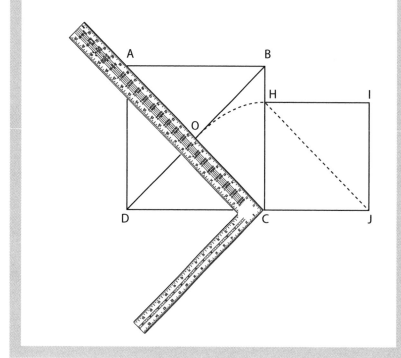

Problem 13-13. Halving the Area of a Square

A square hot-air duct coming from the furnace is to be split into two smaller square ducts, each with one-half the area of the large one.

Solution 13-13

1. Draw the starting square ABCD, the size of the large duct (see **Figure 13-13**).

2. Use the steel square to draw diagonals AC and BD with center O.

3. Use the steel square to measure the distance AO and, starting at C, swing the distance AO to the new point H.

4. Use the square to construct square HIJC.

5. This square will have one-half the area of the original square ABCD.

Why It Works

As in **Problem 13-12**, triangle CHJ is one-half of the smaller square HIJC, but one-fourth of the larger square ABCD. Therefore, the small square is one-half the area of the large square.

Problem 13-14. Find a Circle Equal in Area to Two Other Circles

In a dust collection system, there is a Y joint where a 4-inch pipe and a 6½ -inch pipe converge. (See **Figure 13-14a.**) If the area of the converging pipe does not closely match the two entering pipes, the efficiency of the system will be reduced at that point. What size exit pipe will have the same area?

Solution 13-14

1. Using the steel square, measure the diagonal distance between the 4-inch and the 6½-inch marks. (See **Figure 13-14b.**)

2. The answer to the problem is 7⅝ inches.

Math

The area of pipes A and B are:

Pipe A Area = $\pi\, r^2$

$$\text{Area} = 3.14 \times 2^2$$

$$\text{Area} = 3.14 \times 4$$
$$= 12.57 \text{ square inches}$$

Figure 13-14. Find a Circle Equal in Area to Two Other Circles

Find the diameters of the two given circles on the blade and tongue of the steel square, and measure the distance between them.

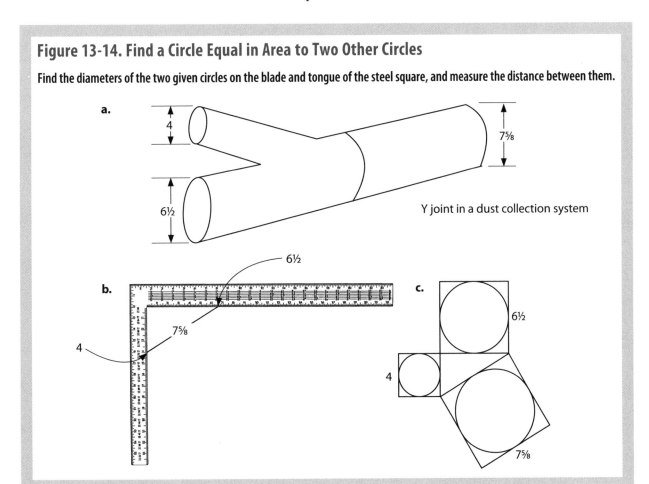

a.

4

7⅝

6½

Y joint in a dust collection system

b.

6½

7⅝

4

c.

6½

4

7⅝

Pipe B Area = πr^2

Area = 3.14 x 3.25^2

Area = 3.14 x 10.56

= 33.17 square inches

Combined Pipe Area:

A + B = 12.57 + 33.18

= 45.75 square inches

Pipe C Area = πr^2

Area = 3.14 x (7.625/2)^2

Area = 3.14 x (3.81)^2

Area = 3.14 x 14.52

= 45.59 square inches

The error is:

45.75 - 45.59

= 0.16 square inches

0.16 ÷ 45.75

= 0.4%, less than 1% error

Why It Works

In any right-angled triangle (Chapter 3, "A Close Look at the Steel Square"), the sum of the squares of two sides equals the square of the hypotenuse. That is shown in **Figure 13-14c**, where three squares are drawn with sides equal to 4, 6½, and 7⅝. The sum of the areas of the two smaller squares equals the area of the larger square. The relationship also is true of circles drawn inside the squares. Thus, when 4 is placed on one arm of a steel square and 6½ is placed on the other arm, the length of the diagonal between those two points equals the equivalent areas.

Problem 13-15. Find a Circle Equal in Area to Two or More Other Circles

A dust collection system has three pipes joining together: a 4-inch, a 5-inch, and a 6-inch pipe. What size exit pipe will have the same area?

Solution 13-15

Solve the problem by the same method given in **Problem 13-14**:

Find the combined area of two of the pipes, and then use that number to find the combined area of the third pipe.

1. Using the steel square, measure the distance between the 4-inch and the 5-inch marks, as shown in **Figure 13-15a**.

2. The length of the diagonal is 6⅜ inches.

3. Measure the distance between 6⅜ inches and the third pipe, 6 inches.

4. The length of the diagonal is 8¾ inches. (See **Figure 13-15b**.)

Therefore, make the large pipe 8¾ inches in diameter.

Why It Works

The same logic applies here as in **Problem 13-14**.

Figure 13-15. Find a Circle Equal in Area to Two or More Other Circles

When multiple ducts join together, the resulting duct must be large enough to carry the flow. Use a steel square to quickly combine two ducts at a time, and thus to find the diameter of the new pipe.

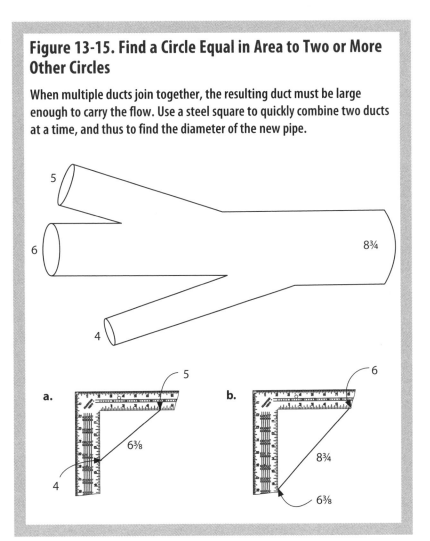

Problem 13-16. Find the Length of the Diagonal of a Square

Find the length of the diagonal of a square that is 70 inches on a side. The problem is often encountered when a diagonal measurement is needed, but the square is too large to measure, or only side lengths are available.

Solution 13-16

1. Use a steel square with an adjustable-arm fence. (See **Figure 7-4**.) Set the diagonal arm to 10⅜ on the tongue and to 15 on the body (see **Figure 13-16a**), or to any other two numbers that are related as 0.708: 1. See Why It Works for an explanation of why the numbers were chosen.

2. Lock the setting.

3. Move the fence along the tongue of the square until the diagonal is at 7 (one-tenth of 70).

4. Read 9⅞ where the diagonal touches the body. (See **Figure 13-16b**.)

5. The diagonal of a 70-inch square is 98¾ inches (ten times 9.875).

Math

Diagonal = $\sqrt{(70^2 + 70^2)}$
= $\sqrt{9800}$ = 99 inches

Why It Works

In any square, the ratio of the length of the diagonal to the length of any side is 0.708. The ratio of the numbers set on the square (10.375 and 15) is 0.708. That pair of numbers is chosen for convenience—any two numbers related to each other by the same ratio would do as well, for example, 7¹⁄₁₆ and 10 (0.7063), 14⅛ and 20 (0.7063), etc.

When the proportion is set on the adjustable arm, sliding the arm to any other side length will find the length of the corresponding diagonal.

Figure 13-16. Find the Length of the Diagonal of a Square

To find the diagonal length of a 70-inch square, use the adjustable-arm fence and set it at 15 and 10⅜ on the steel square. Slide the fence to the square side length, 7 inches (70 ÷ 10), and read the diagonal length, 9⅞ inches. The diagonal of the 70-inch square is 98¾ inches (9⅞ x 10).

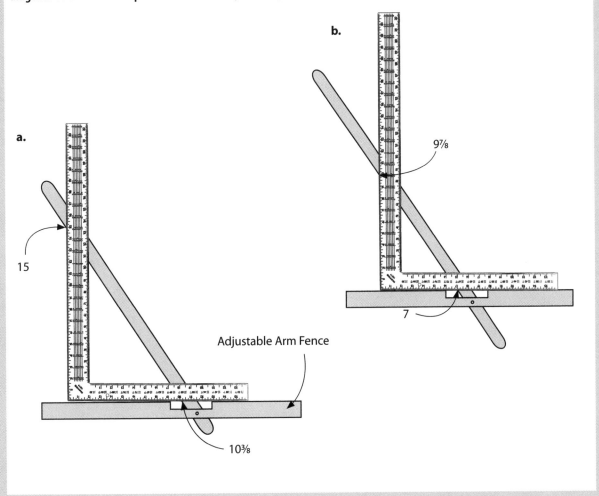

Problem 13-17: Bisect an Angle

Install a window seat and cut edge molding. For a neat fit at each joint, the two connecting pieces should join at the same angle.

Solution 13-17

1. Make a full-size cardboard template for the seat. (See **Figure 13-17.**)

2. To bisect the angle at A, draw a new line parallel to line AB.

3. Draw another line midway between the two lines.

4. Place a steel square with its heel on the midline and its body and tongue at points A and A'.

5. Line AO bisects angle A.

6. To bisect angle C, draw a line parallel to line CD.

7. Draw a line midway between the two lines.

8. Place a steel square with the heel on the midline and body and tongue at points C and C'.

9. Line CO bisects angle C.

10. The angles at B and D can be found in a similar manner.

11. Using a bevel gauge, transfer the angles from the template and cut each piece of molding to fit.

Math

In a circle when a chord (A'B) is divided (at O) and a perpendicular is erected (OC), the triangles A'OC and BOC are equal; thus, angle A'CB has been bisected (see **Figure 13-17b**).

Figure 13-17. Bisect an Angle

Strike two equally spaced lines parallel to one side of the angle, and use the steel square to bisect the angle.

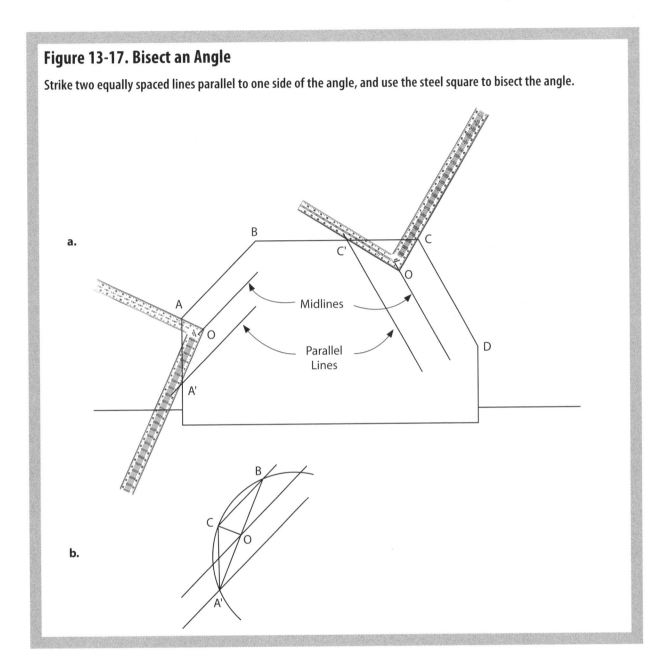

Chapter 14

Laying Out Angles

The body and the blade of the steel square are used in stairbuilding to mark unit rise and unit run at 90° to each other (see Chapter 9, "Stairs"). In like manner, the two 90° arms are used in roofing to set plumb lines and seat lines, once the slope is known (Chapter 11, "Laying Out the Rafters"). In "Laying Out Angles," we will use the diagonal of the steel square.

In such problems, the rise and run are used to find the slope. By setting appropriate numbers on the body and blade of the square, an angle of any number of degrees (including fractions) can be laid out. The values (numbers) to be set on the square can be found mathematically using the tangent of the desired angle, or by consulting the chart in **Figure 14-5**.

Figure 14-1. Reference Lines on the Table Saw

Use the steel square to scribe a line at 90° to the miter gauge slot, (a). Then use the square to scribe the two 45° lines, (b).

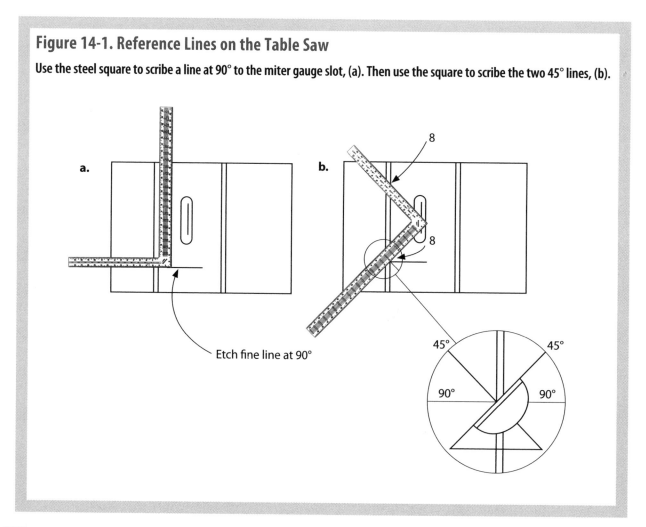

a.

Etch fine line at 90°

b.

8

8

45° 45°

90° 90°

Problem 14-1. Reference Lines on the Table Saw

Use the steel square to scribe accurate 45° and 90° reference lines on the surface of the table saw. The lines make it easy to set the miter gauge for accurate crosscuts and miters.

Solution 14-1

1. Clamp a steel square at a right angle to the miter gauge slot, and score a fine line with a steel scriber, as shown in **Figure 14-1a**, for a 90° reference line.

2. Move the square so the blade and the body are equally long when measured at the miter gauge slot.

3. Clamp the square in place.

4. Scribe a 45° line (see **Figure 14-1b**).

5. In a similar manner, scribe the alternate 45° mark in the other direction.

6. Use these lines to set the miter gauge at the three most common angles: 90°, 45° left, and 45° right.

Math

On a right triangle:

$$\text{Tan} = \text{Rise} \div \text{Run} = 8 \div 8 = 1.0$$

$$\text{Atan } 1.0 = 45°$$

Why It Works

When the square is placed on the miter gauge slot at 8 on the blade and 8 on the body, the square is at 45° to the slot and to the saw blade. Using the same number, any number, on both the arm and body will always give a 45° right triangle.

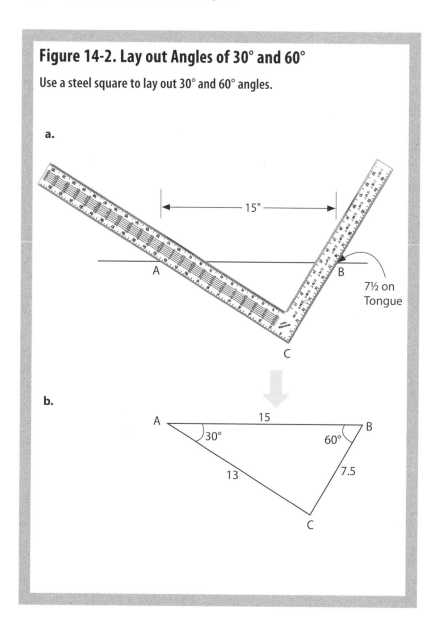

Figure 14-2. Lay out Angles of 30° and 60°

Use a steel square to lay out 30° and 60° angles.

a.

15"

A

B

7½ on Tongue

C

b.

A   15   B

30°   60°

13   7.5

C

Problem 14-2. Lay Out Angles of 30° and 60°

Lay out a 30° angle using the steel square. Along with 45°, angles of 30° and 60° are common in furniture design as well as in carpentry and building. Columns often are built from 12-sided hollow forms, which are sawn at these angles.

Solution 14-2

1. Draw a straight line and mark off 15 inches; mark points A and B (see **Figure 14-2a**).

2. Lay the steel square on the line so 7½ on the tongue touches point B, and the body of the steel square touches point A.

3. Draw lines AC and BC. (See **Figure 14-2b**.)

4. Angle ABC is 60° and angle BAC is 30°.

Math

Side 1 (BC) = 7.5, Hypotenuse AB = 15, Side 2 AC = X

$$AB^2 = AC^2 + BC^2$$

$$AC = \sqrt{(AB^2 - BC^2)}$$

$$= \sqrt{(15^2 - 7.5^2)}$$

$$= \sqrt{(225 - 56.25)}$$

$$= \sqrt{168.75} = 12.99 \approx 13$$

$$Sin = Opposite \div Hypotenuse$$

$$= 7.5 \div 15 = 0.5$$

$$Asin\ 0.5 = 30° \text{ and}$$

$$Sin = Opposite \div Hypotenuse$$

$$= 13 \div 15 = 0.8667$$

$$Asin\ 0.8667 = 60°$$

The equations prove the method works. Remember, in any 30°-60° triangle, the shortest side is half the length of the longest side.

Why It Works

By setting Side 1 = 7.5 and the diagonal = 15, we constructed right triangle ABC.

$$Sin = Opposite \div Hypotenuse$$

$$= 7.5 \div 15 = 0.5$$

$$Asin\ 0.5 = 30°$$

Any two numbers can be picked as long as the diagonal is twice the length of one side.

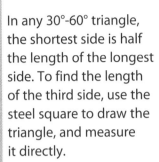

Rule of Thumb

In any 30°-60° triangle, the shortest side is half the length of the longest side. To find the length of the third side, use the steel square to draw the triangle, and measure it directly.

Figure 14-3. Lay Out a 45° Angle

Use a steel square to lay out 45° angles. As long as the measurements on both arms are the same, the diagonal will be at 45°.

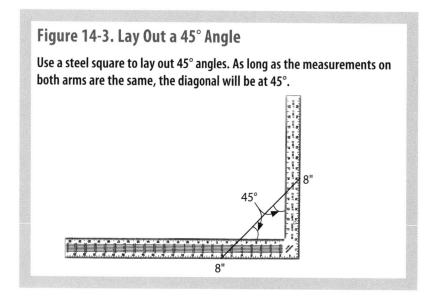

Problem 14-3. Lay Out a 45° Angle

The 45° angle is used for mitering square constructions such as frames and doors. Lay out a 45° angle.

Solution 14-3

1. The diagonal line connecting equal measurements on both arms of the square forms angles of 45° with the blade and tongue, as shown in **Figure 14-3**.

Math

Hypotenuse² = Side1² + Side2²

$$\text{Hyp}^2 = 8^2 + 8^2$$

$$\text{Hyp} = \sqrt{128} = 11.31$$

$$\text{Sin} = \text{Opposite} \div \text{Hypotenuse}$$

$$= 8 \div 11.31 = 0.7073$$

$$\text{Asin } 0.7073 = 44.98° = 45°$$

Why It Works

In a right triangle, when Side 1 = Side 2, the inner angles are 45°, 90°, and 45°. That remains true no matter how large or small the triangle.

Problem 14-4. Lay Out Any Angle

Lay out a 22.5° angle and a 39° angle. Unusual angles come into play when installing stairs and trimming around them.

Solution 14-4a

A calculator with trigonometry functions or a book of trig tables will be needed. With a computer connected to the Internet, the tables are available through Google. Use the trig functions to set the adjustable-arm fence (see **Figure 7-4**) on the steel square.

1. For 22.5°, enter 22.5 in the calculator and then punch "tan."

2. Read 0.4142.

3. Multiply the number by some larger number such as 10, 15, or 20.

0.4142 x 20 = 8.28

4. Set the adjustable-arm fence to 20 (or whatever number by which you multiplied) on the body and to 8¼ (or whatever the result of the multiplication) on the tongue, as shown in **Figure 14-4a**.

5. The resulting angle is 22.5°

Solution 14-4b

1. For 39°, enter 39 in the calculator and then punch "tan."

2. Read 0.8098.

3. Multiply the number by some larger number, for example, 10, 15, or 20.

0.8098 x 15 = 12.147

4. Set the adjustable fence to 15 (or whatever number by which you multiplied) on the body and to 12⅛ (or whatever the result of the multiplication) on the tongue, as in **Figure 14-4b**.

5. The resulting angle is 39°.

Math

Tangent = Opposite Side ÷ Adjacent Side = Rise ÷ Run

Tangent = 8.25 ÷ 20 = 0.4125

Atan 0.4125 = 22.42°

Tangent = Opposite Side ÷ Adjacent Side

Tangent = 12.125 ÷ 15 = 0.8083

Atan 0.8083 = 38.95°

Why It Works

The tangent of a right triangle is the opposite side divided by the adjacent side (rise over run). They are the sides of the steel square being used.

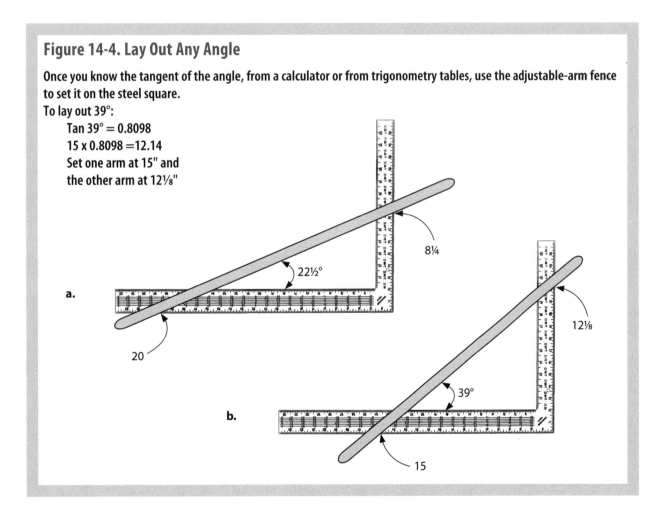

Figure 14-4. Lay Out Any Angle

Once you know the tangent of the angle, from a calculator or from trigonometry tables, use the adjustable-arm fence to set it on the steel square.

To lay out 39°:

Tan 39° = 0.8098
15 x 0.8098 = 12.14
Set one arm at 15" and
the other arm at 12⅛"

a.   22½°   8¼   20

b.   39°   12⅛   15

Problem 14-5. Lay Out Any Angle from 1-45°

Lay out an angle from 1° to 45° using the steel square. For example, find 37°.

Solution 14-5

The table (see **Figure 14-5**) gives numbers to be set on the square to lay out any angle from 1° to 45°. For angles from 45° to 90°, see **Problem 14-8**.

1. Find 37° in the table in **Figure 14-5**.

2. Read Tongue Length = 15 inches; Body Length = 20 inches.

3. Lay the square on a sheet of paper, and draw lines along the outer edges of the tongue and body.

4. On the body line, make a mark at 20 inches.

5. On the tongue line, make a mark at 15 inches.

6. Join these two points to give 37°. (See **Figure 14-5b**.)

7. Because the inside angles of any triangle add up to 180°, the other angles in this triangle are 90° and 53°:

$$90° + 37° + 53° = 180°$$

Math

Tangent = Rise ÷ Run

$$\text{Tan} = 15 ÷ 20 = 0.75$$

$$\text{Atan } 0.75 = 36.87°$$

Why It Works

The ratio set on the square is 15:20 or 15 ÷ 20 = 0.75.

Tan = Opposite Side ÷ Adjacent Side

$$= 15 ÷ 20 = 0.75$$

The arctangent of 0.75 = 36.87° ≈ 37°

All the values in the table are set using this principle.

Figure 14-5. Angle Table for Steel Square

Use the table to find the steel square body lengths and tongue lengths for any angle from 1° to 45°. Join the numbers on the tongue and body of the square to lay out the angle. For angles 46° to 90°, see Problem 14-8.

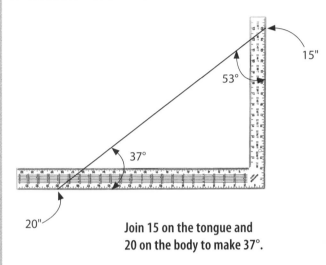

Join 15 on the tongue and 20 on the body to make 37°.

Angle Table for Steel Square

Degrees	Tongue Length (inch)	Body Length (inch)
1	⅜	21
2	¾	21
3	1¼	24
4	1½	21
5	2	23
6	2½	24
7	2½	20
8	3	22
9	3½	23
10	4	23
11	4	21
12	4½	20
13	5	22
14	6	24
15	5	19
16	6	21
17	7	23
18	6½	20
19	8¼	24
20	8	22
21	8	21
22	8½	21
23	8½	20
24	10¼	23
25	10¼	22
26	9¾	20
27	12¼	24
28	12¾	24
29	12¾	23
30	12⅛	21
31	12	20
32	15	24
33	13	20
34	13½	20
35	14	20
36	15¼	21
37	15	20
38	18¾	24
39	17	21
40	16¾	20
41	20	23
42	18	20
43	20½	22
44	21¼	22
45	24	24

Figure 14-6. Lay Out Half Angles

Use the values in Figure 14-5 to set 8½ inches on the tongue and 20½ inches on the body of the steel square. The resulting angle is 22½°.

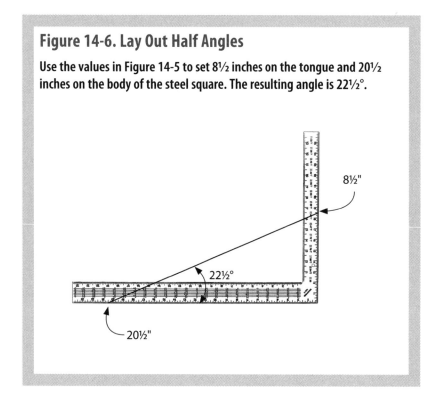

Problem 14-6. Lay Out Half Angles

The chart in **Figure 14-5** can be used to lay out half angles. For example, when making an eight-sided figure with corner angles of 45°, each side piece must be cut at 22½°. Draw this angle using the steel square.

Solution 14-6

1. Use the chart in **Figure 14-5** to bracket 22½°; 22° is 8½ inches on the tongue and 21 inches on the body, and 23° is 8½ inches on the tongue and 20 inches on the body.

2. For 22½°, set 8½ inches on the tongue and 20½ inches on the body.

Math

Tan angle = 8.5 ÷ 20.5 = 0.4146

Atan 0.4146 = 22.52°

Why It Works

The logic is the same as in **Problem 14-5**.

The technique will work when either the setting on the tongue or the setting on the body, for successive degrees, is the same. When it is not, the simplest solution is to draw both angles on paper, from the same vertex, using the steel square. Then, find the half angle halfway in between, by eye or measurement. Use a bevel gauge to transfer the angle to the workpiece.

Problem 14-7. Lay Out Degree Fractions

When making a sixteen-sided figure with corner angles of 22.5°, each side piece must be cut at 11.25°. Find this angle using the steel square.

Solution 14-7

If the degree needed is not in the chart in **Figure 14-5**, use the formula below to calculate the body and tongue lengths. Try lengths of 20 inches to 24 inches until a value close to ⅛ inch is found.

1. Find Tan of degrees wanted.

   Tan 11.25 = 0.1989

2. Multiply this number by 22:

   0.1989 x 22 = 4.376"

3. Set marks at 22 inches on the body and 4⅜ inches on the tongue for 11.25°.

Math

Tongue Length = Tangent of the Angle x Body Length

   0.1989 x 22 inches = 4.38 inches
   ≈ 4⅜ inches

The triangle could also be drawn with side lengths of 20 and 4.

   0.1989 x 20 = 3.98 inches

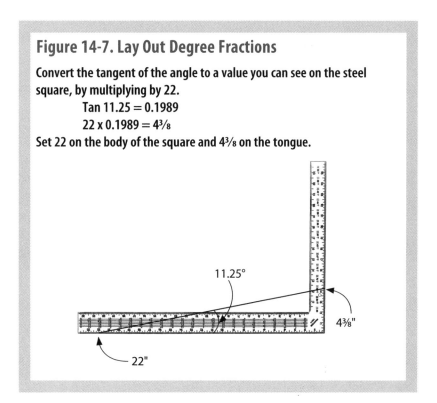

Figure 14-7. Lay Out Degree Fractions

Convert the tangent of the angle to a value you can see on the steel square, by multiplying by 22.

   Tan 11.25 = 0.1989
   22 x 0.1989 = 4⅜

Set 22 on the body of the square and 4⅜ on the tongue.

11.25°

4⅜"

22"

Figure 14-8. Lay Out Any Angle from 45-90°

When any angle more than 45° is laid out, its complement may be found by completing the right triangle. The numbers 20 and 14 are found in Figure 14-5 for 35°.

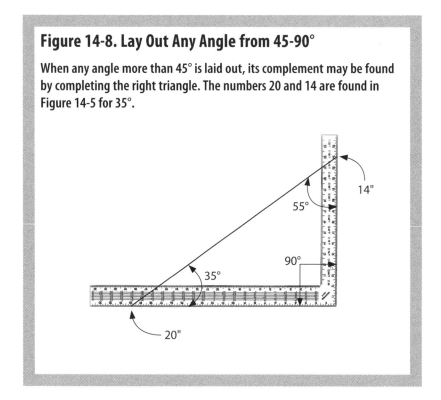

Problem 14-8. Lay Out Any Angle from 45° to 90°

Lay out 55° using a steel square.

Solution 14-8

The table in **Figure 14-5** gives values for measurements on the tongue and body of the steel square such that by joining the points, any angle may be laid out for 1° to 45°. To find angles greater than 45°, find the complementary angle, which is 90° minus the angle in question.

To lay out 55°:

1. 90° − 55° = 35°

2. Find 35° in the table in **Figure 14-5**.

3. Read Tongue Length = 14 inches; Body Length = 20 inches.

4. Lay the square on a sheet of paper, and draw lines along the outer edges of the tongue and body.

5. On the body line, make a mark at 20 inches.

6. On the tongue line, make a mark at 14 inches.

7. Join the two points to give 35° and 55° (see **Figure 14-8**).

Why It Works

The sum of the three angles in any triangle is 180°. In the example, they are 90° + 35° + 55° = 180°

Problem 14-9. Find Angles for Segmentation Turning

Segmented bowl turners must cut the segments carefully and with great accuracy. An angle off by only a half degree for a 12-sided bowl (24 cuts) will result in a total error of 12 degrees—enough to cause a serious gap. A steel square used with a dial caliper or vernier caliper can give any angle with an accuracy of $\frac{1}{10}°$. Once the angle has been set on the square, use the bevel gauge to transfer it to the work.

For example, draw the miter angle for a 14-segment ring.

Solution 14-9

1. Because there are 360° in a circle, the corner angle is:

    360° ÷ 14 sides = 25.71°

2. The miter cut is one-half of the corner angle, therefore:

    25.71° ÷ 2 = 12.86°

3. Set the body of the steel square to any convenient number of inches; the longer the measurement, the more accurate the angle will be—20 inches is convenient. (See **Figure 14-9**.)

4. Multiply 20 times the tangent of the angle in question (0.2283) and get 4.56.

5. Set 4.56 inches on the blade of the square. For accuracy, use the dial caliper or vernier caliper set at

4.56, or measure 4 inches and use the caliper to set the 0.56.

6. The resulting angle is 12.9°.

Math

Tangent of the Angle = Opposite Side ÷ Adjacent Side

    Tan 12.857° = 0.228

    and Adjacent Side = 20.

Opposite Side = Adjacent Side x Tan Angle

    Opposite Side = 20 x 0.228 = 4.56 inches. (See **Figure 14-9**.)

Why It Works

Choose a large number for the body, and then calculate the number to be set on the tongue of the square by multiplying the tangent of the angle times the chosen large number. Once the two numbers have been found, a line drawn across them on the square will describe the desired angle. In the example, choose 20 and calculate 4.56. The measurements for 22 inches and 5.02 inches also could have been used.

Figure 14-9. Find Angles for Segmentation Turning

Use the steel square to form a right triangle and set 20 on the body; use a dial caliper to set 4.56 on the tongue. Connect the two marks to find 12.9°—the miter angle for a 14-sided ring.

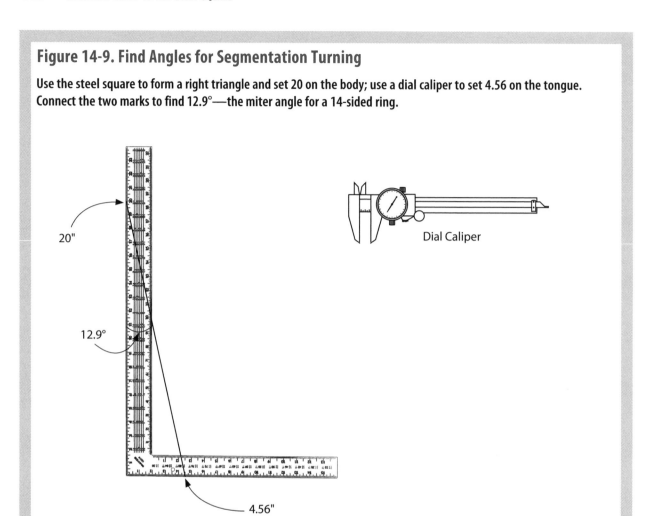

Problem 14-10. Cutting Crown Molding

Crown molding is often cut by tilting it against the fence of a miter box or of a chop saw. However, some molding is too large for that and must be cut flat. To do that, you will need to find the miter and bevel angles.

The crown molding in the example is 6½-inches-wide and will be installed flat to the ceiling and to the wall, using the angles that are milled into its edges.

Solution 14-10

1. The first step is to find the molding angle. Cut a 4-inch-long piece of molding for the measurement.

2. Hold the molding to the inside of a steel square, and measure distance A and distance B.

3. In **Figure 14-10**, A = 5⅛ inches (5.125) and B = 3⅞ inches (3.875).

4. Measure line C (6.5 inches), or calculate it using the properties of the right triangle (see Math on page 144).

5. Find the slope of the molding from vertical, that is, the angle the molding makes with the wall.

  Slope = Tangent of Rise ÷ Run
  = B ÷ A

  Where A = 5.125 and B = 3.875.

  Atan 3.875 ÷ 5.125 = 0.7561 = 37.1° ≈ 37°

6. Find the miter angle.

Figure 14-10. Cutting Crown Molding

Hold the molding to a steel square and measure distances A and B. Distance C can be measured or calculated. Use the dimensions to calculate the miter and bevel angles needed to saw the molding.

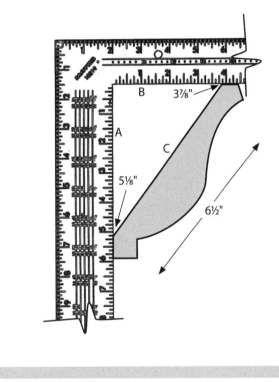

B 3⅞"

A

C

5⅛"

6½"

Miter Angle

= Atan (1 ÷ Sin Slope)

Miter Angle = 1 ÷ Sin 37.1

= 1 ÷ 0.6032

Atan = 1.6578 = 58.9° ≈ 59°

7. Find the bevel angle (blade tilt).

Blade Tilt (Bevel Angle)
= Atan (Sin Miter Angle x
Cos Slope)

Bevel Angle = Atan (Sin 59 x
Cos 37)

Bevel Angle = Atan (0.8572 x
0.7986) = Atan 0.6846

Bevel Angle = 34.4° ≈ 34°

8. Set the chop saw at 59° miter
and 34° bevel. As long as you use
molding with these dimensions,
the saw settings will work in any
four-cornered room.

9. Because the miters and bevels are

so difficult to envision, make some
"golden samples," that is, left-side
and right-side pieces for both
inside and outside corners. Label
these 12-inch sections of molding
clearly: "left inside" with edges
marked "ceiling," "wall," etc.

Math

Length C = $\sqrt{(A^2 + B^2)}$

C = $\sqrt{(5.125^2 + 3.875^2)}$ = $\sqrt{41.27}$
= 6.43 ≈ 6.5 inches

Note: The length of 6½ inches was
also measured on the steel square.

Problem 14-11. Sawhorse with Splayed Legs

Construct a sawhorse to use on the job that will fit on joists set 16 inches apart. The horse is to be 24 inches high with legs that splay for stability.

Solution 14-11

1. **Figure 14-11a** shows the sawhorse 24-inches-high with legs spread 16 inches on-center. The side view shows the legs are also splayed 2 inches toward each end.

2. Mark a 2x4, as shown in **Figure 14-11b**. The height of 24 inches and the half-spread of 8 inches (on-center) are shown on the steel square.

3. Draw the cut lines for the end splay, as in **Figure 14-11c**.

4. Cut the 2x4 according to the cut lines.

5. Use the first piece as a pattern for laying out the other three legs, but be careful— the 2-inch splay means there are two right legs and two left legs.

Why It Works

The solution uses mechanical drawing techniques with the steel square to transfer the elevation views and angles of the sawhorse to the 2x4.

Figure 14-11. Sawhorse with Splayed Legs

Use the steel square to draw the cut lines for the sawhorse.

a.

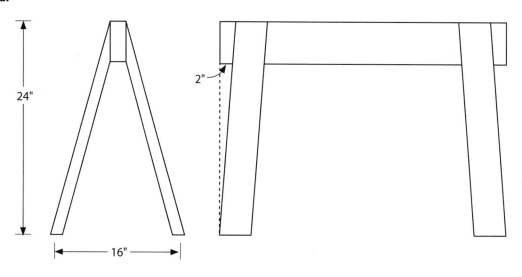

b.

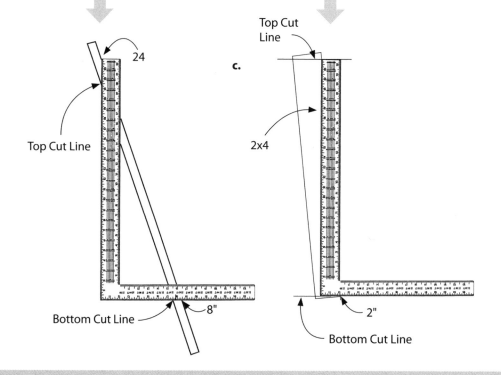

CHAPTER 15

Proportioning Problems

In "Proportioning Problems," all of the problems can be solved using the steel square as a right triangle. In math, any two right triangles having the same angles are related. They are known as similar triangles, and all of the sides and all of the angles are proportional—no matter what size. By knowing or measuring two sides of the steel square (a right triangle), the dimensions of a larger or smaller object can be found.

We can set known values on the arms of the square and draw the triangle on paper, make proportional lines on a board, use a sight line, or employ an adjustable-arm fence (see Chapter 7, "Problem-Solving Techniques"). Using proportions, a rectangle can be resized, the height of a distant object found, or the length of a brace determined.

Problem 15-1. Equal Division

Divide a wide plank into four equal widths in order to rip it into narrower boards.

Figure 15-1. Equal Division

Lay the steel square diagonally across the board to make four equal divisions across the width.

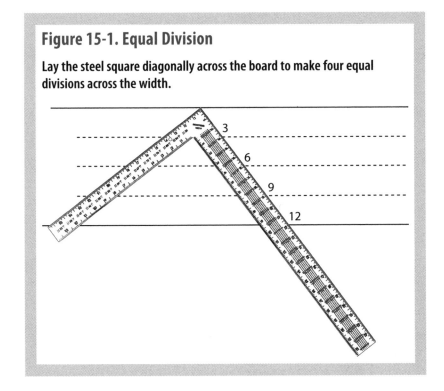

Solution 15-1

1. Lay the steel square diagonally on the board so any four convenient but equally spaced numbers can be used to divide the width.

2. The numbers can be 1, 2, 3, 4 or 2, 4, 6, 8 or 3, 6, 9, 12, as in **Figure 15-1**.

3. Use a marking gauge or a chalk line to lay out the saw cuts.

Math

According to geometry, when a straight line (the edge of the steel square) passes through two or more parallel lines, exterior and interior angles are equal. The right triangles produced also will be equal provided the parallel lines are all equally spaced.

Why It Works

Any number of equal divisions on the steel square can be transferred to the plank, and once marked, lines parallel to the edges can be drawn.

Problem 15-2. Proportioning

A piece of cardboard is 18 inches x 13 inches. Reduce it proportionally so the long side is 11 inches. What is the length of the short side?

Solution 15-2

1. Draw a rectangle 13 x 18 and label points A, B, and C, as in **Figure 15-2**.

2. Draw a diagonal from A to C.

3. Lay the steel square on the piece so the body is on the 18-inch side (AB).

4. Move the square so 11 inches is at corner A. The heel will be at D.

5. Draw a line on the blade side from D to E. Note this is 8 inches.

6. Draw a line from E to F to complete the new rectangle with dimensions of 8 inches x 11 inches.

Math

Find the ratio, or proportional reduction number, between the two sides, and multiply the known dimension by it, to find the unknown dimension:

$$11 \div 18 = 0.611$$

$$0.611 \times 13 = 7.94 \text{ inches}$$

$$\text{Error} = 8 - 7.94 = 0.06 \div 8$$
$$= 0.0075 \text{ or less than } 1\%.$$

Why It Works

Right triangles ABC and ADE are similar, and all sides and all angles are proportional.

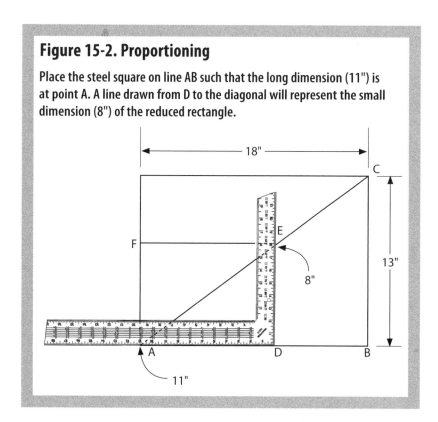

Figure 15-2. Proportioning

Place the steel square on line AB such that the long dimension (11") is at point A. A line drawn from D to the diagonal will represent the small dimension (8") of the reduced rectangle.

Problem 15-3. Proportioning Line

If 1,000 board feet of lumber costs $900, what will be the cost of 1,300 board feet?

Solution 15-3

1. Select a board with a straight edge or draw a straight line, as in **Figure 15-3**.

2. Position the steel square so the 9 on the body (representing $900) and the 10 (representing 1,000 board feet) of the blade are on the line, **Position 1**.

3. Mark the proportioning line AB along the outside edge of the blade.

4. Keeping the blade on line AB, move the square until 13 (representing 1,300 board feet) is on the line, **Position 2**.

5. Read the number 11¾ (or 11.75) on the body of the square.

6. If 1,000 Bf of lumber costs $900, then 1,300 Bf of lumber will cost $1,175.

Math

1000 : $900 = 1300 : X

1000X = 900 x 1300

X = (900 x 1300) ÷ 1000

X = $1170

Error = 1175 - 1170 = 5 ÷ 1175

= 0.4%

Why It Works

In **Figure 15-3b**, right triangle ABC is similar to right triangle ADE. In such triangles, all sides and all angles are proportional. That means as side AB is increased from 10 to 13 to give side AD, the length of side BC (9 inches) is increased to 11¾ inches (side DE). The proportional lengths of lines AC and AE also could have been used.

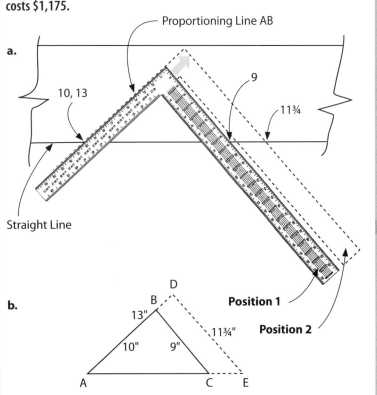

Figure 15-3. Proportions

Place the steel square so 10 on the blade and 9 on the body touch the straight line. Draw the proportioning line AB and slide the square to 13 on the blade. Read 11¾ on the body of the square. Therefore, 1,300 Bf costs $1,175.

Problem 15-4. Finding Tree Height

Determine the height of a tree (barn, silo, water tower, building, whatever). Use the steel square to construct a pair of similar triangles, one of them having the tree height as a side.

Solution 15-4

1. Measure off 100 feet from the tall object, as shown **Figure 15-4**.

2. Place a piece of white tape alongside the 12 mark on the body of a steel square. Make a black mark exactly at 12.

3. Place the square on a table and make sure it is horizontally plumb.

4. Sight across the square to the top of the object, and line up the black mark with the tongue of the square.

5. If the top of the object just catches the black mark on the body of the square and the 12 mark on the tongue, then the object is exactly 100 feet tall.

6. Otherwise, line up the top of the object with the black mark and note where the line of sight hits on the tongue of the square. In the example, the top of the tree and the black mark on the body of the square line up with 10½ on the tongue of the square.

7. Use this equation to find the height of the object:

Height = (12 x 100) ÷ Reading on the Tongue

Height = 1200 ÷ 10.5 ≈ 114 feet

Remember to add in the height of the table where the square is placed, for example 3 feet.

Height = 114 + 3 = 117 feet

Math

A simple proportion is set up:

12 : X = 10.5 : 100

X = (12 x 100) ÷ 10.5

X = 1200 ÷ 10.5 = 114

Why It Works

In similar triangles, all sides and all angles are proportional:

10½ is to 100 as 12 is to the tree height.

100 ÷ 10.5 = 9.5

9.5 x 12 = 114

Figure 15-4. Finding Tree Height

Measure 100 feet to the tree; then line up the 12-inch mark on the square and the top of the tree and note where this line of sight crosses the tongue of the square. The ratio shown, 10½ and 12, determines the tree to be 114 feet tall—plus the height of the table where the square sits.

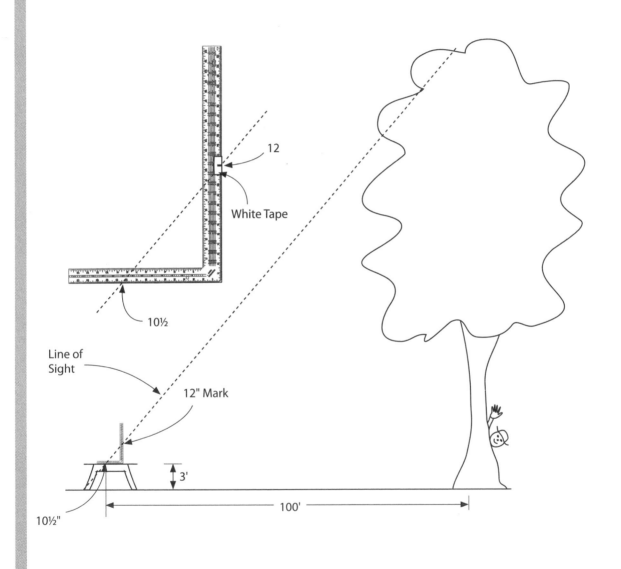

Problem 15-5. Square Yards from Square Feet

An area that measures 16 feet x 12½ feet is being carpeted and the area in square yards is unknown. There's no electronic calculator nearby, but a steel square is available.

Solution 15-5

1. Set an adjustable-arm fence on the steel square (see **Figure 7-4**) at 9 on the tongue and at 16 on the body. The number 9 represents the number of square feet in one yard; the number 16 represents one dimension of the room in feet.

2. Lock the arm at this angle.

3. Move the fence so that the number 12½ is on the square's blade.

4. Read 22¼ on the body.

5. Thus, there are 22¼ square yards in an area 16 feet x 12½ feet.

6. You can get the same answer if you set 9 on the tongue and 16 on the blade against the straight edge of a board, draw a proportioning line, and slide the square along the line so 12½ falls on the board edge. Then read the answer, 22¼, where the blade crosses the board edge.

Math

The calculator has been found:

16 x 12.5 = 200 square feet

200 ÷ 9 = 22.22 square yards
≈ 22¼ square yards

Why It Works

You are using the right triangle represented by the steel square as a proportioning device to solve the equation:

16 ÷ 9 = X ÷ 12.5

Figure 15-5. Square Yards from Square Feet

Use the adjustable-arm fence to set two of the known values on the steel square. Then slide the fence along the square to the third known value, and read the unknown on the square's body.

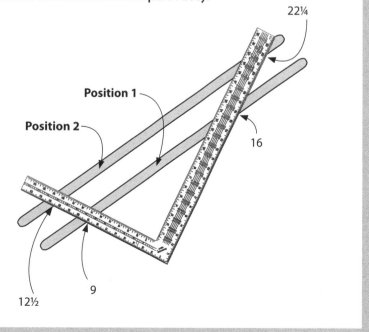

22¼

Position 1

Position 2

16

9

12½

Problem 15-6. Find Length of a Brace

Cut and fit a brace between two basement posts that are 8 feet 9 inches high and spaced 38 inches apart. (See **Figure 15-6**.)

Solution 15-6

1. Use the steel square as a right triangle.

2. Scale the post height of 105 inches to 10.5 (divide 105 by 10).

3. Scale the spacing distance of 38 inches to 3.8.

4. Use a steel ruler and measure the distance between 10½ and 3¹³⁄₁₆.

5. Find 11⅛ inches. (See **Figure 15-6**.)

6. Scale up by multiplying by 10 to find the length of the brace: 11.125 x 10 = 111.25 inches.

Math

$\text{Diagonal}^2 = \text{Side1}^2 + \text{Side2}^2$

$\text{Diagonal} = \sqrt{(105^2 + 38^2)}$

$\text{Diagonal} = \sqrt{(11025 + 1444)}$
$= \sqrt{12469} = 111.66 \text{ inches}$

Error = 111.66 − 111.25
= 0.41 inches

Why It Works

One side of a right triangle was set to the rise (10.5) and the other to the run (3.8). A diagonal was set across the steel square, and the length of the diagonal was measured.

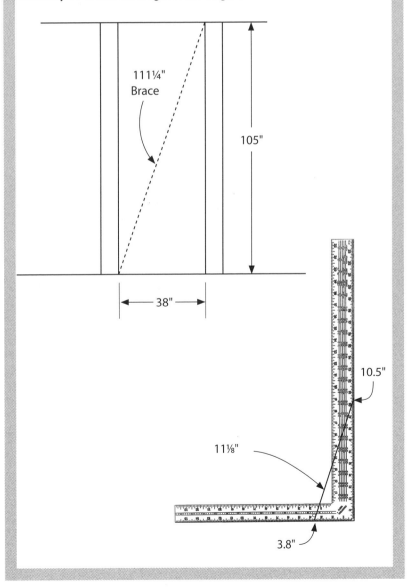

Figure 15-6. Find Length of a Brace

Scale the problem by dividing by 10, and set the adjustable-arm fence at 10.5 inches and at 3.8 inches. Multiply the distance between the two marks by 10 to find the length of the diagonal.

111¼"
Brace

105"

38"

10.5"

11⅛"

3.8"

Problem 15-7. Cut a Leaning Post

Cut a diagonal brace (leaning post) where the post height is 46½ inches and run is 25½ inches.

Solution 15-7

1. The given dimensions (46½ and 25½) are too large for the steel square. To reduce the numbers, divide both by the same constant, for example, 4. The dimensions will remain proportionately the same:

    46.5 ÷ 4 = 11.625 = 11⅝ inches

    25.5 ÷ 4 = 6.375 = 6⅜ inches

2. Set the adjustable-arm fence (see **Figure 7-4**) to 11⅝ inches and 6⅜ inches (see **Figure 15-7a**). Measure the diagonal, 13¼ inches.

3. Select a beam of sufficient length and place the square on one end, as shown in **Figure 15-7b**.

4. Make a mark at the top and cut the beam along the line to establish the heel of the brace.

5. Multiply by the constant to find the length of the brace:

    13.25 x 4 = 53 inches

6. Measure down the beam 53 inches and use the square to mark the bottom angle. That locates the toe of the brace.

7. Cut the foot angle.

Math

The length of the beam can be calculated thus:

$$a^2 + b^2 = c^2$$

Where a = 46.5, b = 25.5, c = unknown

$$c = \sqrt{(a^2 + b^2)}$$

$$c = \sqrt{(46.5^2 + 25.5^2)}$$

$$c = \sqrt{(2162.25 + 650.25)}$$

$$c = \sqrt{2812.5} = 53.03 \approx 53 \text{ inches}$$

Why It Works

The problem is represented on the steel square with the length 25½ set as 6⅜ and 46½ set as 11⅝, each 1:4 scale. A fence placed between these numbers gives the cutting angles. The length of the brace is found by measuring the distance between these two numbers and multiplying by 4:

    13.25 x 4 = 53

Figure 15-7. Cut a Leaning Post

The run and height are represented on the steel square by 6³⁄₈ and 11⁵⁄₈—both to one-fourth scale. Use the steel square with the adjustable-arm fence to transfer the cut lines to the beam.

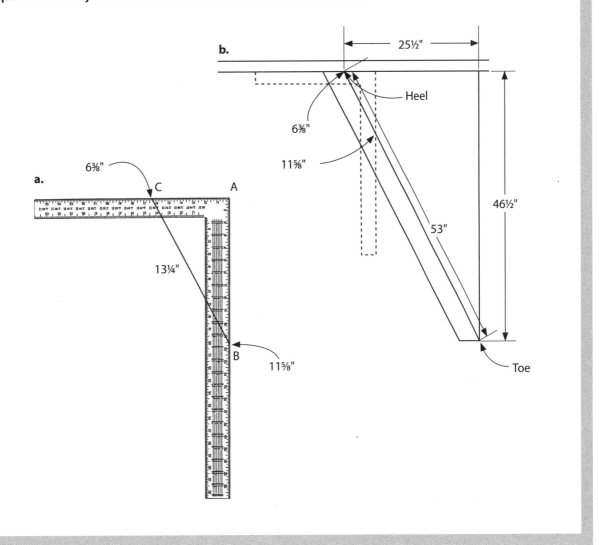

Chapter 16

Arch, Arc, and Ellipse Problems

An arch is usually constructed in the shape of a partial circle (an arc), or of a partial ellipse. To lay out an arc, we need to find the radius of the corresponding circle to set trammels or a compass, and the steel square is used here. The ellipse is a complex figure and is best drawn with a square and a scribing stick, as shown in **Figure 16-3**. The drawing may then be used to construct a pattern for setting out the arch. Both shapes can be laid out quite easily with the steel square.

Problem 16-1. Find the Radius of an Arc

Construct an arched doorway based on a rough drawing of the arc on a sheet of plywood. (See **Figure 16-1a**.) Find the arc radius to set trammels for the router. The width and the height of the arc are unknown—and immaterial.

Solution 16-1

1. Mark the ends of the arc, A and B (see **Figure 16-1b**).

2. Mark the top midpoint of the arc, C.

3. Draw lines from A to C and from B to C.

4. Place a square on line AC so the heel is at A.

5. Draw a line along the square body extending to D.

6. Reverse the square and draw another line from B to D.

7. The point where the lines cross (D) is the other end of a diameter of the circle that includes the arc.

8. One-half of the distance CD is the radius of the circle, and the distance to set the trammels.

Why It Works

Angle CBD is 90°. Angle CAD is 90°. By geometry, lines BD and AD intersect on the circumference of the circle.

Figure 16-1. Find the Radius of an Arc

Use the steel square to locate the ends of a diameter of the circle, and then find its midpoint to determine the radius.

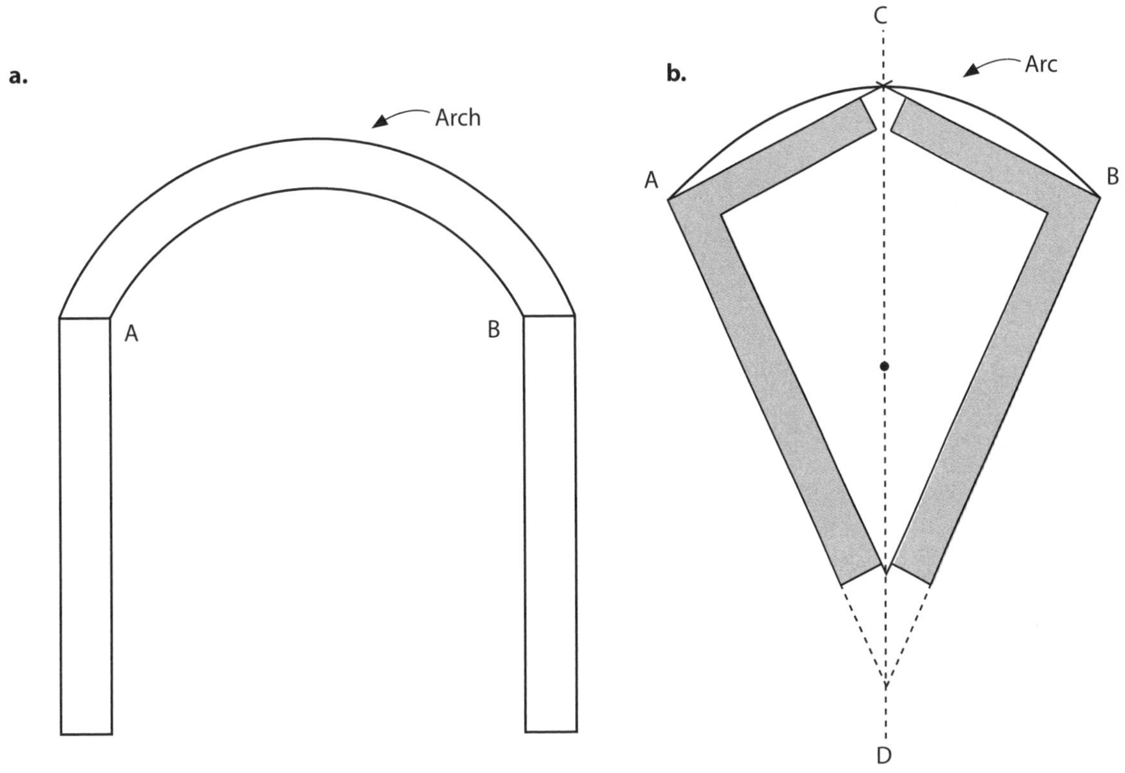

a.

Arch

A

B

b.

C

Arc

A

B

D

Figure 16-2. Lay Out a Large Arch

Draw a rectangle that represents the height and width of the arch, (a); then use the steel square to locate its center, (b). Connect A to F and B to F. Draw perpendiculars from midpoints G and H, (c). Their intersection, I, is the center of the arch, (d).

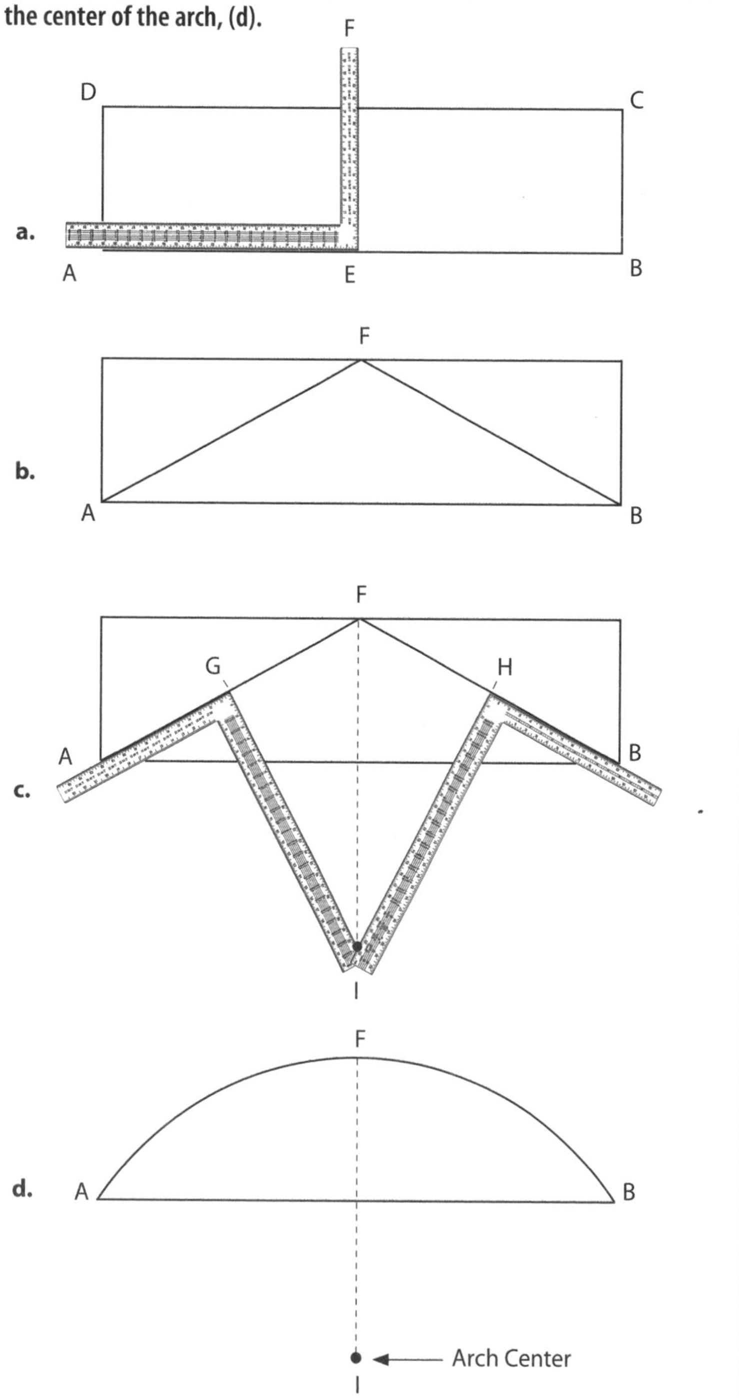

a.

b.

c.

d.

Arch Center

Problem 16-2. Lay Out a Large Arch

Construct a large arch over the gate leading from the patio to the garden. Use homemade trammel points and a large piece of plywood.

Solution 16-2

1. Draw rectangle ABCD on a piece of plywood using the arch span as distance AB and arch height as distance AD, as shown in **Figure 16-2a**.

2. Mark E at the center of AB, and use the steel square to raise a perpendicular to point F.

3. Using the square or a straight board, draw lines AF and BF, as shown in **Figure 16-2b**.

4. Measure and mark the center of line AF at G, and the center of line BF at H.

5. With a steel square, draw perpendiculars from G and H to intersect at point I. (See **Figure 16-2c**.)

6. Set the trammels to distance FI (the radius of the arc) and draw the arch AFB. (See **Figure 16-2d**.)

Why It Works

A chord is any line drawn across a circle that is not a diameter. In geometry, a perpendicular (right angle) through the center point of a chord is a diameter of the circle, and two such diameters will cross at the center of the circle.

Problem 16-3. Lay Out an Ellipse

Build an elliptical picture frame. The inside dimensions are to be 10 inches by 20 inches.

Solution 16-3

The given dimensions, 10 inches and 20 inches, are the minor axis and the major axis of the ellipse. Half of each axis is called the semi-axis. Knowing the minor semi-axis (5 inches) and the major semi-axis (10 inches), you can use a scribe stick with the steel square to draw a quadrant of the ellipse. The quadrant may be used as a pattern for drawing the full ellipse.

The method is fast to set up and easy to use, and every woodworker should be familiar with it (see **Figure 16-3**). Because of the size of the steel square (16 inches x 24 inches), the scribe-stick method cannot be used if one semi-axis is longer than 16 inches, unless you make extensions for the square itself.

1. Construct and use the wood scribe stick, as shown in **Figure 16-3a**. Make the scribe stick of lightweight wood and drill holes at points A, B, and C, with AB equal to the minor semi-axis of the ellipse (5 inches) and AC equal to the major semi-axis (10 inches).

2. Draw perpendicular lines representing the length and height of the quadrant.

Figure 16-3. Lay Out an Ellipse

Make a scribe stick with a pencil and two nails. Set the nails at 5", the minor semi-axis, and 10", the major semi-axis, away from the pencil, as shown at (a). Draw perpendicular lines, place the square, and trace the ellipse by keeping both nails pressed tight against the square, (b).

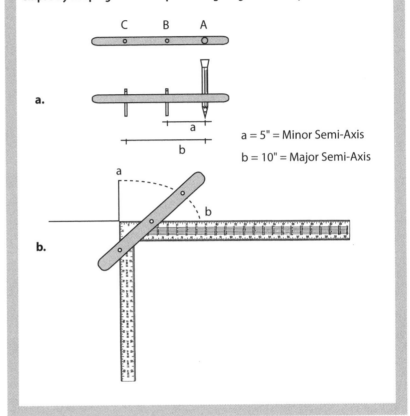

a = 5" = Minor Semi-Axis

b = 10" = Major Semi-Axis

3. Hold or clamp the steel square tightly on the drawing along the major and minor axes, as shown.

4. Hold the scribe stick firmly against the steel square and move the stick so that the pen in hole A scribes one quadrant of the ellipse (see **Figure 16-3b**). Keep both nails in contact with the square as you move the stick.

5. Repeat the procedure to complete the ellipse, or cut out the quadrant and use it as a pattern.

Why It Works

Where a circle has a single center, an ellipse has two focal points (foci), both lying on its major axis. The definition of the ellipse is that the sum of the distances from any point on the curve to the two foci is a fixed length. We are constructing a quadrant where the focal point is the heel of the square. The scribe stick has two fixed lengths (the major semi-axis and the minor semi-axis), which travel at 90° to each other always at a fixed distance; as one gets further from the focal point, the other gets nearer.

Problem 16-4. Construct an Elliptical Arch

Build an elliptical arch above the doorway leading from the living room to the dining room. The arch itself will be 2-feet-high and 7-feet-wide. For appearances, the wooden wedges shown above the arch in **Figure 16-4** must be specially shaped and placed in an elliptical pattern.

Solution 16-4

It is a complex problem. It requires two ellipses: one for the arch itself (minor semi-axis = 2, major semi-axis = 3.5) and another ellipse to determine the angles of the wedges above the arch (minor semi-axis = 3.5, major semi-axis = 6⅛). The two ellipses must be proportional to each other for the construction to work.

To draw the large ellipses, construct a large square.

Small Ellipse

1. On a large piece of plywood, draw one-half of the elliptical arch full size. The half-width is 3½ feet and the height is 2 feet. (See **Figure 16-4c**.)

2. Draw the quarter-ellipse using methods from **Problem 16-3** or **Problem 16-5**.

Figure 16-4. Construct an Elliptical Arch

First, construct the small elliptical arch (2 x 3.5), and then use the steel square to find a proportional ellipse (3.5 x 6⅛) to make the wedges above the doorway.

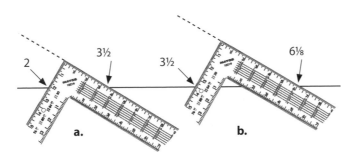

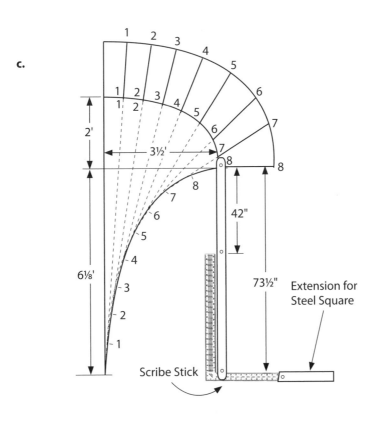

Large Ellipse

1. You know the minor semi-axis will be 3.5; you need to find a corresponding major semi-axis. Lay the steel square on the edge of a board so 2 on the blade and 3½ on the body are on the edge. (See **Figure 16-4a**.)

2. Draw a proportioning line on the board, and move the square up the line until 3½ on the blade touches the edge of the board. (See **Figure 16-4b**.) Read 6⅛ on the body. As the height of the small arch (2 feet) is to the major semi-axis (3½ feet), then so is 3½ of the large ellipse to 6⅛.

3. The measurement 6⅛ feet is equivalent to 6 feet 1½ inches (73½ inches), and is the length needed for constructing the large elliptical pattern.

4. Make a scribe from a stick with two nails and a pencil at one end. (See **Figure 16-3**.) The minor semi-axis is set 42 inches (3½ feet) from the pencil, and the major semi-axis is set 73½ inches (6⅛ feet) from the pencil.

5. The blade of the square is not long enough to guide the last pin of the scribe; make an extension by clamping on a strip of wood. Use the steel square (with extension), as shown in **Figure 16-4c**, to draw a new quarter-ellipse with the major semi-axis of 73½ inches and a minor semi-axis of 42 inches.

6. Divide the quadrant into the same number of units as there are wedges in the half-arch (eight) and number the units 1 through 8.

7. Number the wedge junctions in the arch from 1 to 8.

8. Draw lines from similar numbers on the lower pattern to the bottom of the arch above.

9. Extend the lines on the plywood to indicate the shape of the wedges.

10. Cut out the wedge shapes, and use them as patterns for making each piece.

Why It Works

The steel square can be used any time proportions are needed. The small ellipse had values of 2 and 3.5. The square was used to find a proportional ellipse with values of 3.5 and 6⅛. The relationships hold whether you are working with inches or feet, or with numbers that are scaled up or down by a common factor.

The same logic as in **Problem 16-3** applies to drawing the ellipses.

Problem 16-5. Draw an Oval

Construct an oval (egg-shaped) figure. An oval is one-half ellipse and one-half circle.

Solution 16-5

An oval can be laid out with a steel square by using the inner part of the heel and the minor semi-axis to draw the circle portion. (See **Figure 16-5b**.) The elliptical portion of the oval is then drawn as at **Figure 16-5c**, using the scribe stick shown in **Figure 16-5a**.

1. The scribe stick has two nails and a pencil. Distance a is the minor semi-axis, and distance b is the major semi-axis of the ellipse. The minor semi-axis of the elliptical portion of the oval equals the radius of the circle portion. (See **Figure 16-5a**.)

2. Draw two perpendicular lines AB and CD intersecting at point O.

3. Place the inner heel of the steel square on point O, and use the scribe stick to trace a quarter-circle using the minor semi-axis as the center point. (See **Figure 16-5b**.)

4. Reverse the square and place the body on line AB with the outer point of the heel at point O. Hold the scribe stick firmly against the square, and move the stick (keep both nails tight against the square) so the pencil

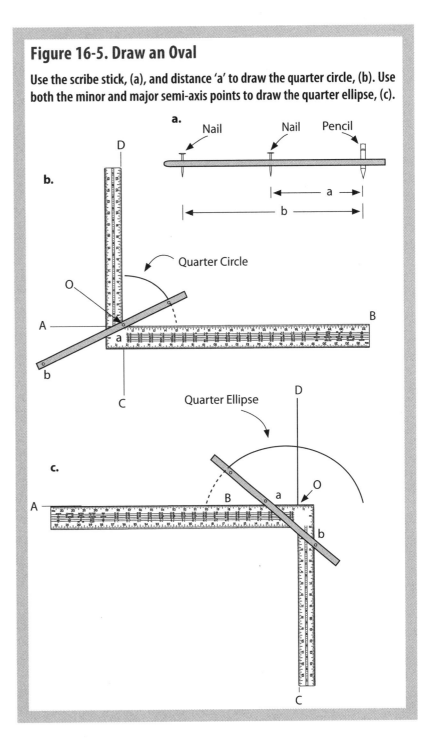

Figure 16-5. Draw an Oval

Use the scribe stick, (a), and distance 'a' to draw the quarter circle, (b). Use both the minor and major semi-axis points to draw the quarter ellipse, (c).

scribes one quadrant of the ellipse. (See **Figure 16-5c**.)

5. Use the half-pattern to draw the whole oval.

Problem 16-6. Bending Boards by Kerfing

One method of bending boards without heat or lamination is to cut a series of saw kerfs side by side on the back side to make the material flexible enough to bend smoothly. The kerfs are cut almost through the wood, leaving a thin layer of undisturbed wood on the top surface. The board is then bent to give a smooth curve, and the kerfs are filled with glue.

For example, a ¾-inch piece of pine must be bent around the end of a cabinet, as shown in **Figure 16-6b**. The arc is 90° and the radius (R) is 12 inches. How many kerfs are needed, and what is the spacing?

Solution 16-6

The simple answer is:

1. Select a test board similar to the piece that is to be bent, and cut a kerf to within ⅛ inch of the other side of the wood.

2. Measure the radius of the curve, and cut the board to this length (kerf to end of the board).

3. Clamp the end of the board to the workbench.

4. Bend the board up until the kerf closes. (See **Figure 16-6a**, Inset.)

5. Use a steel square to measure the distance H between the end of the board and the bench top.

6. Cut a series of kerfs at spacing H for the length needed.

Why It Works

To show why this works, four values are needed:

(1) The radius R of the curve, (2) the curve length L, (3) the bending height H, and (4) the size of the arc in degrees.

1. Make a full-size drawing.

2. Measure radius (R = 12 inches), length (L = 18⅞ inches) and the arc (90°), as shown in **Figure 16-6b**.

3. Use the following formula to find the degrees of the angle:

   Tan = H ÷ R

   Where R = 12 inches and H = 1.25 inches

   Tan = 1.25 ÷ 12 = 0.1042

   Atan 0.1042 = 5.9° ≈ 6°

That means each kerf moves the board 6° around the 90° curve.

4. The number of kerfs can now be determined:

Kerfs = Arc Degrees ÷ Kerf Degrees

   Where Arc = 90° and Kerf = 6°

   Kerfs = 90 ÷ 6 = 15

This means it will require 15 kerfs to move the board around 90°.

Rule of Thumb

Try kerf-bending on a test piece first. If the wood fibers break, dampen the face of the wood for a few minutes before bending.

If the face of the board shows facets, cut more kerfs spaced closer together.

Figure 16-6. Bending Boards by Kerfing

Saw a test kerf the distance R from the end of the wood, as at (a). Tip the board until the kerf closes and measure H at the end of the board. This distance determines how far apart to space the kerfs.

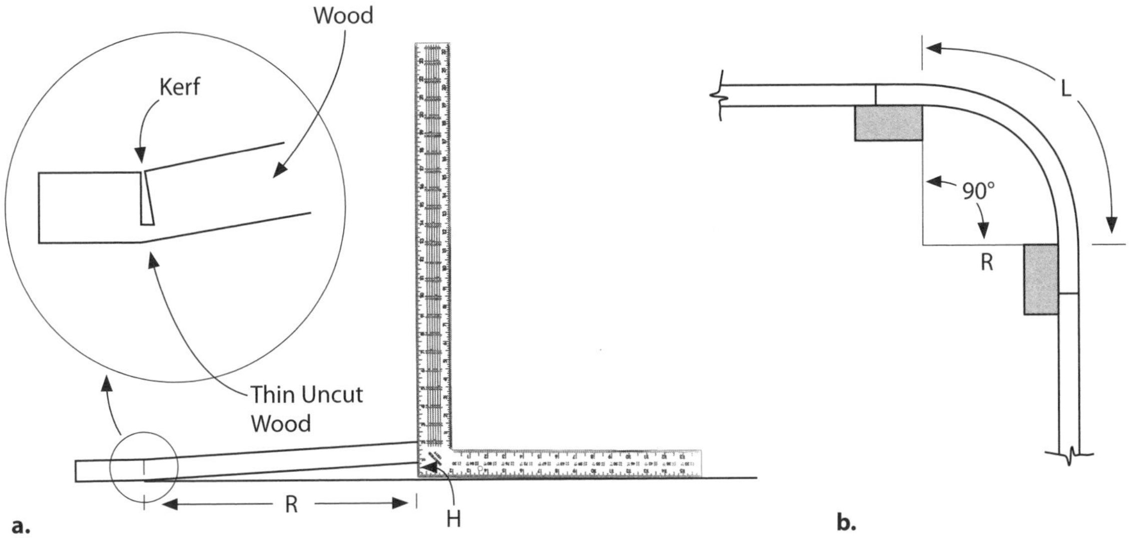

a.   **b.**

5. There will be 15 kerfs over a distance of about 19 inches (L = 18⅞ inches). The spacing will be:

   19 ÷ 15 = 1.27 ≈ 1¼ inches

Note: This spacing also was determined as H.

6. Cut 15 kerfs in the wood and space them 1¼ inches apart. That is the least number of kerfs necessary to make the curve when each kerf closes.

Chapter 17

Cylinders and Cones: Sheet Metal Problems

The problems in "Cylinders and Cones: Sheet Metal Problems" come from the sheet metal trade. The old sheet metal "tin-knocker" is almost out of business today; most ducts and pipes are stock sizes. Sheet metal workers still exist and use the described techniques to bend sheet metal to shape. Sheet metal problems employ standard mechanical drawing techniques to draw square, rectangular, and round exhaust pipes, and to extend the views to make stretch line patterns. Try one of the techniques, which are most interesting and almost magical.

The raised-cone problem is the most intriguing. The steel square is used first to find the radius of the cap, which then is used to figure the circumference of the needed circle. The difference in circumference between the pipe and the cap is directly related to the size of the wedge to be removed. A rather complicated problem is easily solved.

Problem 17-1a. Raised Conical Cover

Make a conical cover for a round ventilating pipe that is 14 inches in diameter. The cap is to be the same diameter and 3 inches high. It will be made of sheet metal and soldered to the top of the pipe.

Solution 17-1a

1. On a steel square locate 3 (the height of the cover) on the tongue, as shown in **Figure 17-1a, Step 1**.

2. Find 7 (the radius of the pipe) on the body of the square.

3. Measure the distance between these two points (7⅝ inches).

4. Set trammels or a compass to this radius (7⅝ inches) and draw a complete circle, **Step 2**.

5. Measure the diameter of the cover blank (15¼ inches) and subtract the diameter of the pipe from it:

   $$15.25 - 14 = 1.25 \text{ inches}$$

6. Next, find the amount of material to be cut out of the circular blank to form the cone.

   $$C = \pi d = 3.14 \times 1.25 = 3.93$$
   $$\approx 3\tfrac{7}{8} \text{ inches}$$

7. Starting at any convenient point on the circumference, step off 3⅞ inches for the width of the wedge to be cut out.

8. Draw lines to the center of the circle to complete the pattern.

9. Allow for a seam and cut out the wedge.

When the 15-inch circle with the 3⅞-inch cutout is bent and soldered together, it will be 14 inches in diameter with a 3-inch rise.

Figure 17-1. Raised Conical Cover

Use the steel square to find the radius of the circle that will be bent to form the conical cover, Step 1. Then calculate the width of the wedge to be cut out, and step it off around the circle, Step 2. Connect these points to the center of the circle to complete the pattern.

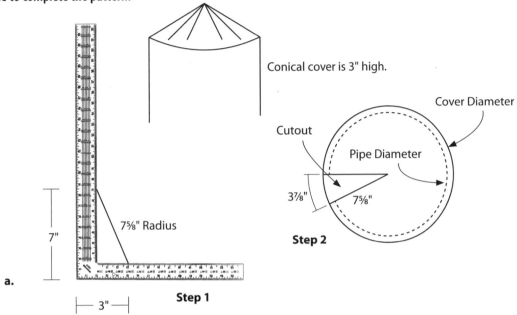

Conical cover is 3" high.

a.

Step 1

Step 2

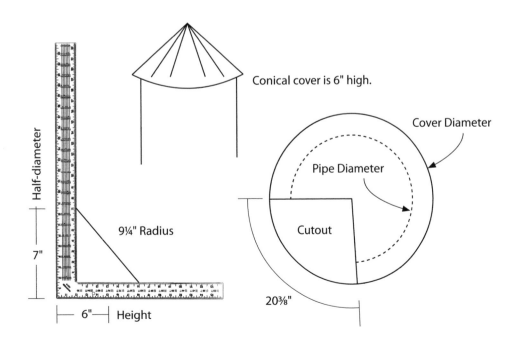

Conical cover is 6" high.

b.

Why It Works

The dimensions of the desired cone (radius = 7, rise = 3) are put on the steel square and the length of the slant (hypotenuse) is measured (7⅝). The distance is also the radius of the circle needed to make the cone.

We now need to find the amount of circumference to remove to reduce the size of the new circle back to the size of the pipe. The figure will be the size of the wedge:

> Circumference of Pipe
> = 14 x π = 43.96

> Circumference of Cone
> = 15.25 x π = 47.89

> Difference = 47.89 – 43.96
> = 3.93 inches ≈ 3⅞"

We found the number on the job by multiplying the difference in diameters (15¼ – 14 = 1.25) times pi (3.14) and found we had to remove a 3⅞-inch wedge.

The method is mathematically sound.

Problem 17-1b. Raised Conical Cover

For a variation on this problem, consider a round ventilating pipe 14 inches in diameter. Cut a conical cover with a 6-inch rise and a 1-inch lip all around.

Solution 17-1b

The solution is similar to **Problem 17-1a**. The conical cover height is 6 inches and the cover radius is 9¼ inches plus the lip, or 10¼ inches. (See **Figure 17-1b**.)

The diameter of the cover is:

> 10.25 x 2 = 20.5 inches

The difference in diameters of the pipe and the cone is:

> 20.5 – 14 = 6.5 inches

The cutout distance is:

> 3.14 x 6.5 = 20.41 inches

That will give a cover 16 inches in diameter and 6 inches high. (See **Figure 17-1b**.)

Problem 17-2. Round Pipe through Pitched Roof

Cut an opening for a round stovepipe through a pitched roof. The pipe is 6 inches in diameter. The architect shows the roof as having 2-3 pitch (slope = 16-in-12). It is obvious the hole will not be round, but an ellipse.

Solution 17-2

Pitch is the angle the roof surface makes with a horizontal plane, the ratio of the rise to the span.

Span is the distance from the outside of one wall to the outside of the opposite wall.

Rise is the distance from an imaginary line at the height of the top plate to the roof peak.

A roof with 16-foot rise and 24 foot span has a 2-3 pitch:

16 ÷ 24 = ⅔

The same roof has a 12-foot run:

Span ÷ 2 = Run

24 ÷ 2 = 12

See Chapter 10, "Roofs," for a discussion of roof pitch, rise, width, run, and span.

1. Draw a line from 12 on the steel square tongue (the run) to 16 on the body (the rise). The line represents the roof angle. (See **Figure 17-2**.)

Figure 17-2. Round Pipe through Pitched Roof

Use the steel square to find the dimensions of the required ellipse; AB is the length of the minor semi-axis and AC is the length of the major semi-axis. The roof has a pitch of 2-3, or 16 inches of rise per foot of run.

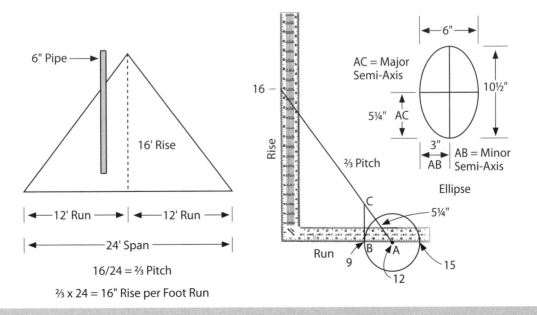

2. Draw a 6-inch circle with its center at 12 (point A) to represent the diameter of the pipe.

3. Draw perpendicular line BC from the edge of the circle at 9 to intersect the pitch line. Measure line AB and line AC.

4. Now AB represents the minor semi-axis (3 inches) of the required ellipse, and AC represents the length of the major semi-axis (5¼ inches).

5. Draw the ellipse full size and make a pattern to cut the hole in the roof. See **Figure 16-3**, page 159, for a method of drawing an ellipse using the steel square.

Why It Works

We used a steel square to represent the rise and run of the roof, with the rise (16 feet) on the body and the run (12 feet) on the blade. The slope of the roof was drawn between the two numbers. We drew the diameter of the pipe (6 inches) on the blade (from 9 inches to 15 inches). We read the ellipse minor semi-axis (3 inches) off the square and read the ellipse major semi-axis as the length of line AC (5¼ inches). All of the data is easily read off the square.

Problem 17-3. Lay Out a Square Exhaust Pipe

Cut a square exhaust pipe for a sloped roof out of sheet metal. The square pipe should be vertical.

Solution 17-3

1. Draw the exhaust pipe and its flange with dimensions, as shown in **Figure 17-3a**.

2. Draw the front elevation view of the job at full scale (see **Figure 17-3b**) using height H, side S, and the angle of the roof.

3. Draw the plan view of the sleeve directly above the front elevation (see **Figure 17-3c**), and number the corners 1, 2, 3, and 4 with the seam numbered 0.

4. Draw a stretch-out line the length of the four sides, as in **Figure 17-3d**.

5. Mark the length of the sides on the stretch-out line and lay out the sides, marking them 0, 1, 2, 3, 4, and 0, as in **Figure 17-3d**.

6. With a steel square, draw lines at right angles to the front elevation, projecting the ends of the edges to the corresponding numbered edges on the stretch-out.

7. Connect the points with straight lines to create the sheet-metal pattern. (See **Figure 17-3e**.)

Figure 17-3. Lay Out a Square Exhaust Pipe

Use the elevation drawings to construct a stretch-out line for the exhaust pipe. Use the steel square to project the roof slope to the corresponding corners of the exhaust pipe.

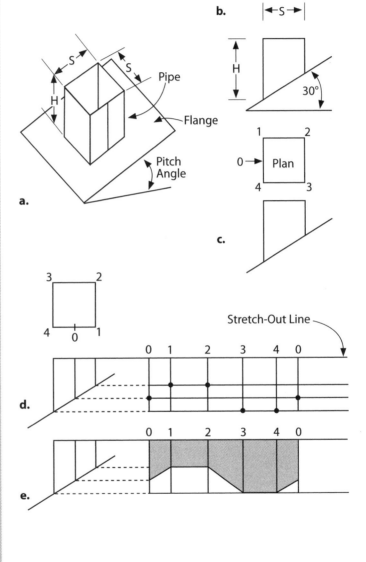

Why It Works

We have used mechanical drawing techniques with the steel square to extend the sides and the pitch angle to the stretch-out line.

Figure 17-4. Lay Out a Flange for the Square Exhaust Pipe

The top view (a) shows the square figure to be extended. In (b), distances AB and MN are extended according to the slope of the roof. The final plan (c) shows how a rectangle must be cut to accommodate the square pipe.

a. Plan

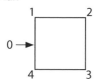

b. Front Elevation

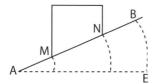

c. Flange Pattern

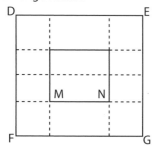

Problem 17-4. Lay Out a Flange for the Square Exhaust Pipe

Lay out and cut a flange to fit the square exhaust pipe from **Problem 17-3**.

Solution 17-4

1. Draw the plan view of the square exhaust pipe, as in **Figure 17-4a**.

2. Draw the front view and extend the roof line AB to intersect with a horizontal line.

3. Use a trammel, or the heel of the square, to swing points B, M, and N onto the horizontal line. (See **Figure 17-4b**.)

4. The horizontal distances 1 to 4 and 2 to 3 do not change because of the slope of the roof.

5. Draw the flange full size as in **Figure 17-4c**.

Why It Works

We have used mechanical drawing techniques with the steel square to extend the sides and the pitch angle onto the flange pattern.

Problem 17-5. Lay Out a Rectangular Exhaust Pipe

Cut a rectangular roof-mounted exhaust pipe from sheet metal.

Solution 17-5

1. Draw the exhaust pipe and the flange with dimensions, as shown in **Figure 17-5a**.

2. Draw the front elevation view of the job at full scale. (See **Figure 17-5c**.) Use height H, side S1, side S2, and the roof slope.

3. Draw the plan view of the sleeve directly above the front elevation (see **Figure 17-5b**) and number the corners 1, 2, 3, and 4, with the seam numbered 0.

4. Draw a stretch-out line the length of the four sides, as in **Figure 17-5c**.

5. Mark the length of the sides on the stretch-out line, and lay out the sides, marking them 0, 1, 2, 3, 4, and 0, as in **Figure 17-5c**.

6. With a steel square, draw lines representing the vertical corners or folds in the metal at right angles to the stretch-out line.

7. With a steel square, project the ends of the edges (at right angles

to the elevation view) to the corresponding numbered edges on the stretch-out.

8. Connect the points with straight lines to create the sheet metal pattern.

9. Make the flange, as in **Problem 17-4**.

Why It Works

We have used common mechanical drawing techniques with the steel square to extend the sides and the pitch angle onto the sheet metal pattern.

Figure 17-5. Lay Out a Rectangular Exhaust Pipe

Use the elevation drawings to construct a stretch-out line for the rectangular exhaust pipe. Use the steel square to project the roof slope to the corresponding corners of the exhaust pipe pattern (shaded area).

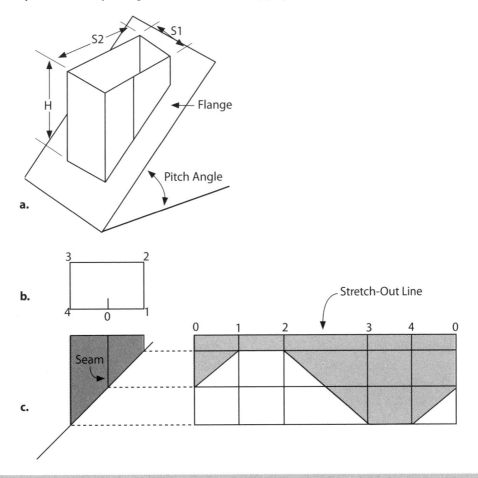

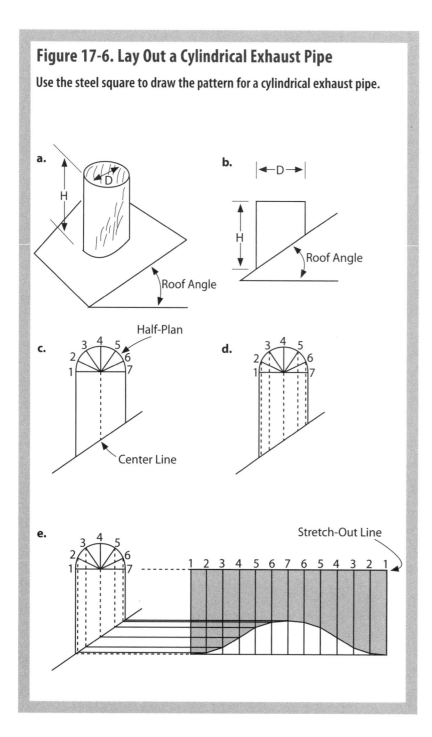

Figure 17-6. Lay Out a Cylindrical Exhaust Pipe

Use the steel square to draw the pattern for a cylindrical exhaust pipe.

Problem 17-6. Lay Out a Cylindrical Exhaust Pipe

Cut a cylindrical exhaust pipe from sheet metal. The pipe will go through a slanted roof.

Solution 17-6

1. Draw the exhaust pipe and the flange with dimensions. (See **Figure 17-6a**).

2. Draw the front elevation view of the job at full scale. (See **Figure 17-6b**.) Use height H, diameter D, and the roof angle.

3. Draw a half-plan view of the sleeve directly above the front elevation. (See **Figure 17-6c**.)

4. Divide the half-plan into six equal sectors and number them, as in **Figure 17-6c**.

Note: The number of sectors depends on the size of the job. The sectors are numbered so that the corresponding elements in the elevation and plan views can be extended to the stretch-out and easily identified.

5. Using a steel square, set the straight edge at right angles to line 1-7, and draw vertical lines from points 2, 3, 5, and 6 of the half-circle to the flange (see **Figure 17-6d**).

6. Draw a stretch-out line the length of the circumference, as in **Figure 17-6e**. The circumference of the pipe is the diameter times pi:

    C = π D.

7. Use the steel square and dividers to transfer the vertical lines onto the stretch-out line. Lay them out as verticals and number them as 1 through 7 and 7 through 1, as in **Figure 17-6e**.

8. With a steel square, project the roof ends of the verticals horizontally across to the corresponding numbered edges on the stretch-out.

9. Connect the points and smooth the line into a curve, as in **Figure 17-6e**.

Why It Works

We have used the steel square along with common mechanical drawing techniques to extend the plan and elevation views of the cylindrical pipe onto a stretch-out line.

Problem 17-7. Lay Out a 60° Y

The previous problems were warm-ups. Now build a dust collection system for the workshop, and make a 60° Y-shaped connector from sheet metal. Both arms of the Y will be the same diameter as the main pipe.

Solution 17-7

1. Draw the Y (see **Figure 17-7a**).

2. Draw the front elevation view of the job at full scale, with center lines. (See **Figure 17-7b**.)

3. Draw the half-plan view of the Y, as shown in **Figure 17-7c**.

4. Divide the half-plan into six equal sectors and number them, as in **Figure 17-7c**.

Note: The number of sectors depends on the size of the job. The sectors are numbered so the corresponding elements in the elevation and plan views can be extended to the stretch-out and easily identified.

5. Using a steel square, draw vertical lines from points 2, 3, 5, and 6 of the half-plan to the flange. (See **Figure 17-7c**.)

6. Draw a stretch-out line the length of the circumference of the pipe, as in **Figure 17-7c**. The circumference of the pipe is the diameter times pi:

    C = π D.

Figure 17-7. Lay Out a 60° Y

Use the steel square to draw the pattern for all three sections of a 60° Y.

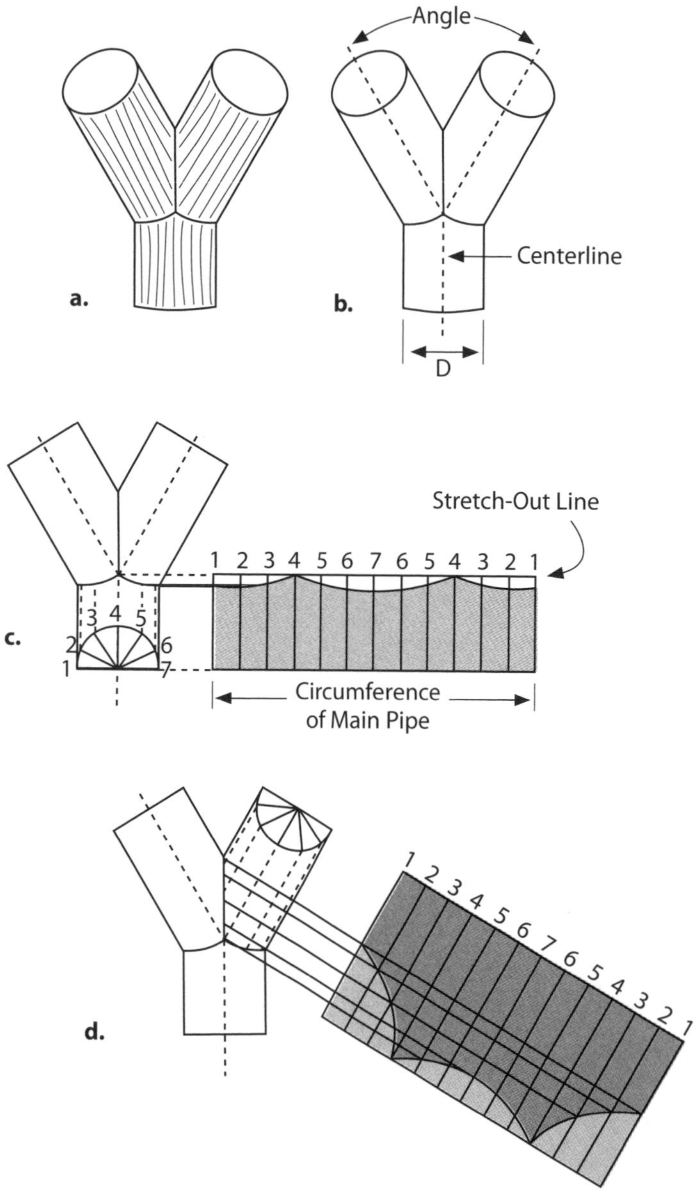

a.

b.

c.

d.

7. Transfer the length of the sides from the elevation view to the stretch-out line and lay out the sides, marking them as shown in **Figure 17-7c**.

8. With the steel square, draw vertical lines at right angles to the stretch-out line.

9. With a steel square, project the ends of the edges to the corresponding numbered edges on the stretch-out.

10. Connect the points with curved lines as in **Figure 17-7c**.

11. Repeat the procedure to lay out the cutting pattern for the top portions of the Y (see **Figure 17-7d**).

Why It Works

We have used mechanical drawing techniques with the steel square to extend the plan and elevation views of the Y-shaped pipe onto a stretch-out line, creating a flat pattern for each section of the Y.

Problem 17-8. Pipe through a Sloped Roof

Cut an opening in a sloped roof for a pipe. The slope of the roof is unknown. Also the diameter and shape of the pipe are unknown, although it appears to be roundish. Fortunately, a steel square and plumb bob up are available.

Solution 17-8

1. Set the pipe to be used in its final position on the roof, as shown in **Figure 17-8**.

2. Make sure it is plumb by using a plumb bob, and prop it in place. The drawing shows a way to use the plumb bob (while up on the roof) by mounting the plumb line on a length of 2x4.

3. Move the square around the pipe, and make marks about one inch apart.

4. Join the marks.

5. Follow the outline to cut through the roof.

Why It Works

Whether the through-pipe is round, square, or polygonal, the method will transfer an outline of its shape onto the sloping roof. It is using the square as a layout tool rather than as a calculating engine.

Figure 17-8. Pipe through a Sloped Roof

Use the plumb bob hung on a 2x4 to set the pipe in a vertical position on the roof. Use the steel square to transfer its outline onto the sloping roof. The size and shape of the pipe are immaterial.

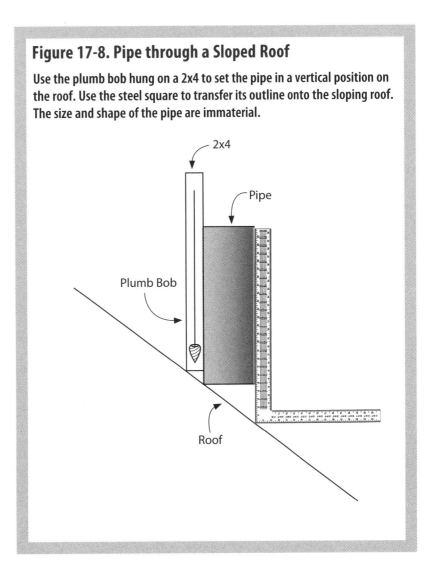